CARING FOR AMERICAN INDIAN OBJECTS

A Practical and Cultural Guide

EDITED BY SHERELYN OGDEN

MINNESOTA HISTORICAL SOCIETY PRESS

 For information, write to the Minnesota Historical Society Press, 345 Kellogg Blvd. W., St. Paul, MN 55102-1906.

www.mhspress.org

Proceeds from the sale of this book will be used by the Minnesota Historical Society to support its programs.

The Minnesota Historical Society Press is a member of the Association of American University Presses.

Manufactured in China

10 9 8 7 6 5 4 3

∞ The paper used in this publication meets the minimum requirements of the American National Standard for Information Sciences—Permanence for Printed Library materials, ANSI Z39.48-1992.

International Standard Book Number
ISBN 13: 978-0-87351-505-4 (paper)
ISBN 10: 0-87351-505-6 (paper)

Library of Congress Cataloging-in-Publication Data

Caring for American Indian objects : a practical and cultural guide / edited by Sherelyn Ogden.

p. cm.
Includes bibliographical references and index.
ISBN 0-87351-505-6 (pbk. : alk. paper)

1. Indians of North America—Antiquities—Collection and preservation. 2. Indians of North America—Material culture. 3. Indian museums—North America. 4. Museum conservation methods—North America. 5. Museum techniques—North America. 6. United States—Antiquities—Collection and preservation. I. Ogden, Sherelyn.

E77.C28 2004
973.04′97′0074—dc22

2003025877

Contents

Foreword

Our Obligation to Our Past

JOSEPH D. HORSE CAPTURE ***(A'ANININ [GROS VENTRE])***

All across Indian country, cultural centers and tribal museums are forming to address the need of cultural preservation. The primary purpose of this book is to aid tribes by providing additional methods to preserve their past for future generations.

The tools of our ancestors, the *objects* that they created and used, are invaluable to the understanding of ourselves. On the Plains, women took care of the family and created most of the things that were worn. When objects were created and adorned, women would get together and work on a project together. This would provide an opportunity for the women elders to pass on their knowledge to the younger women, who would then pass it on to the next generation. In turn, men would work together to provide for their close-knit community. Hunting, warfare, and most of the religious matters were their responsibility. They were also fathers, husbands, and sons, who protected the community and land from hostile peoples and provided the much needed resources to insure their survival. These are the stories that an item can tell. It connects us to our past.

The decoration that adorns an item tells us about the artistic style and the ingenuity of our people. Whether they were carved of cedar, formed with clay from the earth, or woven with reeds, these articles of our ancestors bring the past in front of us. Under close examination, they provide clues to how our people gathered and processed the materials that they used. The construction of the item provides insight into how they created the things that were important to them for function and durability.

The future is changing for Native people. Many tribes are devoting resources to construct museums and cultural centers, which gives them an opportunity to preserve and foster their history and culture. When a tribal museum or cultural center acquires an object, it can be a focal point for elders to pass knowledge to young people and share information with each other. Other important resources like historical photographs, documents, and a library provide educational opportunities for young Native people to learn more about their cultural traditions. When properly cared for, items that are held within the community can revitalize and reinforce cultural traditions.

I believe that it is our responsibility, as Indian people, to preserve our culture, including the items that were used by our ancestors. The role of preservation is a very important part of this responsibility. Because most of these items were and continue to be made of animal and plant materials that degrade, they can easily be lost by neglect or improper preservation techniques. Special care and storage are vital. With more and more tribes taking a proactive approach to building facilities to house items from their tribe and building collections, the future of these important materials is promising. Once these items are gone, this important physical link to our ancestors, the items that they wore or held in their hands, is gone forever.

Preface

When I began work on this project, I had no idea it would prove to be so special. My collaboration with the American Indians involved in the project was enlightening and enjoyable, and I met remarkable people whom I would not have had the opportunity to meet otherwise. They taught me much, and I am grateful.

As a paper and book conservator, I have occasionally been asked to provide assistance in the care of paper-based American Indian cultural items, such as treaties and drawings. The methods and techniques I suggested were always based on standard museum practice. As the years went by and I changed jobs, I provided assistance, with the help of my colleagues, in the care of other types of American Indian cultural items. Again my response was always based on standard museum practice. But often, it seemed, my suggestions did not meet the cultural needs of the items and were impractical given the situation in which these items existed. I was glad that tribal methods of care were still practiced. I hope American Indians succeeded in caring for items when my suggested methods did not suffice.

Yet there appeared to be a need for additional practical information on caring for these items, especially as tribal museums and cultural centers grew in number. Since much of standard museum practice is practical, easy to accomplish, and relatively low in cost, it seemed like a good idea to at least make the information available to the people who needed it, and who could perhaps adapt some of it to their particular needs. Also, some of standard museum practice is analogous to tribal care practices. Since non-Indians who are inexperienced in Indian cultures cannot judge which standard museum practices are compatible with various Indian cultural priorities, it seemed best to make a body of basic information available to the Indian people who wanted it. Providing this information in book form also seemed best.

When I first thought about doing this project, I interviewed several American Indian people. I asked if a book like this would be useful, and I asked what topics they would like addressed and what questions they wanted answered. I was concerned that this book might be unnecessary; items clearly have lasted for generations by tribal care methods, so standard museum methods and techniques might not be needed. But the American Indians I consulted felt it was useful for the people who make decisions about care of items to have as much information as possible, and that the book would be helpful. I continued to seek the advice and guidance of American Indian people throughout this project, and their suggestions were gratefully incorporated into the book.

I have another reason for undertaking this project. Much of my initial training as a paper and book conservator involved drawings by and about American Indians. I was privileged to rehouse and treat hundreds of items from Chicago's Newberry Library's Edward E. Ayer Collection. As I treated these drawings I was absorbed by the images I saw, and I wanted to learn more about the cultures they represented. About twenty years later I prepared a book similar to this one on the care of library and archival materials. The enthusiastic response to the practical approach of that book encouraged me to respond to requests for practical information from American Indians and consider this project. Now, about thirty years after my first work as a conservator, I feel I have come full circle in preparing this book, and I am able to draw on the aspects of my work and experience that I enjoy the most.

This book is not perfect. Every effort was made to be as accurate as possible, but in projects like this mistakes inevitably happen. Neither does the book include the information some people will think it should, nor in the way they think is best. But, as I write this preface, what I hope is that the book will prove useful and be accepted as it is intended—as an offering of additional information. I am aware of the tension between predominantly Western museum standards of practice and tribal cultural practices and of the barriers to which this tension can lead. I am also aware of the unpleasant connotations museums hold in the hearts of some Indian people. There is no intent in this book to impose standard museum practice on the care of American Indian items. In fact, I hope the opposite will happen. I hope the book will somehow lead to a greater exchange of information about tribal care practices so that some of these can be incorporated into standard museum practice. I hope further that an open collaboration can develop between American Indian people and non-Indian museum professionals that will maintain Indian cultures and enrich standard museum practice.

Acknowledgments

This book would not have come about without the grace, guidance, knowledge, and assistance of many people. This has proven to be a truly collaborative project, and I am grateful to the dozens of American Indians, colleagues, friends, and other interested parties who provided help and support. Of course, any errors or omissions are my responsibility. All those who participated in the project are too numerous to cite individually. Many, however, should receive special recognition.

Before the project was undertaken, several people were interviewed about the advisability of producing such a book and its usefulness. Their valuable opinions helped shape the book so it would be as relevant as possible. For this I thank particularly Kathryn "Jody" Beaulieu (Anishinabe / Ojibwe), Director and NAGPRA Representative, Red Lake Tribal Library and Archives; Victoria Raske (Anishinabe / Ojibwe), Museum Project Coordinator, Grand Portage Band of Ojibwe; Marcella Cash (Sicangu Lakota), Director / Archivist, Sicangu Heritage Center; Nancy Odegaard, Conservator / Head of Preservation, Arizona State Museum and Professor, Department of Anthropology, University of Arizona; and Marian Kaminitz, Head of Conservation, National Museum of the American Indian.

Without the hard and dedicated work of the authors, the book would not have been written. These committed individuals believed in the book and in the importance of sharing and disseminating information in a respectful way. For taking on this challenging task, I am grateful to: Faith G. Bad Bear (Crow / Sioux), Assistant Curator of Ethnology, Science Museum of Minnesota; Thomas J. Braun, Objects Conservator, Minnesota Historical Society; Gina Nicole Delfino, Central Registrar, Minnesota Historical Society; Ann Frisina, Textile Conservator, Minnesota Historical Society; Sven Haakanson Jr. (Alutiiq-Sugpiaq), Executive Director, Alutiiq Museum and Archaeological Repository; Joseph D. Horse Capture (A'aninin [Gros Ventre]), Associate Curator, The Minneapolis Institute of Arts; Brian M. Kraft, Registrar, The Minneapolis Institute of Arts; Pollyanna Nordstrand (Hopi), Exhibit Planner, National Park Service; Nancy Odegaard; Nokomis Paiz (Anishinabe / Ojibwe), School Teacher, Red Lake, MN; Alyce Sadongei (Kiowa / Tohono O'Odham), Assistant Curator for Native American Relations, Arizona State Museum; Paul S. Storch, Objects Conservator, Minnesota Historical Society; Laine Thom (Shoshone / Goshiute / Paiute), Park Ranger (Interpretation), Colter Bay Indian Arts Museum, Grand Teton National Park; Joan Celeste Thomas (Kiowa), Registrar, Gilcrease Museum; and Marjorie Waheneka (Confederated Umatilla Tribes), Exhibits and Collections Manager, Tamástslikt Cultural Institute. The individuals who allowed themselves to be quoted are: Kathryn "Jody" Beaulieu; Felton Bricker Sr. (Mohave Indian Tribe), Mohave Valley, Arizona; Marcella Cash; Randall J. Melton (Creek / Seminole), Registrar, Tamástslikt Cultural Institute; and Char Tullie (Diné / Navajo), Registrar, Navajo Nation Museum. For more information, see the list of contributors.

Once the manuscript of the book was written, several individuals gave generously of their expertise, time, and energy reviewing it and making textual and editorial suggestions. The book is much better as a result of their considerable efforts, and I thank them. They are: Marcia Anderson, Head of Museum Collections / Chief Curator, Minnesota Historical Society; Kathyrn "Jody" Beaulieu; C. J. Brafford (Oglala Sioux), Director, Ute Indian Museum; Thomas J. Braun; Ann Frisina; Andrew Gulliford, Director, Center of Southwest Studies, Fort Lewis College; Marian Kaminitz; Nancy Odegaard; Victoria Raske; Alyce Sadongei; Paul S. Storch; Christy Sturm, Director, Poeh Museum; Allan Thenen, Paper Conservator, St. Paul, MN; Char Tullie; Larry Zimmerman, Head of Archaeology, Minnesota Historical Society.

The use of illustrations and information from outside sources is gratefully acknowledged. The Buffalo Bill Historical Center in Cody, Wyoming, and The Minneapolis Institute of Arts allowed illustrations from their collections to be used. The Northeast Document Conservation Center, the Upper Midwest Conservation Association, and the Graduate School of Library and Information Science at the University of Illinois at Urbana-Champaign allowed copyrighted information to be used. Margaret Holben Ellis, Director of the Thaw Conservation Center, the Morgan Library, allowed information to be included from her unpublished "Glossary of Paper Conservation Terms."

Several people should be acknowledged for the special assistance they provided. Tatiana Lomahaftewa Slock, Assistant Curator of Collections, Institute of American Indian Arts Museum; Lynn Brittner, Director, Southern Ute Indian Cultural Center; Jeanne Brako, Curator, Center of Southwest Studies, Fort Lewis College; Susan Barger, Small Museum Development Consultant, TREX, Museum of New Mexico; and Susan Thomas Harden, Curator, Anasazi Heritage Center, generously gave time and information when I visited them during a research trip early in this project. Andrew Gulliford shared invaluable insight and experience gained during his research and writing of *Sacred Objects and Sacred Places* and provided assistance throughout the project. Nancy Mithlo, Assistant Professor of Anthropology, Smith College; Malissa Minthorn, Research Library and Archives Manager, Tamástslikt Cultural Institute; and Susan Heald, Senior Textile Conservator, National Museum of the American Indian, were helpful in providing important information and guidance. Miriam Clavir, the author of *Preserving What Is Valued,* and Jean Wilson, the editor of that book at the University of British Columbia Press, arranged for me to have page proofs of that book to assist me in the preparation of the manuscript for this one. Joan Celeste Thomas and Faith G. Bad Bear graciously and patiently explained general ways of their people to me so that I could convey information more accurately in the book and provide information that was more appropriate. Nancy Odegaard and Alyce Sadongei provided guidance and information throughout the project without which the book would have turned out very differently.

Many of my colleagues at the Minnesota Historical Society deserve special recognition. I especially thank my colleagues in the Conservation Department for their support, patience, and helpful suggestions throughout this project. Their good-spirited cooperation and unfailing encouragement were an important factor in carrying the project to fruition. I am grateful to them all. In particular I would like to thank the authors Thomas J. Braun, Ann Frisina, and Paul S. Storch; John Fulton, Conservation Technician, who worked extensively with the authors in editing the text; Eric Mortenson, whose expertise and experience are evident throughout the book in his fine photographic work, which greatly enhances the text; Jean Moberg, whose sound technical assistance was a help in many aspects of the project; and Timothy Herstein, Paper Conservation Assistant, Bryan Johnson, Book Conservation Assistant, and Bridget White, Photo Lab Clerk, whose assistance with the photography and other matters is especially appreciated. Several members of the Museum Collections Department were crucial. I thank particularly Marcia Anderson, whose extensive knowledge and experience were of inestimable value throughout the project. Her ongoing guidance and support and her willingness to answer endless questions and provide input are greatly appreciated. I am grateful to Cynthia Hall, Museum Project Specialist, for showing me collections items, helping me select appropriate ones for photography, moving them as necessary, and answering questions. I also thank Diane Adams-Graf, Museum Project Specialist, for providing information as needed throughout the project. I am grateful to Gina Nicole Delfino, Central Registrar, who clarified details regarding registration issues. I am also grateful to Terence Vidal, Site Manager, Jodell Meyer (Ojibwe), Assistant Site Manager, and Kenneth Weyaus Sr. (Ojibwe), Site Technician, Mille Lacs Indian Museum and Trading Post, for their great assistance in selecting items for photography and providing information and insight on both traditional and museum storage techniques. I wish to thank the members of the Society's Indian Advisory Committee (IAC) for their valuable input. In particular, I would like to thank those who agreed to take time from an IAC meeting to be photographed for the book: Jeff Savage (Ojibwe); Victoria Raske (Ojibwe); Kathryn "Jody" Beaulieu (Anishinabe / Ojibwe); David Aubid (Ojibwe); and Joseph Campbell (Dakota).

I would like to thank the Minnesota Historical Society Press for their fine work in publishing this book. Many members of the staff contributed to the project, and their efforts are greatly appreciated. I am particularly grateful to Gregory Britton, Director, and Ann Regan, Managing Editor, and Will Powers, Design and Production Manager, for encouraging and supporting the project. The experience and expertise of Sarah Rubinstein, Editor, enabled the manuscript to move through the publishing process smoothly, and her suggestions and guidance throughout the process are greatly appreciated, as is her good judgment.

Special thanks are due to Allan Thenen for his assistance in repeatedly reviewing and editing the manuscript and for his encouragement throughout the project. I am grateful for his help, support, and willingness to serve as a sounding board for ideas.

Most notable thanks go to the Minnesota Historical Society and its Director, Nina Archabal, for allowing me to take on this project. I am grateful for the time my colleagues at the Society and I were able to spend on the project and for the financial support the Society provided in carrying out this project. I am especially grateful to my supervisor, Michael Fox, Assistant Director for Library and Archives, who was highly supportive of this project from his first contact with it, and to his predecessor, the late Lila Goff, who initially thought it worthy and approved it.

Finally, I wish to acknowledge the American Indian people who strive to preserve their cultures. In particular, I acknowledge the American Indian ledger artists from the past whose remarkable drawings first inspired me, and the American Indian caregivers whose tribal care practices and techniques have preserved their cultural items for generations.

Introduction

SHERELYN OGDEN

A ledger book filled with delicately colored drawings that tell a story, a hand-beaded bandolier bag that has been worn with pride on many special occasions, and a skin shirt that is painted, pierced, and quilled, proclaiming the considerable accomplishments of a previous owner—these are just some of the items that prompted the writing of this book. American Indian cultural items such as these are important not only as unique expressions of beauty, craftsmanship, and belief but especially as a means of connecting American Indian people today to their past and of continuing their culture.

This book is about the care of these items. More and more cultural centers and tribal museums are being established. Cultural items are being given to these repositories by older members of the tribes, by non-Indians who want to give items back to the community of origin, and through repatriation. The purpose of this book is to share information on proven methods of care used in standard museum practice. American Indian people have used tribal methods to care for their cultural items for generations. The intent of this book is *not* to replace any of these techniques. Instead, it is to offer Indian caregivers information they may not already have to aid them in making decisions.

In general this book is intended to be used by people who have little or no training or experience in standard museum practice but who seek additional information. The primary audience for this book is the American Indian people who are charged with the care of their cultural items. A secondary audience is the staff of cultural institutions of all sorts who seek introductory information on how to care for American Indian collections. The word *you* is used throughout this book to address both these audiences—American Indian caregivers and Indian and non-Indian staff of cultural institutions. It may refer to both these audiences collectively, or it may refer to just one.

Several excellent books are available on the care of collections, but none of these is devoted to American Indian cultural items. The goal of this book is to make available a body of practical information that focuses exclusively on the care of these items. Other sources of information are mentioned within the text or are listed in the bibliography at the back of the book. These should be seen as tools to be used in implementing the suggestions made in this book.

In addition to American Indian cultural items, Indian people have many family items that are not traditional to their culture but are traditional to other cultures, such as a white wedding dress, a military uniform, or a china teapot. The care of items such as these is not included here, although the issues and principles are the same. The care of such items has been well covered in other publications, which are listed in the bibliography.

This book encompasses the general needs of cultural items of all American Indian people, not just people of specific regions, cultures, or language groups. Of course the contributors to this book recognize the vast diversity of Indian people and their cultures, but a broader approach has been taken in the hope that by addressing general issues at an introductory level, this book will be of use to Indian people everywhere. Likewise, I hope that staff of cultural institutions, wherever they are, will find it helpful.

This book is repetitious. This is because it is not expected to be read from beginning to end but will instead probably be used mostly for reference, like a manual, with the table of contents and index guiding readers to the specific information they need.

Every attempt was made to provide the most up-to-date and accurate information possible. Every mailing and e-mail address, Web address, and contact number was checked for accuracy prior to inclusion in this book. Nevertheless, by the time this book appears in print, some of this information will probably be outdated. I decided when producing this book that providing as much useful information as possible was best, even though some of it might become outdated relatively soon.

A book like this can never answer all questions. If readers have questions about the application of the information to their particular situation, they should not hesitate to contact the contributors, whose addresses are listed at the back of the book, or other preservation professionals, who are available by contacting the American Institute for Conservation, listed in appendix 5.

The care of American Indian cultural items presents special challenges. These items are more often than not *composite objects*, made up of several different materials. Each material has different care needs, requiring that compromises and creative solutions be developed. Even more challenging, the care of these items raises questions about their spiritual and cultural nature and how to ensure that this aspect is respected and protected. I hope that an active dialogue can develop between Indian people and preservation professionals in order to discover ways to meet these challenges. Mostly, however, I hope that some of the basic information presented in this book will contribute, in a small way, to the care of these wonderful items and to the continuation of the American Indian cultures.

Just as the suggestions made in this book are derived from standard museum practice, so is the terminology. The word *preservation* as it is used here refers to "the protection of cultural property through activities that minimize chemical and physical deterioration and damage and that prevent loss of informational content."[1] Some of the activities referred to include keeping items and their storage areas clean, displaying items under appropriate conditions, and choosing storage containers and mounts that are chemically stable and that adequately support items.

These general activities are usually carried out in museums by *preservation professionals* who can include curators, collections managers, registrars, conservators, scientists, teachers, and administrators. They have extensive specialized training that enables them to plan and implement preservation activities, conduct research, and perform treatments. They practice *conservation,* "the profession devoted to the preservation of cultural property for the future. Conservation activities include examination, documentation, treatment, and preventive care, supported by research and education."[2] These are the definitions suggested by the American Institute for Conservation of Historic and Artistic Works, which is the leading professional organization in the United States for preservation professionals. Other countries have similar organizations. The International Institute for Conservation of Historic and Artistic Works serves members from all over the world. Most of these organizations use similar definitions. An attempt has been made to avoid the use of technical terminology in this book as much as possible. Nevertheless, technical terms are sometimes used. These are defined where they appear in the text or in the glossary at the back of the book.

Notes

1. American Institute for Conservation of Historic and Artistic Works, *Directory* (Washington, D.C.: American Institute for Conservation of Historic and Artistic Works, 2001), 22.
2. Ibid., 21.

PART I

CULTURAL CONSIDERATIONS OF PRESERVATION

American Indian cultural items, like most things, deteriorate over time, and the deterioration cannot be stopped. It can take place slowly or rapidly, depending on the materials from which the items are made, the conditions under which they are stored, and how they are handled. Standard museum practice suggests several procedures to slow deterioration of all types of items. Standard practice, however, often fails to take into account cultural considerations. Museum staff, and conservators in particular, tend to apply the same standard procedures to all items regardless of the lifeways of the culture from which they come. The items are seen as artifacts, separate from their culture, rather than as cultural links between the past, present, and future. This can lead to strained relations between museum staff and American Indian people and, worse still, to inappropriate treatment and display of items. A general understanding of various cultural practices and points of view and a respect for these on the part of everyone involved are key to the appropriate care of American Indian cultural items.

For this reason, part 1 of this book is devoted to the cultural considerations of preservation. All the chapters in part 1 are written by American Indians. As they point out in the following pages, these considerations are relevant to Indians and non-Indians alike, although Indian people surely come to this topic with a greater understanding of it than do most non-Indian people.

1

Why Should American Indian Cultural Objects Be Preserved?

SVEN HAAKANSON JR. *(ALUTIIQ-SUGPIAQ)*

> *American Indians have been viewed as a vanishing people. What if our cultural objects had not been preserved? Memories are sparked by them, and we learn through the oral history of our elders. Objects assist in having memories flourish. Elders see objects, and then stories flow from them, and younger Indians learn.*
>
> *Museums as well as other institutions have stored and preserved not only cultural objects but the remains of our ancestors. We have been seen as a thing of the past. While there is absolutely no justification for desecrating human remains, what if the cultural objects had not been preserved? We all have the responsibility now to restore the dignity that has been denied to us as a people and to breath life into the cultural objects that have been preserved.*
>
> **KATHRYN "JODY" BEAULIEU** *(ANISHINABE/OJIBWE)*

The preservation of American Indian cultural objects from the past, present, and future will always challenge their owners, collectors, and makers. Who legally owns the objects, their copyright, and the knowledge? This is a question that continues to plague museums and Native communities across our country. I do not know if we will ever solve this issue, but in my opinion it depends on what we, as individual people, agree to do. It has been my experience over the past fifteen years of working in museums that it takes human connections to make positive changes happen. No one wants to see their history forgotten or destroyed, while everyone wants to see their material culture and human remains given proper respect and treated in a way that follows their traditional path.

When the Native American Graves Protection and Repatriation Act (NAGPRA) was signed into law by President George Bush on November 17, 1990, over five thousand museums were obligated to reexamine, catalog, and inform Native Americans about the objects they held in their collections. Museums were required to offer to return certain types of objects to Indian people. At first, staff and administrators at museums were angered. Then they were confused and frustrated because they did not know what types of objects they held in their collections. They did not know whether their objects fit the definitions of NAGPRA—if, for example, they were associated or unassociated funerary objects, sacred objects, or cultural patrimony. Also, many scientists and curators felt it was a loss to science for human remains to be returned for reinterment and an even greater loss to repatriate sacred objects. Now, thirteen years later, museums that undertook this process have learned a tremendous amount about contemporary American Indian cultures and about how they can respectfully handle human remains and cultural objects. Because of NAGPRA, collaborative efforts between museums and American Indians began and discussions followed about future exchanges, exhibitions,

and long-term projects that could educate the public and Natives themselves about their own histories.

But a major portion of objects held in museums does not fall under NAGPRA. During the past five hundred years, and especially in the past two hundred years, museums systematically built collections. Ritual objects, clothing, tools for hunting and transportation, and household utensils were collected to document as curiosity pieces what was assumed then to be the disappearing primitive societies of America. Little did the collectors or museums realize that their collections would hold far more value than just Native-made items of a disappearing people. Their collections would embody American Indian history, heritage, and cultural knowledge.

These collections, if realized and understood, contain implicit information and knowledge about how each Native group made and used its material culture. Most American Indian groups have lost much of this knowledge and can learn about it only from collections of items that are usually found in American and European museums. This is why museums play a very important role in the preservation of American Indian history. They are caretakers of objects that have proven to be a way for us to learn and understand our past traditions. Without these collections Natives would have an even harder time demonstrating their links to their prehistory and the heritage of their people.

I was asked why some objects should be preserved and to demonstrate what we can do to build long-lasting relationships with museums that allow for exchanges, loans, and more. Currently, as a director of a Native-run museum, my mission is to promote our traditional heritage, history, language, and cultural knowledge. The Alutiiq Museum and Archaeological Repository in Kodiak, Alaska, was founded in 1995, and within the past seven years we have had several archaeological collections returned. We now house over one hundred thousand items and manage four programs: *Alutiiq Word of the Week, Community Archaeology, Rural Schools Art Show,* and *Carving Traditions.* The first three received the Institute of Museum and Library Services 2000 National Award for Museum Service. We currently have a national traveling exhibition, *Looking Both Ways,* in a partnership with the Arctic Studies Center of the Smithsonian Institution, and we are working with several European museums on Alutiiq collections from the 1800s. We have benefited in a positive way from NAGPRA. More importantly, the Alutiiq people now know more about their heritage than ever before and understand the importance of preserving traditional knowledge, culture, and objects held in museums.

Russians occupied our region from 1784 to 1867, and the Alutiiq people were nearly exterminated during the first twenty years of this occupation. From 1784 to 1804 our population dropped over 80 percent, and we lost much of our cultural and traditional knowledge at that time. Then in 1867 the United States purchased Alaska. It was during the 1800s that Russians, Europeans, and Americans made collections of Alutiiq objects. Many were private collections, but over the years the items made their way into museum collections. The collections that are housed in museums across Europe, Canada, and the United

States have added a tremendous amount of information to the revitalization of our cultural knowledge and material culture. These objects are invaluable links to the understanding of our history.

For the past thirty years archaeological excavations have been conducted on Kodiak Island. These have allowed us to learn the depth of our history and have given us a broader understanding of what this type of research can do. One excavation in particular recovered over 35,000 objects, including wooden bowls, kayak parts, masks, baskets, human remains, bows, arrows, harpoons, and wooden shields. While extremely important, these collections of items are only fragments of what were hunting kits, tools, kayaks, household utensils, and buildings. We can only make educated guesses about the specific function and role that each object held within our culture and how it was constructed. Nevertheless, these fragments give us still more clues to our cultural past.

In the past ten years many Native groups across the United States have planned, developed, and built their own cultural centers and museums to care for and house the objects that fall under NAGPRA and to take pride in their own heritage. This has allowed Natives not only to promote and share their knowledge but to learn more about their history. For example, through a grant from the National Endowment for the Humanities, the Alutiiq Museum and the Arctic Studies Center of the Smithsonian Institution undertook a six-year collaborative project. They developed the traveling exhibit mentioned earlier titled *Looking Both Ways,* published a catalog, and produced educational packets and a compact disc on Alutiiq heritage. This was not a typical exhibition where curators displayed ethnographic objects and told us with written display labels what they were. Instead, the voices of our elders narrated what the objects are and what they mean to them as Alutiiq people. This linked the items to our living culture and history, giving life to what would otherwise be a snapshot from the past. My father, Sven Sr., is quoted in the exhibit, saying "you've got to look back and find out the past, and then you look forward." This statement embodies what *Looking Both Ways* has done as an exhibition and for us. We have examined our past, through ethnographic objects, oral histories, and archaeological data, learned from these sources, and are building a deeper understanding of our history for our future.

Are Natives and museums to argue over the objects that do not fall under NAGPRA as they have previously over those that do? I pray not, because this will only further divide our abilities to work together in preserving and protecting our national, cultural, and local histories for our future generations. What is important is that we continue to develop relationships that are win-win situations. We need museums to continue caring for and promoting our heritages, and they need us to inform them about the objects they house, what they symbolize, and how they were made, used, and treated.

We have several challenges to meet and goals to achieve in the future. We need to convey that American Indian cultural items are more than objects of art or representations of primitive peoples. They are cultural links between the past, present, and future for specific groups of people. Additionally they may be

the only history we have for these Native peoples. The items contain implicit information about how traditional materials were made into objects that were used everyday to fulfill both practical and ceremonial needs. What we can learn from these items is how our ancestors viewed their world, how they treated animals, and how they respected their ancestors. Most important, we can use these items to preserve our culture and to bring this knowledge into a living context that continues to be passed on from generation to generation, rather than tucked away in a book, archived, or hidden in a museum collection.

2

Handling Considerations: One Person's Story

JOAN CELESTE THOMAS *(KIOWA)*

As a museum professional I have been taught the standard museum way to handle the collections in my care. For example, always use two hands when carrying an item, and never pick up a framed work of art with one hand, and the list goes on. But as both a museum professional and a member of the Kiowa Tribe, I bring another element into how I interact with items—the cultural element. Looking at items from a cultural aspect is an important part of who I am as an American Indian woman from the Plains.

I grew up listening to stories my grandmother told of the old ways. She was brought up by her grandmother, who was very traditional and lived through a time of great change for our people during the late nineteenth century and the early part of the twentieth. She instilled in me a respect and deep appreciation for our Kiowa traditions. I was taught respect for my elders and to listen and use the information they wished to pass on to me. She also stressed aspects of our culture of which only certain individuals should possess knowledge. This has always made me a little different from my non-Native colleagues, as I do not automatically assume I should be given all the cultural information regarding an item in a collection. Also, I question why an item has become part of a museum or personal collection, thus removing it from its cultural context, and why it is now being used in ways it was never intended.

My grandmother also made sure I was aware that traditions and ways of doing things varied with each tribal group. I was never to assume that everyone did things as we Kiowa did. She always said to be respectful of other cultures when among them, and to observe their ways and listen carefully when told how to conduct myself. I believe this to be true whether you are working with an American Indian collection or any collection outside your own cultural group.

While I was growing up, I did not realize how much a part of my life these teachings were, and how these ways of doing things would affect the way

I relate to my profession. When I started working in museums, the Native American Graves Protection and Repatriation Act was only a dream, and working in a museum could be like walking through a cultural minefield when working directly with collections. In fact, for a time I was reluctant to work with ethnographic items because of past experiences coming across items that should never have left their cultural group, or that I as a Kiowa woman had no business knowing about, let alone being asked to handle. In those days few people knew what traditional care of objects was, or could even be bothered with the concept. This has changed. Now before an item is handled, questions are asked about who should move it, how it should be moved, and how it should be stored. Most importantly, Native people are being asked to make suggestions as to how we in the museum profession can better work with Native items in our care.

As a museum professional of Kiowa descent, my first question is always, Should I even be involved in handling this particular object? If for cultural reasons I feel uncomfortable, I will discuss this with an appropriate tribal member and also relay my concerns to my supervisor. I have been fortunate in my career to work with culturally sensitive individuals who understand my reason for concern when I come into contact with certain items in museum collections.

What the museum professional can give to the tribal caregiver is suggestions on handling objects, such as providing support when moving an item, or keeping it away from light and dust. Most Native caregivers are already doing this for their own collections. I am not going to suggest here the standard museum methods for handling objects, as other chapters discuss these. Rather I will offer some guidelines I use when handling items that may be culturally sensitive.

With regard to storing objects and handling them, always try to find out as much as you can about their origins. Even if you know only the general area or cultural group from which a particular object originates, this will give you a better idea of how to interact with it. If you know that a particular cultural group prefers that only males handle or move this type of item, you have the opportunity to find the appropriate staff person to move the item. For example, in the event the item must be moved or handled, I find a male staff member to do this for me. To my mind this is the best solution. I also believe very strongly that by relating to the items in your collection within their cultural context, you are enriched as a museum professional and, more importantly, as a person.

It is vital to follow guidelines from various tribal groups in the proper handling of their objects. To that end I always try to be open when colleagues ask me about my own tribal traditions and how we view handling certain objects. There are, of course, some items I will not discuss, and in a gentle way I let my colleagues know this is something about which I cannot comment.

Much of what we learn as museum professionals in the care and handling of objects comes down to what my grandfather referred to as "horse sense," and I have found this to be true. Follow your common sense and you will rarely go wrong. Whether you are dealing with a delicate portion of beadwork or a sturdy wooden bowl, you should always be aware of how the item is made and its condition. Are there loose strings on the beadwork, and will it lie flat? Are there any visible cracks in the wooden bowl? In most cases, taking the time to visually inspect the object with which you are working will give you the answers to your questions on how to move or store it.

In one museum, I worked with a beautiful basket collection. When moving the baskets, we made sure they were fully supported on the bottom and, if needed, along the sides. We were careful not to abrade the surface materials of the basket. In the case of an especially important basket, we created a custom box to house it with supports inside to maintain the basket's shape and prevent damage when moving it. I usually wear either cotton gloves or some type of nitrile or latex gloves when working with collections. I have seen what oils from hands can do even over a short period of time to basket fibers and especially metals.

Another example of cultural considerations for handling American Indian items is illustrated in the following experience my colleagues and I had when preparing to install a large project involving many items of both historic and contemporary southeastern American Indian origin. At the museum our primary goal in our collections management program was to interact with items in our care in a culturally correct manner. This meant we observed certain rules where appropriate when handling items. Because my Indian colleagues and I had been provided information in the past that did not seem culturally correct to us, we now chose to consult several people who were familiar with the cultural norms for these particular items. We consulted with members of the tribe of the items' origin and surrounding area who we thought would give us culturally accurate information. We felt it was crucial that all the items be looked at from their own cultural context.

Since we had outside workers making the mounts for all the items going on display, we needed to relay to them the cultural sensitivities we had learned about. Once we explained the cultural concerns we had, they had no problem following our recommendations regarding how they would interact with certain materials. One of the requests we made was that no premenopausal women come into direct contact with certain items. We also asked as a sign of cultural respect that no abrasive language be used around the items. We were open to discussion and tried to answer all the questions they had. We listened and had a free exchange of ideas about how they felt about these restrictions and how we would work together. To a person they indicated that they believed they learned more and had a better appreciation for the items they came into contact with than they had experienced on any other "job." This project had become more than just a job for them. They felt invested in trying to do the right thing when looking at and handling these particular American Indian objects.

It is important to note here that the cultural rules we followed in this situation apply only to items from a specific tribe. Other tribes may have different rules that need to be followed. Always contact the tribe of an item's origin

to determine the appropriate way to handle it. By going to the source in a respectful way, you will usually get the accurate information you need.

The museum and collector should always be aware when adding to their collections that the items they are handling are from a living and vibrant culture. No object exists within a cultural vacuum. There are people who care deeply about how you are handling, displaying, and storing the cultural material in your care. I can speak only as a Kiowa in the profession, but I have been enriched as a human being by working with tribal elders and historians to learn how they wish their items to be treated. I come from a specific background as a Plains Indian woman, and I know I cannot speak for other tribal groups, and it would be inappropriate for me to do so.

When handling museum items, I always try to use the principles I have discussed here, which enable me both to do my job and show respect for the cultural materials with which I come into contact.

The Voice of the Museum: Developing Displays

POLLYANNA NORDSTRAND ***(HOPI)***

While collections are often a museum's greatest resource, people experience museums primarily through their displays. The general public probably has little understanding of the museum's role in collections care and views the museum as a place to see things. And so a display's most important role is as a tool for communicating with the public. In an attempt to demystify museums, the current trend in exhibit development is to present information that supports a "big idea" and has a point of view. This is a dramatic shift from the past method of displaying a huge selection of a collection simply organized by group, especially when it comes to American Indian collections. Indian communities had a part in this change of attitude toward displays. Even before the Native American Graves Protection and Repatriation Act (NAGPRA), less formal consultation processes allowed for Indian perspectives to inform the shape of exhibits. The recent growth in the number of tribal museums reflects the need for alternative perspectives to American Indian exhibits in mainstream museums. Museums, as public places, provide us all with an opportunity to experience things that we might not otherwise in our personal lives.

Why Is It Important to Display American Indian Objects?

We experience inspiration and wonder by seeing American Indian objects. They may represent a personal or spiritual expression, a connection to our past, a distant landscape. In the context of an exhibit, objects take on importance because they provide evidence of these things and are seen as the truth. Museums have a voice. In fact, we often hush as we enter. Is it so that we can hear the stories that are there?

I delight in finding the juxtaposition of a fine Hopi ceramic vase and early-twentieth-century American glass. I feel the buoyant rise of pride. And now I am not so quiet. The exhibit gives me the chance to share my feelings

with the friend who accompanied me to the museum. I kneel down to see the name on the bottom of the vase (so glad it is displayed on a glass shelf). This potter's mother was the renowned Nampeyo. And my grandmother used to play on their front step. Perhaps other visitors (not Indian) see a vase like the one in their grandmother's collection. They remember a story she told them. The two vases seem so different. Yet both represent a refined beauty. Maybe my grandmother had a glass vase like one of these. Maybe our grandmothers had an occasion to meet.

I leave the case thinking of the journey of this vase from the Southwest desert to this East Coast museum. I wonder about the role of the Indian Arts and Crafts Board in the lives of artists. What role did the Museum of Modern Art's early exhibit of American Indian art have in the development of museum collections? That may be the first time Indian items were exhibited in an art context rather than an ethnographic one. This vase is the only American Indian object that I find separate from the primary display of American Indian objects (all labeled as art). I remember its shape distinctly (unusual, but I had seen one like it before). It also gave me an important story.

What Are Some Considerations in the Display of American Indian Objects?

The selection of objects for display needs careful consideration. What cannot be ignored in the discussion of the display of American Indian objects is the balance of cultural considerations and the museum's goals. This is especially important in light of the not-so-balanced approach museums have historically taken. What first comes to mind is the conflict between culturally sensitive information protected by Indian communities and a museum's role as a public institution. In many Indian communities, some knowledge is seen as a privilege for the few, not a right for all. Objects as well as images are integral to this knowledge, especially in ceremonial use. Too often museums have not respected this tradition and have recklessly displayed sensitive items that were never created for public view. This has led to suspicion within Indian communities, even of their own tribal museums. Exhibits that rely heavily on sacred material have also led to suspicion within Indian communities.

When beginning an exhibit project, you may want to approach the selection of objects by first analyzing your own point of view. Do you see this object as a work of art? As a historic artifact? As a living being? What was the maker's intention in creating this object? Did he or she intend for it to be displayed? Or even preserved beyond its original use? You may also want to consider how your point of view influences the story you are telling the audience. If a ceremonial item is displayed for its aesthetic qualities, are you providing accurate information to the audience?

Many tribes have developed guidelines for the display of sensitive items. These guidelines may call for special mounting, removal at certain times of the year, or exclusion from display altogether. Some items may require special care while on display, such as feedings. The guidelines can be requested from tribal councils, cultural preservation officers, or repatriation coordinators. Some tribes also request copies of exhibit plans for review. It is not safe to assume that all tribes share the same understanding about object care and handling.

Consultation and Collaboration

During exhibit development projects, museums have the opportunity to gain community support by increasing awareness of the museum's function. For instance, members of the community may avoid the museum because they fear the possibility that human remains are being housed in the building. The introduction of an exhibit project at a community meeting allows the museum staff to provide accurate information about the museum's collection. Further community participation offers opportunities for learning about collections care and the importance of museums for preservation. This awareness is especially important for tribal museums that require the financial support of their communities.

There is a great difference between consultation and collaboration. Your museum should establish goals of consultation before beginning a project. A simple method of consultation is to provide written statements of the museum's intention and exhibit plans to the tribal leadership. Even though this method is sound and may avoid some future conflicts, it may not lead to a fruitful relationship. If the goal is to build a long-lasting relationship with the community, a more involved collaborative process should be developed.

Members of the Minnesota Historical Society's Indian Advisory Committee meet with the Society's Head of Museum Collections. *Left to right:* Jeff Savage (Ojibwe), Victoria Raske (Ojibwe), Marcia Anderson, Kathryn "Jody" Beaulieu (Anishinabe/Ojibwe), David Aubid (Ojibwe), Joseph Campbell (Dakota).

A collaboration is a mutually beneficial process and begins by identifying how the desired outcomes will be accomplished for all involved, not just the museum. Museum employees may have access to resources that tribal members do not. The process should be sensitive to limited resources. The process should also provide ample time for appropriate review to take place. Some tribes may require the tribal council to review and approve a plan; the council may meet infrequently. The most appropriate person to review may be difficult to reach. Travel may be difficult to coordinate at certain times of the year due to weather or ceremonies.

Collaborative projects that are widely inclusive allow for a diversity of perspectives to be represented in the museum. When conflicting interests impede inclusiveness and collaboration, you might approach the problem by acknowledging the diversity of perspectives. A common conflict is between scientific explanation and oral histories. These can easily be placed side by side to allow the audience to compare and evaluate for themselves.

The realities of tribal politics cannot be ignored. It is important to seek out the official tribal representative for certain types of consultation. This person has usually been authorized by the elected tribal government and may

change with new administrations. At times the perspective of the current official may differ from the past official. New decisions may have been made regarding sensitive items. Tribes and tribal members may have disputes beyond the scope of an exhibit project. Your museum may need to seek separate consultation with each tribe or individual.

Interpretation of Collections

Museums use several methods for interpreting their collection. Think back to the vase. There are a number of stories that it could tell in a variety of exhibits: the design could tell the migration story of a certain clan; the artist, a personality within the story; the object, a work of art to be enjoyed for its form; the artifact, a record of a point in time. Interpretation offers a way for the audience to become engaged in your collection. Your perspective in developing the exhibit offers a point of view for the audience to approach the subject. Just as you give careful consideration to the selection of objects, you should think with sensitivity about the information that is being conveyed. There are many stories to tell about Indian communities that do not violate the sacred.

Exhibits organized around themes or specific stories rely on specific types of objects. Collections have their strengths and weaknesses. Some museums have had to acquire new collections in order to develop exhibits about contemporary American Indian communities, since their collection may not have contained objects from later than around 1930. Tribal museums have the opportunity to involve their communities by borrowing objects and images from them for display. Images and oral histories are valuable resources in the telling of stories.

Your museum also has a primary audience. The exhibit you develop for the local tribal community might be very different than the exhibit for the tourist audience. In developing an exhibit, begin by considering what it is that you want to communicate to your audience. Museums of all kinds are now seeking ways to encourage their communities to become involved. Exhibits offer an opportunity to build bridges with these communities. They offer an opportunity for the community to share in the process and find value in their own collections (objects, images, and stories).

Additional Reading

Raphael, Toby. *Exhibition Conservation Guidelines: Incorporating Conservation into Exhibit Planning, Design and Fabrication.* Washington, D.C.: National Park Service, Division of Conservation, 1999.

Wedll, Joycelyn. "Learn about Our Past to Understand Our Future: The Story of the Mille Lacs Band of Ojibwe," in *The Changing Presentation of the American Indian: Museums and Native Cultures,* 89–98. Washington, D.C.: Smithsonian Institution, 2000.

Welsh, Peter H. "The Way to Independence: A New Way to Interpret Native American Collections," in *Ideas and Images: Developing Interpretive History Exhibits,* edited by Kenneth L. Ames, Barbara Franco, and L. Thomas Frye, 31–64. Nashville, Tenn.: American Association for State and Local History, 1992.

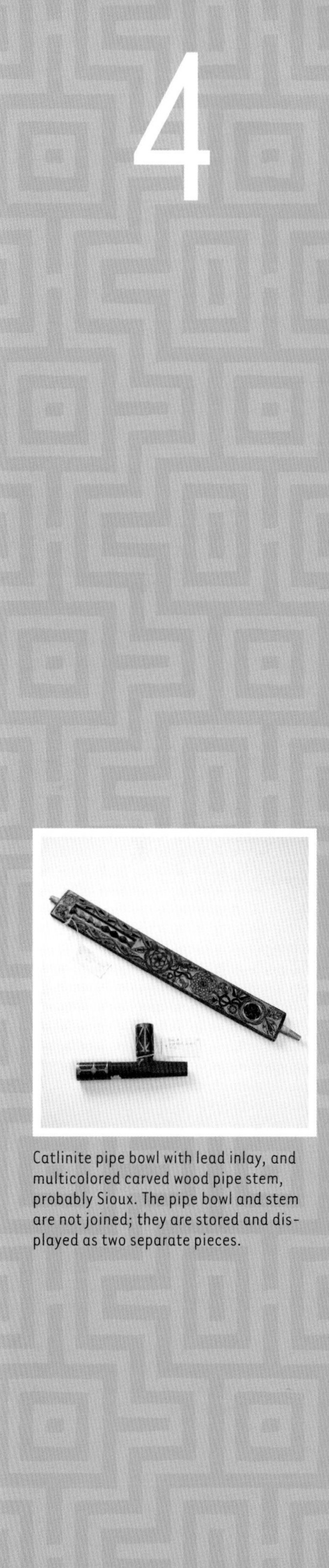

Catlinite pipe bowl with lead inlay, and multicolored carved wood pipe stem, probably Sioux. The pipe bowl and stem are not joined; they are stored and displayed as two separate pieces.

Display in a Proper and Respectful Way

INTERVIEW WITH LAINE THOM *(SHOSHONE/GOSHIUTE/PAIUTE)*

What do you think people should know about displaying American Indian cultural items? What is most important?

American Indian cultural items should be combined with historical and contemporary photographs and graphic text of Native peoples, narrative and commentarial, relevant to the themes of the exhibit. The result of such an exhibit would be an important method of learning the ways of life of Native peoples, historically and now. It is important to display items in such a way that their past history and current use are understood in the context of the lifeways of Native peoples.

What does it mean to be displayed with respect?

Ceremonial items that do not meet the definitions of the Native American Graves Protection and Repatriation Act (NAGPRA) should be displayed in specific ways and with respect. These are items that are ceremonial but not sacred. Generally, sacred items should not be displayed, in my opinion. The fact that items are "ceremonial" and were and are used as such should serve as a guideline in terms of defining "respect" and "specific ways." As in the case of pipes, the bowl and stem should be separated; the only time the pipe is connected is when it is used in ceremony.

How do American Indian cultural items differ from non-Indian items with regard to display and tribal use? Are there some pieces that are on display that would be returned or loaned back to Indian people to be used in certain ceremonies?

Among Native Americans, there is no word for *art*. The items we are discussing were not created for artistic purpose. There is no separation between what is beautiful and functional.

When most non–Native American persons view these items behind glass, they think that what they are looking at is from the past and frozen in time.

However, they aren't, because much of the time many of the items are still used by contemporary Native people. People who own heirloom pieces often bring out the pieces and use them for social gatherings and for religious purposes as well, as I do with my own personal collection. I have quite a large collection of Shoshonian material. There are a few museums that want what I have, but I'm not ready to let go of them as I still utilize these items ceremonially.

Possibly in the future, when I get older, I'd like to will out what I have to a tribal museum. If you can use heirloom pieces that you have inherited, I don't believe that you should turn over those pieces to a cultural museum yet. Maybe on short-term loan, but not to be given.

If people are unsure of how to display items properly and with respect, perhaps they should contact appropriate tribal members.

Right. I think people would *have* to contact the tribes to get their input on how these items should be displayed. What I'm talking about here is contacting Native American elders, museum specialists/curators, advisory boards, and community representatives of various tribes, and if possible the tribe associated with the specific item that one has questions about.

Do you think this is a good idea? Do you think people should do this?

I think so. I think it's *very* important. And I think tribes should always be contacted to work with the displays in the museums.

This puts the burden of responsibility on tribal members to respond to requests for help and to provide guidance. Would tribal members be willing to do this?

I think so. If you contact them repeatedly and in a respectful manner, most would be more than happy to help an individual in a museum.

Why do you think it is important for American Indians to display their cultural items?

A museum is a place where all people can learn about a culture and its ways of life—can learn the ways of life of Native Americans in the past and the way it is now.

I believe that because Native American culture is dynamic and always changing, Native ways of thinking in the past, present, and future are connected. Items used in ceremonies from the past are still utilized by contemporary Native American people today. Whatever the item is, it is "alive" and full of spirit. These items connect past, present, and future.

Museums are a way to preserve our culture and for our younger generation to learn about this culture too.

5

What About Sacred Objects?

ALYCE SADONGEI *(KIOWA/TOHONO O'ODHAM)*

The presence of American Indian sacred objects in museums continues to raise questions about their preservation and care for museum professionals and American Indian communities. These questions, which relate to standard collections management and conservation, speak to the diversity of tribal cultural practice and acknowledge the tensions that exist between predominately Western standards of collections care and tribal cultural practices. How should these objects be cared for while in museums, and who prescribes the care?

In the years following the passage of the Native American Graves Protection and Repatriation Act (NAGPRA), museum professionals have become increasingly aware of the significance that some cultural objects have for American Indian communities. Through consultations, museums have had the opportunity to hear directly from tribal representatives about their preferences for storing, displaying, and caring for tribal objects. The steady growth of tribal museums and cultural centers over the past ten to fifteen years has also presented these organizations with similar challenges of how to care for objects. In this chapter I discuss some of the issues regarding the care of sacred objects in museum collections.

Museums, by their very nature, isolate objects from human societies in order to preserve them for future generations. Some may argue that museums are changing, especially in light of the collaboration and increased communication that NAGPRA has led to among tribal communities and museums, and the unique methods of museum practice that tribes are employing in their own cultural institutions. The removal of objects from their original contexts, however, is key to this discussion, and it continues to be an underlying tenet of the museum field. Sacred objects in museum collections have been lifted from their original context to further the museum's goal of preservation or education, not to further their fulfillment as sacred objects.

Recent research into the nature of sacred collections suggests that it is possible to view sacred objects in light of their original purpose by using the following general categories of use: Physical Use, Symbolic Use, and Life End-

ing Use. Physical Use implies that the sacred object requires handling or physical touch by a knowledgeable religious or cultural practitioner to engage the object's sacred attributes. Symbolic Use suggests that the object may not possess sacred attributes but is culturally significant to the tribal community based on its age, association with a ceremony or a historic tribal leader, or even craftsmanship. Life Ending Use is employed by religious or cultural practitioners to ritually end the life of an object in order to cease its sacred attributes.

Undoubtedly tribal and non-tribal museum professionals have been able to observe some of these different categories of use in the museum, especially if they have engaged in consultations with tribal representatives. Tribal museum professionals may recognize these types of special use from their own tribal traditions. The categories are very simple and are outlined here to provide a minimal sense of the different uses or contexts sacred objects have for tribal communities. Museum professionals may find the conceptualizations of use helpful in clarifying different care practices.

Some non-tribal museums have elected to apply tribal cultural practices to their existing collections care policies. In some instances, tribal religious leaders have carefully instructed these museums about the care of objects. In other cases, museum staff have observed or witnessed the practices of tribal representatives who have offered to care for the objects. Regardless of how these practices have been learned, it is important for non-tribal museums to know the difference between *active practice* and *passive accommodation.*

Active practice is reserved behavior that only a knowledgeable religious or cultural practitioner can engage in with regard to formal interactions with the sacred object. It is important to remember that the handling of sacred objects is not arbitrary for tribal communities. Generally, only certain individuals with the proper training and authority can handle objects that are imbued with great religious or supernatural attributes. *Passive accommodation* allows the museum staff to accommodate the active practice of a religious or cultural practitioner.

For example, a group of tribal representatives accompanied by one of their recognized religious leaders asks to see an object in the museum's collection that they consider to be sacred and imbued with its own life essence. Upon seeing the object, the religious leader reaches for it, opens it, and begins to use the contents. Before the object is put away, the practitioner may ask the museum staff if an offering, provided by the practitioner, can be placed near the object for a period of time.

The key to this scenario is that the practitioner, *not* the museum staff, engaged the object or employed active practice. Also, the offering is specifically made *by the practitioner* to the object. The offering is *not made or provided by museum staff.* If the museum staff choose to leave the offering on or near the object, they are passively accommodating the request of the practitioner.

During the past several years, numerous articles and presentations at professional meetings have suggested guidelines for methods of ritual care, such as feeding, the placement of an offering, gender restrictions, and handling guidelines, which can be codified and used by museums. It is appropriate for museums to consider that by incorporating ritual elements of care into existing collections management practices, museum staff are essentially prescribing religious practice that should be relegated to individuals who have knowledge of such rites. In most cases, tribal representatives are requesting that museums offer passive accommodation; they are not asking museum staff to conduct rituals on their behalf once they leave the museum.

Given the wide variety of tribal religious practices and worldviews, it is essential that museums refrain from applying what they learn from specific tribal representatives to other objects in the collection that have not been the focus of consultation. Further, museums should not second-guess the authority or the recommendations of the tribal representatives they are consulting in regard to learning the best way to care for sacred objects. On the other hand, museums should not incorporate tribal methods of care or indicate their willingness to do so if the museum lacks the resources to carry out recommendations.

Tribal museums that are created by and for their communities are in the best situation to provide tribally specific methods of care to sacred and significant objects in their collection. Usually, tribally specific museums hold collections with which they are directly associated, thus eliminating the need to generalize on the nature or purpose of an object. Tribal protocols can prevail and can dictate other methods of museum practice, such as using the tribe's language in accession and catalog records. Consultation with tribal religious leaders and practitioners is the most effective method that museums, tribal and non-tribal, can use to determine what special care an object may require, should it stay in the museum.

Since the passage of NAGPRA, museums have sought to "do the right thing" by engaging in repatriation consultations and opening the door to dialogue that offers alternatives to collections care. Sacred objects, however, often require special care that cannot be reduced to a list of "do's and don'ts." The very notion of sacred is not static and, in fact, is subject to change. While having such a list or guidelines is appealing, it simplifies the profound nature and purpose of these objects.

For virtually all sacred and significant objects in museum collections, tribal or non-tribal, the type of care is subject to the context in which the objects are currently situated. In the post-NAGPRA years, neutrality can be the most important form of respect that museums can demonstrate.

Neutrality takes into account the diversity of human belief and cultural expression and acknowledges that no single belief is privileged over another. For museum professionals, this means providing effective museum standards of care. In those cases where a relationship is established with knowledgeable religious and cultural practitioners and where resources are available, museums should also passively accommodate tribal cultural practice, until such time when the object returns to the community where its purpose is activated and fulfilled.

PART II

GENERAL PRESERVATION CONSIDERATIONS

In part 1 the authors show how cultural considerations can pervade every aspect of an item's care. In part 2 the authors make suggestions for the general care of collections. These suggestions are based on standard museum practice. You will need to consider the cultural priorities of the items in your care and adapt the general care suggestions as needed.

Medicine men often ask those in charge of the care of cultural items to do things that are not part of accepted museum practice. Often medicine men understand this, but they must do some things to preserve the culture. Every tribe is different. This situation should be pointed out; it should be stated so everyone recognizes that this issue exists. In my institution we often make an adjustment or try to strike a balance. For example, we store sacred items separately and allow them to be smudged. It is important to be sensitive to what the local people say because we need to preserve the culture.

MARCELLA CASH ***(SICANGU/LAKOTA)***

6

The Causes of Deterioration and Preventive Care

SHERELYN OGDEN

Our cultural objects are part of our lifeways, which we pass on from generation to generation. Times change. These cultural objects give an idea of what it was like in a previous time. They tell us who we are.

CHAR TULLIE *(DINÉ/NAVAJO)*

Deterioration is a natural process that cannot usually be stopped; it can only be slowed. American Indian cultural items, like everything else, are susceptible to this process.

Several factors contribute to deterioration, and these factors are interrelated, with one increasing the severity of another. Being familiar with the causes of deterioration is the first step in slowing the process. Once the causes are known, ways to reduce deterioration can be incorporated into tribal care practices as appropriate given the cultural needs of the items.

The emphasis in this chapter and in the three that follow is on *preventive care,* the measures that reduce or prevent deterioration. This chapter and the following ones on storage, handling, and housekeeping all focus primarily on preventive care of items in storage, while chapter 11 addresses preventive care of items used for display. Conservation treatment to repair damage caused by deterioration can be costly and is beyond the financial resources available in many situations. Preventive care, however, is a realistic goal. For example, the safe storage and handling of items are easily accomplished and relatively inexpensive. Most of the guidelines described here can be applied to the storage and handling of items in museums, cultural centers, or private homes, and several of them cost little or nothing.

American Indian people have used tribal care practices and techniques to care for their cultural items for generations. Many of these methods and techniques are analogous to the preventive care methods followed in museums. I hope that some of the methods and techniques suggested in this and the following chapters will be useful additions to the tribal care practices already in use by Indian people and will contribute further to the preservation of these important items.

Composite Nature

Many American Indian cultural items are composite objects. As used here, this term means that they are made up of different materials. For example, a dance stick may be made of wood, feathers, fur, sinew, skin, and metal beads. A cradle board may be made of wood, buckskin, glass beads, sinew, and brass tacks. Or a pair of leggings may be made of skin, porcupine quill, shells, bone, beads, and thread. The composite nature of American Indian items often contributes to their deterioration. The various materials of which the items are made have different and conflicting preservation needs. Also the materials frequently interact with each other in damaging ways. This makes their preservation particularly challenging since what is beneficial for one material in an item may not be for another. Preservation becomes a judgment call, a balancing act, a compromise.

I worked with an item once that contained most everything. It was a pipe with a bowl made of pipestone and a stem made of wood covered with buckskin. Brass tacks held the buckskin in place. The pipe had a mallard duck's breast, quill-wrapped sinew, blue glass beads, red and white heart glass beads, brass beads, eagle feathers, and ribbons. The brass tacks corroded, causing a green powder to stain the buckskin, and the mallard breast developed insects.

FAITH BAD BEAR *(CROW/SIOUX)*

Above: Ojibwe black cotton blouse with metal tinkler cones, small round mirrors, five-point metal stars, strung beads, flat shiny buttons, round clear buttons, and brass jingle bells. **Right:** Mandan/Hidatsa scapula hoe made of bone, sinew, and wood, scratched and chipped from normal use.

These two items illustrate the composite nature of many American Indian items.

Natural Instability

Many items deteriorate because they are made of materials that are naturally unstable or incompatible (see sidebar). *Inherent vice* is a term used by preservation professionals to refer to this chemical or structural instability of the materials that compose an item. Little can be done to slow the deterioration caused by inherent vice. The best way to lessen its effect is to control the other causes of deterioration as much as possible, which, in turn, will slow the effects of inherent vice.

Ojibwe birch-bark and basswood wastebasket with unidentified wood rim reinforcement, made for sale at the Mille Lacs Indian Trading Post, Onamia, Minnesota. Notice the splitting, peeling birch bark.

- Many American Indian scrolls, storage containers, boats, and structures are made from birch bark. The layers of this material split and peel over time, causing the items made from it to split, delaminate, and fall apart.
- Iron beads are sometimes attached to items with sinew. The natural oils in the sinew tend to corrode iron beads, resulting in what looks like a powdery rust. This in turn causes the sinew to weaken and eventually break, and the beads to fall off the item to which they were originally attached.
- Certain types of glass beads develop white crystals because of the particular chemical composition of the glass. This is commonly referred to as glass disease and can cause the beads to become completely disfigured or broken.
- Damaging acids form in paper from certain components used in the manufacturing process, especially alum-rosin size and wood fibers containing lignin. This results in paper that becomes weak, brittle, and discolored over time. American Indian drawings in ledger and autograph books as well as paper documents can be susceptible to this.

Temperature and Relative Humidity

Inappropriate levels of temperature and relative humidity promote deterioration. In general, cool and dry conditions are best.

AVOID EXTREMES

High heat and humidity speed deterioration and encourage mold growth and insect activity. Extremely low relative humidity, which can occur in winter in centrally heated buildings and year-round in arid climates, leads to splitting, drying out, or embrittlement of certain materials. While some materials from which American Indian items are made are particularly affected by either high or low extremes of temperature and humidity, a few other materials are affected by both extremes. Skin is one example. It can become hard or soft, dry or sticky, flexible or stiff, depending on its tannage and the levels of temperature and humidity under which it is stored.

AVOID FLUCTUATIONS

Fluctuations in temperature and relative humidity can also be damaging. Many materials are hygroscopic, readily absorbing and releasing moisture. They respond to daily and seasonal changes in temperature and relative humidity by expanding and contracting. These dimensional changes accelerate deterioration and can lead to visible damage. It is important to note that relative humidity is dependent on temperature; if one changes, the other changes as well.

Ojibwe wood and skin hand drum. The torn skin drumhead is a result of differential dimensional changes caused by temperature and humidity fluctuations.

MATERIALS SENSITIVE TO HIGH RELATIVE HUMIDITY

Materials that are especially sensitive to high relative humidity include textiles, skin and skin products, metal, paper, wood, and fibers. These are commonly found in such items as garments, ledger books, drawings, baskets, bags, pouches, quivers, footwear, weapons, shields, and parfleches.

MATERIALS SENSITIVE TO LOW RELATIVE HUMIDITY

Materials that are especially sensitive to low relative humidity include quills, wood, skin and skin products, and fibers. These are commonly found in such items as outfits, drums, bags, pouches, shields, and parfleches.

CONTROL CONDITIONS

The ideal storage space has climate controls that are able to maintain generally accepted levels of temperature and relative humidity. Climate control equipment ranges in complexity from a simple room air conditioner, humidifier, and/or dehumidifier to a central, buildingwide system that filters, cools, heats, humidifies, and dehumidifies the air (HVAC [Heating, Ventilation, Air Conditioning] system). If you are able to acquire a buildingwide system, it is advisable to seek the guidance of an experienced climate-control engineer prior to selection and installation of the equipment. Whatever sort of controls you have, it is best to operate them full time. Avoid turning them off nights, weekends, holidays, or other times when people are not in the space. This could lead to fluctuations and damage to the items.

Note that in certain climates generally accepted museum preservation levels of temperature and relative humidity may damage the structure of the building in which the items are housed. Choices and compromises may be unavoidable.

Less costly measures can be taken to control the temperature and relative humidity:

- Keep buildings well maintained.
- Seal cracks in buildings as soon as they appear, particularly in the walls, floors, and windows.
- Attach weather stripping to doors and windows.
- In areas that experience cold weather, seal windows on the inside with plastic sheets and tape.
- In spaces used exclusively for storage, seal windows more completely using both wallboard and plastic.

When it is not possible to control conditions in the entire storage space, highly sensitive items can be kept in a smaller enclosed space, such as a storage cabinet or a box, where conditions can be controlled to a limited extent by the use of humidity-buffering materials. Such a space is commonly referred to as a microenvironment (see chapter 11 for more information). One type of humidity-buffering material is silica gel, a commercially available granular form of silica that can be conditioned to maintain a specific level of humidity in a closed container. Paper (tissue), cloth (muslin, towels, or sheets), and cardboard also work as buffers that limit fluctuations, but to a lesser degree. It is important that these materials meet preservation standards, which are discussed in chapter 7, on storage.

WHAT SHOULD CONDITIONS BE?

The ideal temperature and relative humidity differ for various materials. A frequent recommendation in keeping with standard museum preservation practice that is suitable for mixed collections, like those of American Indian items, is a stable temperature no higher than 70°F and a stable relative humidity between a minimum of 30 percent and a maximum of 50 percent. Research indicates that relative humidities at the lower end of this range are preferable because deterioration then progresses at a slower rate. Some materials, however, such as items made from wood or skin, require a higher relative humidity. In general, the lower the temperature the better. Note that maintaining *stable* conditions is very important. It is better to maintain conditions that are less than ideal but do not fluctuate. If this is not possible, less stringent conditions can be chosen for the most extreme times of the year, such as summer and winter, with gradual changes in temperature and humidity between these times.

An exception to this recommendation applies to those geographic areas where conditions do not often fall within this recommended range. One example is certain parts of the southwestern United States, where the relative humidity is often below 30 percent. Other examples are the Pacific Northwest and the southeastern United States, where conditions are often more humid than recommended. Items that have been kept in the same temperature and humidity conditions since they were made have probably acclimated to these conditions. If the conditions are changed to match more closely the recommendation above, damage may occur to the items. In extreme cases, parts of the items may shrink, crack, or burst.

When deciding on the best temperature and relative humidity range for your collection, consider your geographic area and the average temperature and relative humidity there. Also, examine your cultural items. If they do not appear to have suffered from the effects of extremes of temperature and relative humidity, you can assume that they have acclimated to their environment. It is probably better to keep them in the conditions to which they are acclimated than to change the conditions to match the recommendation. Note that if you expect your items to be sent on loan to another area where the conditions are different, damage may occur to them unless you provide a controlled microenvironment for them while they are on loan. The same is true for items you borrow from another area.

MONITORING IS IMPORTANT

Ideally the temperature and relative humidity should be systematically measured and recorded. These measurements will tell you what the conditions actually are, justify a request you may make to install equipment, or let you know if equipment you already have is operating properly and producing the desired conditions. Various instruments are available that measure temperature and relative humidity. These range in price and complexity. The choice you make depends on your resources and needs. When selecting monitoring equipment, you may want to contact a preservation professional for advice on what would work best in your particular situation.

- The covers of ledger books warp, and the pages cockle (ripple) when humidity increases, and flatten out again when it lessens.
- Skin parfleches expand and contract with changing humidity, causing the skin to cockle (buckle) and warp; in extreme cases, loosely adhered paint can flake off the surface.
- Wood swells and shrinks with fluctuating humidity, even more so than certain skins. This is evident in drums where the wood frame and the skin heads expand and contract differently, and the resulting stress to the materials usually causes the skin to split.
- Metals corrode in high humidity, especially when they are in contact with a material that tends to hold moisture, such as skin or sinew. A skin shirt with metal ornaments is an example.
- Basketry fibers expand and contract with changing humidity, causing baskets made from them to distort, and the fibers to break eventually.
- Birch bark, which has a natural tendency to split and peel, does so more quickly when the humidity fluctuates.

GENERAL RECOMMENDED CONDITIONS

For mixed collections of composite objects in a moderate climate:

- stable temperature no higher than 70°F
- stable relative humidity between 30 percent and 50 percent
- avoid sudden extreme fluctuations

But remember that in some geographic areas collections may have acclimated to conditions outside this range. Be sure to take this into account and adjust conditions accordingly.

MONITORING EQUIPMENT

- The simplest and least expensive instruments are thermometers and certain types of dial hygrometers. The disadvantage of these instruments is that they can become inaccurate after a few years, and the user needs to keep a systematic written record of readings to obtain useful information.
- Humidity indicator strips or color cards are inexpensive and produce reliable *approximate* readings. Again, the readings need to be recorded manually.
- Several types of instruments provide reliable accurate humidity readings, but these cost approximately $100 or more. Only some provide written records.
- Instruments that accurately measure both temperature and relative humidity and record these measurements are best. Different types are available. Until recently recording hygrothermographs were used most frequently. Now data loggers are often used to transfer information to a computer that produces customized charts. Both of these instruments are used primarily by museums and are excellent tools. They range in price from a little under $200 to over $1,000, not including software and cables where needed.

For more detailed information on monitoring equipment, consult the sources listed in the bibliography at the back of this book (Canadian Conservation Institute, *CCI Notes;* National Park Service, *Conserve-O-Gram Series*) or online at

http://www.nedcc.org/plam/tleaf22.htm;

http://www.cr.nps.gov/museum/publications/conserveogram/03-01.pdf;

http://www.cr.nps.gov/museum/publications/conserveogram/03-02.pdf; and

http://www.cr.nps.gov/museum/publications/conserveogram/03-03.pdf.

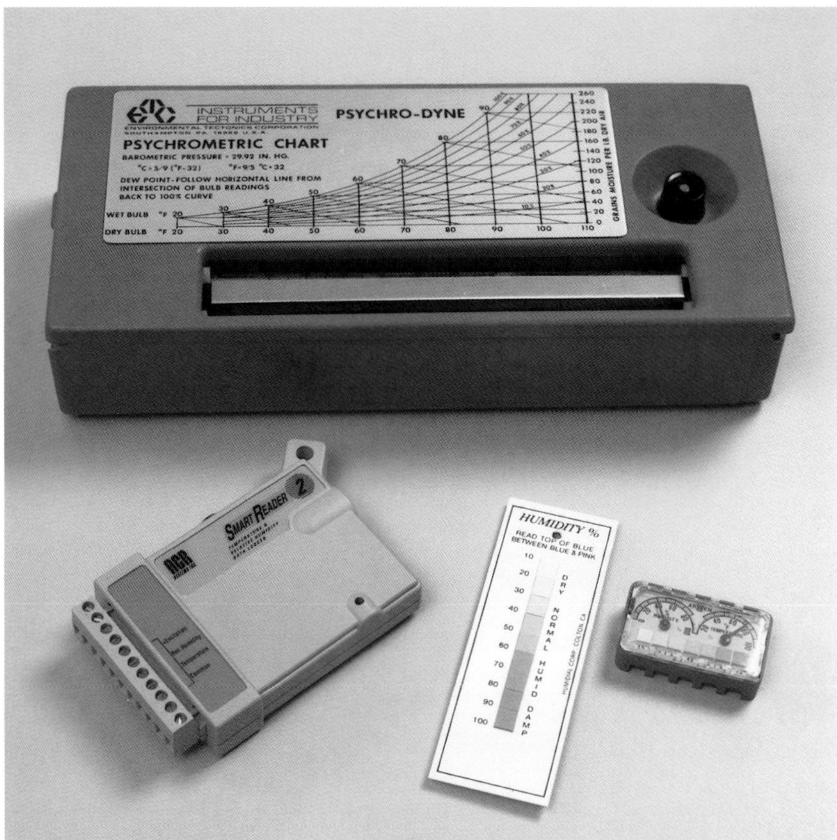

Temperature and relative humidity monitoring equipment. *Clockwise from top:* psychrometer, thermometer and dial hygrometer, humidity indicator color card, data logger.

Light

Light accelerates the deterioration of many materials used in American Indian items by acting as a catalyst in their chemical and physical breakdown. Light also causes natural colors, dyes, and certain pigments to fade or change in color, altering the appearance of some items in a relatively short period of time. Feathers are particularly sensitive to color change from light. Basketry fibers and wood are also sensitive to color change but to a lesser degree. Vegetable dyes are particularly prone to alteration. These dyes were (and sometimes still are) used to color such items as baskets, porcupine and bird quills, horsehair, rawhide for boxes, and textiles. The colors in the vegetable tanned skin used for some ledger bindings also tend to fade.

HOW MUCH LIGHT IS TOO MUCH?

Any exposure to light, even for a brief time, is damaging, and the damage cannot be reversed. Although all wavelengths of light are harmful, ultraviolet (UV) is particularly harmful. One of the most common sources of UV is the sun. Since many American Indian items are still in their original use, they may be exposed periodically to the sun, especially when they are taken outside, and thus are particularly vulnerable to fading. Items can also be exposed to UV light indoors. Certain types of lamps, such as fluorescent tubes, emit high amounts of UV energy and should be avoided. If they cannot be avoided, they can be filtered with relatively inexpensive plastic filtration films that reduce UV emissions.

WHAT IS RECOMMENDED?

As total damage from light is a function of both the intensity and the duration of exposure, standard museum preservation practice calls for illumination to be kept as low as possible and used for the least amount of time. Ideally, items should be exposed to light only while they are on display or being used, if this is in keeping with tribal care practices. At all other times, according to museum preservation guidelines, they should be stored in a light-tight container or in a windowless room illuminated only when the items are being retrieved or replaced, or when the room is being cleaned. Light levels should be kept as low as possible while still enabling location of items and cleaning of the room, and exposure should be for the shortest time that is feasible. Ideally illumination should be by incandescent bulbs. It is important to note that these bulbs generate heat and should be kept at a distance from items. In general, light sources that emit UV energy should be filtered. For more information on light, see chapter 11.

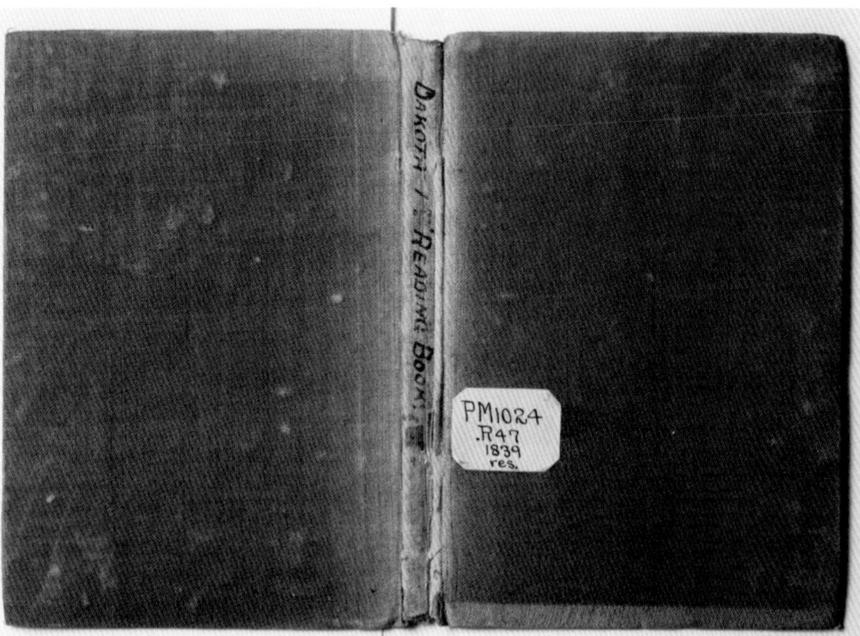

Cloth bookbinding faded along spine from exposure to light while shelved. Note that the front and back covers, which were protected from light, are not faded.

STANDARD MUSEUM PRESERVATION RECOMMENDATIONS REGARDING LIGHT

Several of these recommendations may not be compatible with tribal care practice. It is up to you to decide which measures to implement, as you see fit.

- Minimize exposure to light, especially UV.
- Keep levels as low as possible.
- Use storage rooms that are windowless.
- If storage rooms contain windows, cover these with drapes, shades, blinds, or shutters that completely block the sun. This will also aid in temperature control by minimizing heat loss and limiting the generation of heat by sunlight during the day.
- If skylights allow sunlight to shine directly on items in storage, either cover them to block the sun or paint the skylights with titanium dioxide or zinc white pigments, which reflect light and absorb UV energy.
- Filters made of special plastics also help control UV energy. Ultraviolet-filtering plastic films or rigid sheets can be used for windows to lower the amount of UV passing through them. Because these filters do not provide 100 percent protection against light damage, drapes, shades, blinds, or shutters that completely block the light are preferable. Fluorescent tubes can be covered with ultraviolet-filtering sleeves. An alternative is the use of special low-UV fluorescent tubes, although these are more costly than regular fluorescent tubes. For more information on UV-filtering window films, consult the following online source http://www.cr.nps.gov/museum/publications/conserveogram/03-10.pdf.
- To help limit the duration of exposure of materials, timed light switches can be used in storage rooms.

Air Pollution

Pollutants contribute heavily to the deterioration of all sorts of items, including those of American Indian origin. The two major types of pollutants are gases and particulates. Gaseous contaminants, such as sulfur dioxide, bring about chemical reactions that lead to the breakdown of materials and may, for example, cause some metals to rust or turn green and others to tarnish. Particulates are very fine dusts, often generated by construction, mining, or other earth-moving activities, that can travel long distances. These fine dusts can abrade, soil, and disfigure materials, causing items to become scratched and surface details on them to be hidden.

Controlling the air quality in storage spaces is a difficult and complicated matter that depends on several interrelated factors. Equipment is available to improve air quality. It varies in size, complexity, and effectiveness. Any equipment you have or plan to acquire should be matched to the particular level of pollution in the area where your storage space is located. Before purchasing equipment, you may find it helpful to consult an engineer with experience in air quality control in museums or other cultural institutions for recommendations. Various standards for air quality have been suggested, but until greater experience is gained, the most reasonable recommendation is to reduce the amount of pollutants in the air as much as is feasible.

WHAT MEASURES HELP CONTROL AIR QUALITY?

- In geographic areas that are dusty and windy, keep windows closed and put filters on air registers. Use doormats to help collect dirt at all building entries. Having two doors through which to enter a building at each entry point, an outer and an inner door, with a vestibule between them, is advisable.
- Provide good air exchange in areas where items are stored. Be sure that replacement air is as clean as possible. For example, air intake vents should be located as far as possible from sources of heavy pollution, such as a loading dock where trucks idle.
- Storing items in containers when the use of nontraditional containers is acceptable may help decrease the effects of pollutants. If the storage space is in a highly polluted area, such as an urban or industrial center, you may want to consider containers made from materials that have special agents for trapping pollutants, called molecular traps. These are described in the next chapter.
- Eliminate as much as possible the origins of pollution from inside or near the storage space. While automobiles and industry, major sources of pollution, will probably be beyond control, other sources may be reduced. These include cigarette smoke, photocopying machines, certain types of construction materials (wood, paints, sealants), cleaning compounds, and new furniture and carpets, which can release harmful vapors such as formaldehyde. See http://www.cr.nps.gov/museum/publications/conserveogram/01-11.pdf.

Water and Fire

Protection from *water* damage is essential. Even a minor water accident, such as one caused by a leaky pipe, can result in extensive and irreparable harm.

PRECAUTIONS THAT PROTECT AGAINST WATER DAMAGE

- Regularly inspect roof coverings and flashings over the storage space, and repair them as needed.
- Clean gutters and drains frequently.
- Never store important items under water pipes, steam pipes, bathrooms, air-conditioning equipment, or other sources of water.
- Always store items at least four inches above the floor, never directly on the floor.
- Avoid storage in basements or other areas where the possibility of flooding is great.
- If items *must* be stored in areas that are vulnerable to flooding, install water-sensing alarms to help ensure that water is quickly detected.

Damage caused by *fire* can be even more serious. If items survive at all, they are likely to be charred, covered with soot, brittle from exposure to high heat, wet from water used to extinguish the fire, moldy, and reeking with the smell of smoke.

PRECAUTIONS THAT PROTECT AGAINST FIRE

- Several fire-suppression methods are available. Make sure at least one is in operation in the storage space. If nothing else, make sure every storage area has one or more portable fire extinguishers of the "ABC dry chemical" type, and have everyone trained in their use, preferably by local firefighters.
- Regularly inspect and properly maintain the fire suppression system(s).
- Equip the storage space with an adequate fire detection and alarm system. At the very least, install a smoke detector.
- Wire the detection and alarm systems directly to the local fire department or to another twenty-four-hour monitor if available.

Opinion varies regarding the preferred type of detection and suppression for storage spaces containing important items. Many options are available, and some of the systems are complex and expensive. Before investing in a system, consult an experienced fire safety engineer who is familiar with current developments in the field and with your situation.

PREPARATION HELPS

Being prepared for an emergency is the best way to prevent it from becoming a disaster. If several items are stored together in one location, such as a museum or cultural center, it is advisable to have a plan for protecting these items in an emergency. Many cultural institutions that contain items of value have an emergency plan that covers all hazards that pose a reasonable threat, including water and fire. A systematically organized, formally written plan enables you to respond efficiently and quickly to an emergency, minimizing danger to people and damage to items and the building in which they are kept.

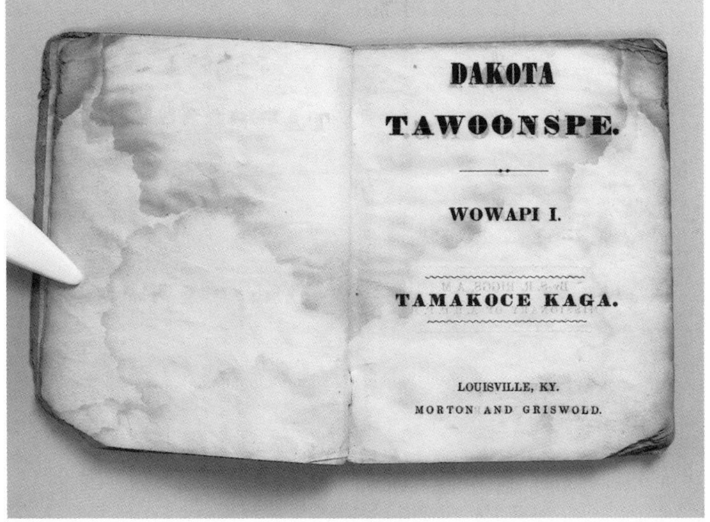

Dakota *Tawoonspe.* Staining on the title page of this book was caused by water.

When preparing the emergency plan, risks to the building in which items are kept should be identified and eliminated if possible; those that cannot be eliminated, such as location in an earthquake zone or proximity to a water main, should be addressed in the plan. Most plans include such information as the names and telephone numbers of staff to call immediately, the telephone numbers of emergency services (fire department, police, recovery services, etc.), floor plans showing the locations in the building of various shut-off valves, the locations of in-house emergency supplies and

equipment, and the names and telephone numbers of outside sources of additional emergency supplies and equipment (flashlights, paper toweling, wet vacuums, dehumidifiers, etc.)

If items are stored in a private home, you should likewise be prepared for an emergency. Check regularly for threats, such as leaky pipes. Make sure smoke detectors function and fire extinguishers are maintained annually. Know where water and fuel pipes are, as well as all shut-off valves. Maintain a list of the items in your care, and keep it in a secure place off-site.

Emergency preparedness plans range in size from long complex documents for large museums to short lists of pertinent information and phone numbers for use in homes. Much has been written on the subject of emergency planning. Consult the bibliography (Canadian Conservation Institute, *CCI Notes;* Rose, Hawks, and Genoways 1995) and the following online sources for further information: http://www.nedcc.org/plam3/tleaf33.htm; http://aic.stanford.edu/disaster; http://www.mnhs.org/preserve/conservation/recovery.html; and http://www.si.edu/archives/report/disaster.

Information on salvage can also be found in these sources and at http://www.veirls.org/flood_recovery/salvage_chart.html. This last source has an excellent chart that tells at a glance how to care for wet materials of all sorts, starting with archival collections and moving on to museum collections. Another useful source of information on stabilizing a variety of materials is the *Emergency Response and Salvage Wheel,* produced by the National Institute for the Conservation of Cultural Property, Inc. It is available for purchase from Heritage Preservation (see contact information in appendix 5) or E-mail at TaskForce@heritagepreservation.org.

Biological Agents

The primary biological agents that cause damage to American Indian items in storage are insects and mold.

INSECTS

Insect damage can be devastating. Insects eat anything from which they derive nourishment. Because American Indian items frequently contain materials rich in protein, they are particularly susceptible. Insects are especially attracted to items containing skin, feathers, textiles, fibers, paper, and wood. As many precautions as possible should be taken to prevent infestations.

Integrated Pest Management

Museums have traditionally relied on pesticides for preventing and solving pest problems. But pesticides often do not prevent infestation, and the chemicals in most pesticides pose health hazards to staff and damage collections. See chapter 10 for more information on this subject. Newer extermination methods, such as controlled freezing, heat, and modified atmospheres, are good alternatives for dealing with existing infestations, but they do not prevent infestation and may not be an acceptable treatment for American Indian cultural items. Prevention can best be achieved through strict housekeeping and monitoring procedures.

Preservation professionals recommend a strategy called *Integrated Pest Management* (IPM). Nonchemical means such as controlling the temperature and relative humidity, food sources, and building entry points are used to prevent and manage pest infestations. Chemical treatments are used only as a last resort when other methods have failed or when serious damage is occurring rapidly.

Wool clothing fragment with feathers and glass beads; Plains Indian. The textile and feathers have been severely damaged by insects.

What Precautions Can Be Taken?

Because insects are attracted by clutter, keep storage areas clean at all times, and do not allow clutter, dust, and dirt to accumulate. Remove trash, especially that which contains food, from the building every day.

Food presents special problems. Since insects are attracted by it, standard museum preservation practice maintains that food should never come in contact with items. Recommendations such as this, however, are often inappropriate for American Indian collections. Food can be a collection item. Dried berries, gourds, and corn are sometimes found in collections and are accessioned items. Further, many American Indian items are still in their original use and may require that food and other substances attractive to insects be used in them.

Tribal practice may also dictate that tobacco or other substances that attract or even contain insects be placed in storage with items. Some museums freeze these substances to kill any insects that may be present before placing them in storage. It is suggested that, when appropriate and in keeping with tribal care practices, any substance attractive to insects be separated from items in storage after use. In addition, regularly examine items and storage areas that contain tobacco or other substances that attract insects so that if insects are present they will be discovered immediately.

In fact, vigilance may be your best all-around protection. Ideally, frequent routine visual checks of storage areas should be conducted. Be sure to look inside containers such as boxes, which can hold several items. Often an infestation destroys every item in a container before it is discovered. For monitoring storage areas, the use of "sticky" traps, a type of insect trap, is recommended. These are available at most hardware and grocery stores. They capture insects, allowing types, locations, and quantities to be determined over a period of time. This information helps in eradicating the problem.

Note that insect problems can be related to rodent problems. Poisoned

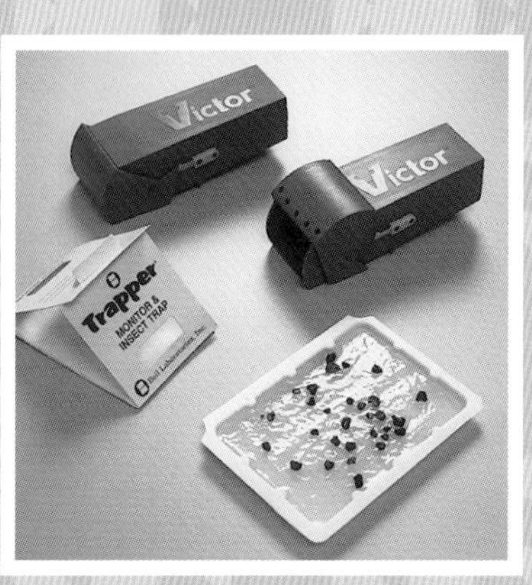

Insect and rodent traps. *Clockwise from top:* non-harming rodent traps, rodent glue board, insect trap.

baits should not be used for rodent control as the animals will get sick from the bait and die in an inaccessible area. This will lead to a secondary infestation of insects feeding on the rodent carcass. So if you have an insect problem, you may want to determine if it is the result of a rodent problem. Glue boards are a useful rodent monitoring and trapping device if used properly and checked regularly. Traps that catch but do not harm rodents are another useful control method.

High temperature and, in particular, high relative humidity encourage insect activity, so control these in storage areas. Since insects enter through windows, doors, and vents in storage areas, keep these closed as much as possible. Cracks or breaks in the building fabric are also points of entry, another reason for buildings that contain storage spaces to be well maintained. Cut back grass and plantings at least eighteen inches from any building that houses items. For more information on control of insects, consult the sources in the bibliography (Canadian Conservation Institute, *CCI Notes;* Rose, Hawks, and Genoways 1995) and the following online sources: http://www.nedcc.org/plam3/tleaf311.htm; http://www.cr.nps.gov/museum/publications/conserveogram/03-07.pdf; and http://www.cr.nps.gov/museum/publications/conserveogram/03-08.pdf.

If possible and in keeping with tribal care practices, check all items that enter the building, and certainly all that enter the storage area, for insects, and then place them in quarantine for three weeks before storing them with the rest of the collections. These items include those that have been out for use, new items for the collection, items that are being returned after a loan, and all equipment, supplies, and packing materials. If after three weeks you do not see any signs of insect activity, the items can be removed from quarantine and put away.

What If You Find Insects?

If you *do* see signs of insects, you need to act fast. The best way to deal with this situation in most instances is to freeze the item following very specific guidelines. These are provided in appendix 3. Be sure to seek the advice of appropriate members of the American Indian community regarding the acceptability of freezing within tribal practice if you are unsure about this. Although the advisability of controlled freezing for certain materials, such as glass beads, has been questioned by preservation professionals because it is not without risk, most agree that this is the simplest, safest, and most practical approach to the problem. This procedure is easy, relatively inexpensive, and effective if done properly.

An alternative to freezing is to heat an infected item, again following very specific guidelines. This method, developed by the Canadian Conservation Institute (CCI), uses the sun as the source of heat and is in the process of being informally field-tested in various climates. It utilizes very little equipment and promises to be inexpensive. For information on this procedure, contact CCI (appendix 5). For a description of a practical application of this procedure, see

the *WAAC Newsletter,* volume 23, number 2, May 2001; or online at http://palimpsest.stanford.edu/waac/wn/.

Another alternative that is employed in several museums is the use of modified atmospheres. This procedure, however, uses specialized equipment and supplies, such as carbon dioxide, nitrogen, and oxygen scavengers, and is more expensive and complicated to accomplish.

If an infestation is discovered in the storage area, isolate the affected items from the rest of the collection and securely wrap them in polyethylene bags or sheeting. Also isolate items adjacent to affected ones. The insect should be identified, as this will aid in extermination and may help determine the source of the infestation. Local and state agricultural extension agents can often identify insects and have useful information on control of infestations. You can take photographs of insects that have been identified or make a roster of the suspects and post it for easy reference.

Avoid the use of over-the-counter spray-type insecticides to remedy the problem; the chemicals may damage items. Instead, call a licensed pest-control operator. Choose one who works with a licensed and bonded service and who is familiar with integrated pest management. In fact, having *regular* pest control service in and around the building where items are stored is a good preventive measure. The extent of the infestation will determine the best way to deal with it. If only a few items are affected, controlled freezing may be the approach to take. If most of the collection is affected, other methods need to be considered.

If you have any questions when faced with an insect infestation, do not hesitate to contact a preservation professional immediately for guidance and for the most up-to-date information.

QUARANTINE PROCEDURES

An enclosed space separate from the storage area should be designated as the quarantine area. A room or large chamber works best. It should be reasonably well sealed so that insects cannot migrate from it to other parts of the building. The area should have similar room conditions to the storage area so items can acclimate to the storage conditions while in quarantine.

Because of varying incubation periods for insects, it is probably best to quarantine items for three weeks. Each item should be double-bagged in plastic (polyethylene, if possible), with each bag closed with a twist tie. Each double bag should contain just one item. If an item is too large to fit in a bag, it should be double wrapped with polyethylene sheeting and tape. If the items enter the quarantine area from outside when the weather is cold or humid, you may want to wait for a short time before bagging the items so you do not trap moisture in the bags from humidity or condensation on the items. After the items have been bagged for three weeks, carefully examine them for any signs of insects.

MOLD

Mold damage can pose a serious threat, especially if the storage space is located in a hot, humid climate or near a large body of water where humidity is high. Mold spores are ever present in the environment, and the higher the temperature and relative humidity, the greater the risk of mold. Items made of skin, textiles, fibers, and paper are particularly susceptible to mold growth, as well as items previously used to hold food.

What Precautions Can Be Taken?

The most important precautions are sustaining levels of temperature and relative humidity that meet standard museum preservation guidelines, as discussed earlier; providing good circulation of air; and maintaining clean, clutter-free storage areas. In most instances mold does not grow below 60 percent relative humidity and also has difficulty growing in areas where there is air movement. Mold prefers humid, still environments. Mary Lou Florian, a researcher in British Columbia, stresses the importance of keeping air moving

around items to ensure that moisture does not settle on them, but moves off so they stay dry. This means the air around an object or display case should circulate. Also, avoid displaying and storing items on or near cold walls, floors, and windowsills, and metal and cement surfaces. Move and inspect items regularly. If you smell mold, improve the environment immediately. If a water-related emergency occurs, such as a flood or fire, tend to wet items right away, before any opportunity for mold growth develops. For more information on precautions that can be taken, consult the sources in the bibliography (National Park Service, *Conserve-O-Gram Series*) and online at http://www.cr.nps.gov/museum/publications/conserveogram/03-04.pdf.

What If You Find Mold?

Once mold growth appears, isolate the affected items from the collection. Disposable rubber or plastic gloves and a particle dust mask, sometimes referred to as a filtering face piece, should be worn when handling moldy items. Select a mask with a rating of N99 or N100 or with the equivalent of a HEPA (high-efficiency particulate air) filtration rating. Also select one with two head straps rather than one because these fit more securely, providing better protection. These are available from safety supply houses and large home improvement stores. Inhaling mold spores can cause serious medical problems that are difficult to remedy and sometimes cannot be cured. Wearing a respirator with a HEPA filter provides better protection than a dust mask. It should be noted that the Occupational Safety and Health Administration (OSHA) requires that employers provide a medical evaluation for employees before they use a respirator and, technically, before they wear a dust mask as well. This evaluation is important as some people cannot safely wear respirators for various reasons. Also, respirators need to be fitted properly to provide adequate protection, and a formal fit-test must be conducted by a qualified person. For more detailed information on respirator use, consult the sources in the bibliography (National Park Service, *Conserve-O-Gram Series;* Ogden 1999) and online at http://www.cr.nps.gov/museum/publications/conserveogram/02-13.pdf; or at www.cdc.gov/niosh/respinfo.html.

Once moldy items have been isolated from the collections, they should be dried thoroughly, and when they are dry, the mold should be removed from them. A preservation professional should be contacted for advice on how best to do all this given the particular circumstances with which you are confronted.

Security

The final topic of this chapter is security. All items of cultural significance, beauty, and high monetary value, regardless of the cultural tradition of which they are a part, may be vulnerable to theft and vandalism. In recent years, American Indian items have become highly valued by collectors and are more

susceptible to theft than ever before. Those charged with the care of these items need to be aware of this situation and should evaluate the amount of risk to which the items in their care are subjected. If necessary, adequate protection should be provided. Also, adequate security may be a requirement of other institutions loaning items to yours (see chapters 11 and 12). Protection can range in complexity from simple locks on cabinets to elaborate buildingwide security systems. In some cases a security specialist should be consulted.

Many measures can be taken, including the following suggestions. Securing the building is important. Standard museum preservation practice maintains that the building that houses items should be well secured during hours when it is closed to the public. Perimeter intrusion alarms and internal motion detectors that are wired directly to the local police department or to another reliable twenty-four-hour monitoring agency work well. During working hours it is best to use only one building entrance and exit, which is used by visitors and staff alike; all other doors should be alarmed so that any unauthorized use can be detected. Keep windows closed and locked. Carefully limit the distribution of building keys, and limit even further the keys to storage areas or to cabinets that contain highly valuable items. Keep the list of key holders current, and require staff members to return keys when they leave the employ of the museum. Keep combinations to safes highly confidential, and give them to the least number of people possible.

Keeping good records of the cultural items you have in the building is also an important security measure. Char Tullie (Navaho), Museum Registrar at the Navajo Nation Museum, explains that "standard museum registration methods should be followed in all museums and cultural centers [see chapter 12]. If a theft occurs, you will need a way to prove ownership of valuable items. Without good documentation you cannot prove anything." Faith Bad Bear (Crow/Sioux), Assistant Curator of Ethnology and NAGPRA Project Manager, Science Museum of Minnesota, agrees. She notes that "any museum that is a repository for American Indian cultural items should follow standard museum registration methods. Museums are legally responsible for the items in their care and are liable if they are lost."

Both Tullie and Bad Bear stress the importance for tribal museums to fashion registration methods after standard museum practice and its strict ethical standards. These methods are discussed in chapter 12. If a theft occurs, you will need to prove ownership of the stolen items. Sound registration methods facilitate this. These methods include marking each item with its own unique accession number or other form of identification. Appendix 1 describes how to do this. Bad Bear cautions that "for Indian items it is important that this number be removable since you do not know how the item will be handled or used in the future. For example, using tags rather than applying the numbers directly to items may be preferable."

If you discover that any items have been stolen, contact the police, your insurance company, and any other relevant organizations. The following organizations are good places to begin:

American Indian Ritual Object Repatriation Foundation at
http://www.repatriationfoundation.org/htm; telephone: 212-980-9441;
e-mail: circle@repatriationfoundation.org

National Antique and Art Dealers Association of America, Inc., at
http://www.naadaa.org/htm; telephone: 212-826-9707;
e-mail: inquiries@naadaa.org

Art Loss Register, a database used by dealers, museums, and collectors, at
http://www.artloss.com; telephone: 212-297-0941;
e-mail: info@alrny.com

Notices can be posted at the following sites:

H-AMINDIAN listserv at
http://www2.h-net.msu.edu/~amind/about.html;
telephone 480-965-3919; e-mail: amind@mail.h-net.msu.edu

American Association of Museums newsletter at
http://www.aam-us.org.htm; telephone: 202-289-1818;
e-mail: aviso@aam-us.org

American Association for State and Local History at
http://www.aaslh.org.htm; telephone: 615-320-3203;
e-mail: history@aaslh.org

In Summary

As you see, many preventive measures can be taken to preserve cultural items, several with minimal expense and effort. The measures discussed thus far have to do with the environment in which items are stored. The containers, supports, mounts, and furniture used to house the items are another important facet of storage. Preventive measures that relate to this are covered in the next chapter.

Checklist: Low-Cost/No-Cost Preservation Measures

Preventive care measures range from those that benefit every item in the collection, such as improving the levels of temperature and relative humidity, protecting against insects, mold, water, and fire, or providing storage furniture made of chemically stable materials, to measures that address the specific needs of individual items, such as supplying suitable storage supports and mounts. Once the causes of deterioration are understood, many preventive care measures become a matter of common sense. Although some of the measures that can be taken are costly, many are not. Incorporating as many measures as possible into tribal care practices will help preserve American Indian cultural items. A little prevention will go a long way toward extending the useful life of these important items for as long as needed.

LOW-COST/NO-COST PRESERVATION MEASURES

1. Keep storage areas clean and clutter-free, and use dust covers as needed.
2. Avoid storing items in attics and basements, or near ventilation ducts, radiators, heat-producing appliances, and fireplaces.
3. Attach weather stripping to doors and windows.
4. In cold climates, seal the inside of windows with plastic sheeting and tape.
5. Use room humidifiers and dehumidifiers if you do not have a buildingwide climate control system.
6. Maintain good air circulation.
7. Put humidity-sensitive items in a cabinet with humidity-buffering materials.
8. Minimize exposure to light, especially UV.
9. Keep light levels as low as possible.
10. Cover windows with drapes, shades, or blinds.
11. Apply filters to lamps that give off ultraviolet light.
12. Inspect roof coverings and flashings regularly and repair as needed.
13. Clean gutters and drains frequently.
14. Seal cracks in the building.
15. Avoid storing items under sources of water such as bathrooms, washing machines, and pipes. Always consider water sources in the room(s) and ceiling(s) above.
16. Store items at least four inches off the floor.
17. Use water-sensing alarms.
18. Have portable fire extinguishers nearby and have them inspected yearly.
19. Install smoke sensors.
20. Inspect regularly for mold and insects.
21. Keep grass and plantings at least eighteen inches from the building.
22. Quarantine all items for three weeks before they go into storage.
23. Provide containers, supports, and mounts for fragile items (see chapter 7).
24. Use only preservation-quality materials for containers, supports, and mounts (see chapter 7).
25. Handle items with care, using gloves as required (see chapters 2 and 8).

7

How Should Cultural Items Be Stored?

SHERELYN OGDEN

Using the appropriate containers, supports, mounts, and furniture for the storage of cultural items is crucial to their preservation and is an important aspect of preventive care. This chapter provides some of the basic information you will need to make sound decisions and selections regarding the housing of your cultural items.

Storage Containers, Supports, and Mounts

Containers, supports, and mounts are used to provide physical protection and support for items while they are in storage. Not all items require this protection, but those that do will benefit greatly from having it, and their useful life can be extended significantly.

WHY ARE CONTAINERS IMPORTANT?

Often the best way to protect an item in storage is to place it in a container. This will help keep it clean, will keep fragments or other detached parts with the item, and depending on the type of container, will protect the item from being broken as well as assist in moving it from one place to another. Containers range greatly in variety and include such enclosures as boxes, bags, and small glass bottles (for tiny loose pieces such as beads).

BOXES

Boxes are probably the most commonly used containers. They should be strong enough to support the weight of the item(s) they contain without buckling, and yet be as light as possible so they do not add unnecessary weight and bulk. All materials used in the construction of boxes should meet preservation standards as much as possible (discussed below). Boxes can be made in-house or purchased from a commercial supplier. It is easier and probably more cost-effective to buy them. Commercially available boxes range from expensive cloth-covered and lined varieties to less costly self-assembly types made of uncovered acid-free cardboard. They are available in custom or standard sizes and vary from ones large enough to hold a dress to those small enough to accommodate a single piece of ball ammunition. Commercially available two-piece boxes of simple construction in standard sizes are probably the least expensive and most practical choice for the majority of situations.

Many museum professionals find small standard-sized boxes to be invaluable in drawer storage. These relatively low-cost boxes can be used to contain round objects that roll, heavy objects that slide, or detached pieces of items that shift and become misplaced when the drawer is opened and closed. They can also be used to hold natural materials, such as fiber cord or strips for weaving, so they will not spill or become entangled in a drawer. The use of boxes makes items easily portable, protects them from physical damage, and prevents them from becoming lost. Finally, boxes can be used to subdivide a drawer to house many small items.

Preservation-quality storage boxes with acid-free tissue

WHY ARE SUPPORTS AND MOUNTS IMPORTANT?

Supports and mounts vary as widely as American Indian items themselves and include such devices as pads, rings, tubes, trays, and hangers. Many items, particularly weak and physically damaged ones, need the protection of a storage support or mount to enable them to be stored safely without losing their shape or suffering further physical damage. Several examples illustrate this.

Above: Ring support to prevent a grass basket with rounded bottom from rolling
Below: Interior flexible support to prevent a grass basket from collapsing

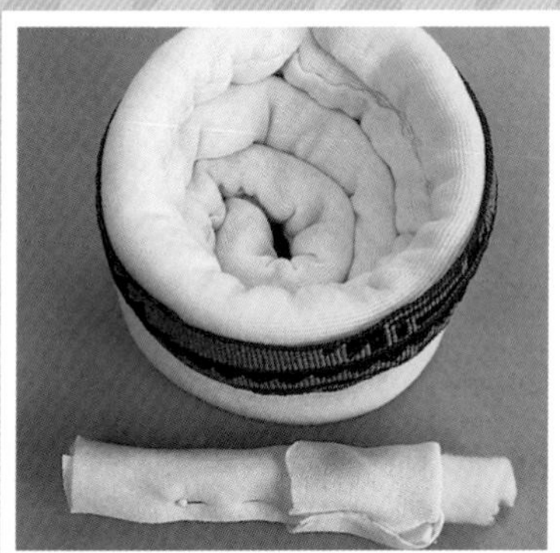

- A buckskin vest needs the benefit of a padded hanger to support the rounded shape of the shoulders when it is hung, so that the skin does not crease or break at the shoulders from the weight of the vest, especially if the skin is weak. If the vest is beaded, it may be too heavy to be hung and need to be stored flat instead. Even when stored flat, without the support of the padded hanger, or other type of padded support, the skin eventually may crack in the area of the shoulders.
- Similarly, a dress with jingles made from dozens of snuff tin covers is too heavy to hang and needs to be stored flat. To prevent the textile from which the dress is made from creasing and eventually breaking where folded, it needs to be stuffed with crumpled acid-free tissue along its folds to avoid sharp creases.
- Woven sashes, because of their length and weight, cannot be hung without becoming distorted. They need to be stored flat, but because of their length they must be folded. To avoid creating creases that could eventually become breaks, the sashes need to be folded over acid-free tubes cushioned with acid-free tissue. If tubes are not available, acid-free tissue can be rolled or twisted into a similar shape and used by itself.
- A woven basket with a rounded base needs a ring support to immobilize it so it does not roll on the shelf where it will be stored. This needs to be shaped to fit the basket from a rolled length of polyester batting wrapped in cotton-knit fabric.

WHAT IS THE BEST TYPE OF CONTAINER, SUPPORT, OR MOUNT?

Selecting the best type of container, support, or mount involves assessing the materials from which the item is made; its construction, size, shape, condition, and use; the availability of space for storage; the need for access to the item; the need to have interns and volunteers make the container, support, or mount; and the cost. In addition, you may want to seek input from the people who made the items or other appropriate members of the American Indian community.

Containers can be custom made to fit a specific item. Often, however, as mentioned earlier, commercially available standard-sized containers are adequate or can be modified to fit a particular item. Unlike containers, most supports and mounts need to be custom made. Sometimes they need to be made to the size and shape of one particular item. Other times, one support or mount can be made to hold several items. For example, a padded acid-free cardboard mount with sets of cotton ties can hold several war clubs that are stored in a drawer. The clubs are held in place on the board with the ties. The padding on the board reduces vibration to the clubs caused by the drawer's movement. The board is made to fit in the drawer in such a way that it does not shift as the drawer is opened and closed, thus protecting the clubs from sliding. This mount has the added benefit that the clubs can be moved on it, such as from the drawer to a research area, being supported while in transit without being handled. Also, custom mounts that hold several items rather than just one make more efficient use of storage space. It should be noted, however, that such mounts, particularly ones that stack, may not show proper respect for certain items. The advice of appropriate members of the American Indian community should be sought prior to making mounts like these.

Several excellent books that provide practical information and simple instructions on the construction of containers, supports, and mounts are available. These are listed in the bibliography (Barclay, Bergeron, and Dignard 2002; Canadian Conservation Institute, *CCI Notes;* National Park Service, *Conserve-O-Gram Series;* Rose and de Torres 1992). Some are also available online, as indicated in the bibliography. Containers and, in particular, supports and mounts are essential to the preservation of some items and should be provided if at all possible.

In all instances, the traditional, originally intended method of storage should be carefully considered and respected. Original containers always should be kept unless tribal practice dictates otherwise.

Rigid shoe mounts for storage, transport, and study of a moccasin collection

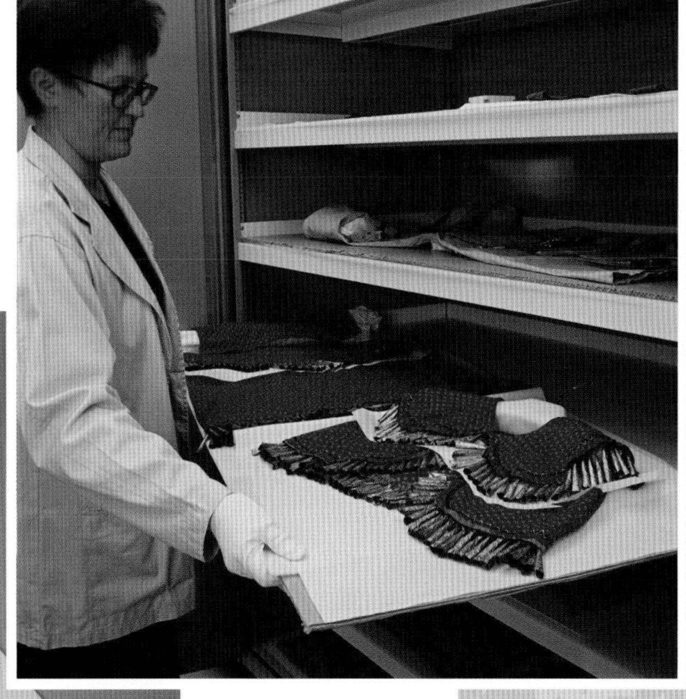

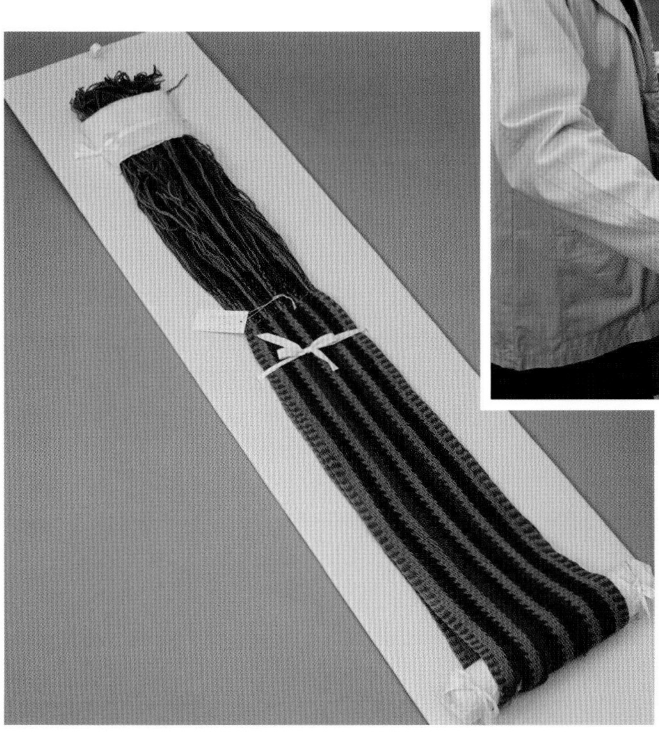

Right: Cynthia Hall, museum project specialist at the Minnesota Historical Society, holds a rigid mount for a blouse with tinkler cones. Note the padded hanger supporting the shoulders.
Below: Rigid mount for Ojibwe woven wool yarn sash folded over an acid-free tube cushioned with tissue

Above: Mannequin head mount to support headdress in good condition. **Right:** Headdress in poor condition stuffed with acid-free tissue and stored flat in a drawer

FROM WHAT MATERIALS SHOULD CONTAINERS, SUPPORTS, AND MOUNTS BE CONSTRUCTED?

Whenever possible, containers, supports, and mounts should be made from materials that meet standard museum preservation requirements. These requirements vary depending on the material. In general the materials should be chemically and physically stable, durable, and non-damaging. Materials that do not meet these requirements can cause irreparable visual, chemical, and physical damage.

WHAT DO THE TERMS "ARCHIVAL QUALITY," "CONSERVATION QUALITY," AND "PRESERVATION QUALITY" MEAN?

These terms have been used over the years to imply that materials meet standard museum preservation requirements. The terms have been loosely used, however, and given a variety of meanings, especially by manufacturers and suppliers of storage materials. For this reason, it is best *not* to rely on these terms but to use specific characteristics, as described in the following pages. Please note, though, that to simplify discussion, throughout this book the term *preservation quality* is used to describe materials with these characteristics.

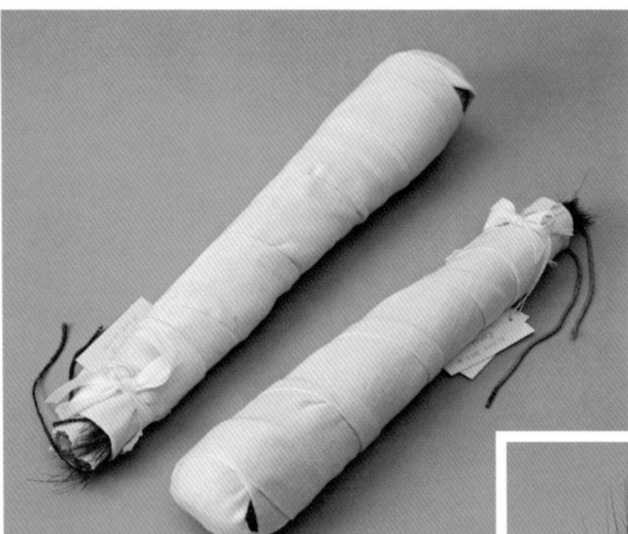

Above: Ojibwe hair roaches rolled on roach sticks and wrapped for storage according to tribal method. This storage method preserves the roaches' shape so they can be worn. **Below:** An Ojibwe braided roach headdress that is too deteriorated to roll and wrap is stored flat on a rigid mount. **Right:** An Ojibwe hair roach with a beaded headband is stored on a mannequin head to protect the beaded band.

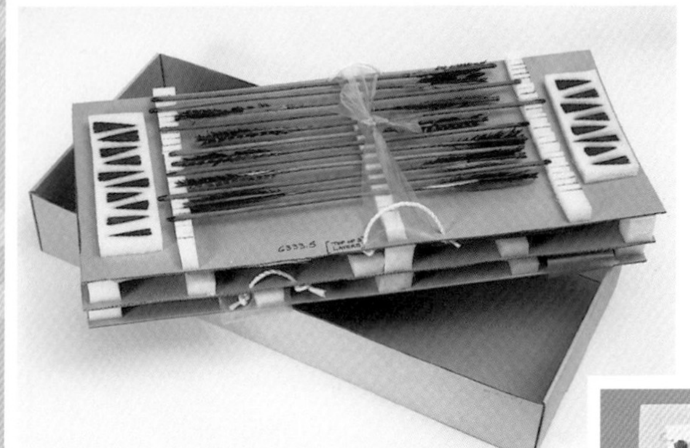

Stacking rigid mounts for arrows. The mounts are designed to protect the feathers on the shafts and to maximize space. Note the points stored in recesses carved in polyethylene.

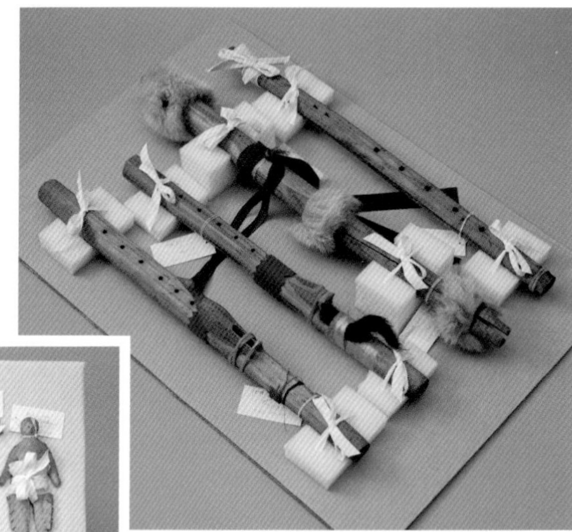

Above: Rigid mount with polyethylene supports and sets of cotton ties to hold several musical instruments in place. **Left:** Rigid padded mount with sets of cotton ties to hold several Ojibwe dolls in place

ARE THERE STANDARDS THAT LIST SPECIFICATIONS FOR STORAGE MATERIALS?

Yes, there are national and international standards. They are produced by such organizations as the American National Standards Institute (ANSI), the National Information Standards Organization (NISO), and the International Standards Organization (ISO). These important standards specify in technical terms the characteristics that are recommended by the organization producing the standard. For example, one standard, ISO 18902.2001, formerly ANSI IT 9.2 – 1998, specifies storage materials for photographic processed films, plates, and papers and can be followed in general for the storage of most non-photographic paper-based materials as well. Although there is still not complete consensus among the organizations, they are moving toward agreement. Very few of these standards are cited in supplier catalogs at the present time. Those that tend to be listed in catalogs are mentioned in this book at the appropriate place. For your purposes, it is probably best to rely on the characteristics discussed below when selecting storage materials.

WHY IS CHEMICAL STABILITY IMPORTANT?

Some of the deterioration that items in storage suffer is caused by the acids and other harmful substances in the containers, supports, and mounts that are used to protect them. These harmful substances migrate from storage materials into the items, causing such problems as discoloration, corrosion, and embrittlement. For example, discoloration caused by an acidic window mat can disfigure and hasten the deterioration of an Indian drawing on paper that has been matted and framed. Similar damage takes place when a textile item, such as a shirt, is wrapped in acidic tissue that discolors the textile and transfers acidity from the tissue to the textile, speeding its deterioration.

To avoid these problems, it is essential for all storage materials to be chemically stable—to *not* generate any harmful substances. If this is not possible, a chemically stable barrier can be used between the storage material and the item. For example, an acidic cardboard tube can be covered with a stable material such as polyester film, which acts as a protective barrier between the acids in the tube and the item rolled on it.

PAPER-BASED STORAGE MATERIALS SHOULD BE ACID-FREE

Paper-based materials are used widely, being readily available commercially and relatively affordable. Paper materials are made from cotton, linen, or wood fibers, with wood being used most often. Wood, however, contains highly damaging impurities that lead to the formation of harmful acids. For this reason, only paper materials made from wood pulp that has been chemically purified to remove lignin and other damaging impurities are safe to use. Paper materials made of 100 percent cotton or linen are also safe to use. Folders, envelopes, tissue, and papers for interleaving sheets should be lignin-free and made of chemically stable fibers. The board for boxes should also be lignin-free and chemically purified. The board used for matting Indian drawings on paper should be a 100 percent cotton or linen rag board or an otherwise lignin-free, chemically purified conservation mounting board. Tapes for making mats, folders, and boxes should be chemically stable, non-staining, and free of damaging components if possible. Such materials commonly are described as *acid-free*. It is important to be aware that *not* all paper-based materials are acid-free. Standard museum preservation practice maintains, however, that only acid-free materials should be used.

WHY IS pH IMPORTANT?

Knowing the pH of paper-based storage materials will tell you whether they are acid-free. The acidity and alkalinity of paper and paper-based materials are expressed by pH, a measurement on a scale of zero through fourteen. Seven is the neutral point, with measurements under seven indicating increasingly acidic, and over seven indicating increasingly alkaline conditions. Although the recommendation varies for what an ideal pH for storage enclosures should be, depending on the item to be stored, a pH of 7.0 through 8.5 is a good general range.

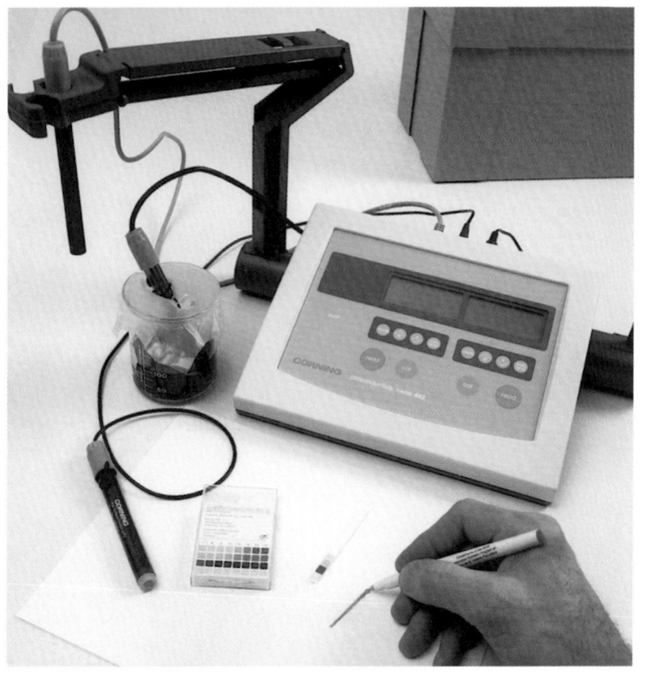

Tools for measuring the pH of paper. *Clockwise from top:* pH meter, pH detector pen, pH indicator strips.

It is advisable to measure the pH of purchased storage materials to ensure that they are acid-free (pH over 7), because sometimes materials do not meet their advertised levels. There are several methods for measuring pH. The simplest is the use of a pH detector pencil or pen, which indicates the surface pH of the material being tested (never to be used on a cultural object). This method is suitable for most situations. These pencils and pens are relatively inexpensive and readily available from conservation suppliers. A more specific pH reading can be obtained by using pH indicator strips. The most accurate readings are those provided by pH meters. These latter two methods are used primarily by museums.

WHAT IS AN ALKALINE RESERVE?

Some paper-based storage materials contain a buffering agent, such as calcium carbonate, added during manufacture. This buffering agent is referred to as an alkaline reserve. The alkaline buffer neutralizes acids as they form in the storage materials and helps keep the materials acid-free long-term. Over time, however, the buffering agent may eventually be depleted.

SHOULD BUFFERED OR UNBUFFERED MATERIALS BE USED?

Buffered materials are appropriate for storing some American Indian items but not others, and you must know which to use. Museums keep supplies of both buffered and unbuffered materials and use whichever is appropriate for the item being stored. It is, however, expensive to keep both types of supplies on hand. Also, it is impossible to distinguish between them visually, so they must be clearly marked. The easier and safer approach for most people is to use acid-free *unbuffered* materials for everything.

WHAT ARE MOLECULAR TRAPS?

One relatively new type of storage material incorporates molecular traps to provide added protection from gaseous pollutants. Molecular traps, such as activated carbon or natural or synthetic zeolites, capture and retain pollutants. These are most suitable for storage materials that will be used in highly polluted areas or for items that are particularly sensitive to pollutants. Storage materials that contain molecular traps are available as paper or board and are sold under the trade name of MicroChamber.

DURABILITY

Items should be stored only in containers that are sufficiently durable to protect them. If containers are not sturdy, the items they contain may become distorted or broken, or the container itself may become damaged or even fall apart. Needlessly strong storage containers may also present problems, adding unnecessary weight and bulk that can lead to handling and spatial difficulties.

ARE PLASTICS SAFE TO USE?

Plastics lend themselves well to constructing containers, supports, and mounts, but they vary greatly in chemical stability and should be used knowledgeably. Some plastics are unstable chemically and produce by-products as they deteriorate that accelerate the breakdown of many materials used in American Indian items. These should always be avoided, even though using them is tempting because they are easily obtained and inexpensive. Three types of plastic meet preservation standards. These are polypropylene, polyethylene, and polyester. These plastics come in many forms with different characteristics—planks or foam, rolls or sheets, hard or soft, thick or thin, opaque or transparent—and are sold under different trade names.

Polyvinyl chloride (PVC) should *not* be used in any form—not as sheeting, a photograph sleeve, or a tube—because of the damaging by-products it emits. The same is true of bubble-pack; do *not* use it, because of possible coatings, physical damage, or harmful by-products. *Avoid* polyurethane, like that commonly found in seat cushions; it turns to powder as it ages and gives off damaging by-products. Finally, do *not* use polystyrene, as this has a tendency to become brittle and yellow as compared to other acceptable plastics. Generally it is important to determine that the plastic materials you use for long-term storage are one of the three safe types.

FABRICS

Several factors determine a fabric's safety for use. One is the fiber from which it is made. Certain fibers, such as silk, are by nature acidic and should not come in contact with items that are vulnerable to acid. Other fibers emit harmful volatiles, such as sulfur compounds. Fabrics and felts containing wool are an example. Wool is also a food source for insects. These fibers should be avoided.

In most instances the safest fiber choice is cotton or linen because these are by nature chemically stable. If these are not readily available, polyester is an acceptable alternative. An unsized fabric is best. Sizings and surface applications are used to stiffen fabrics or make them fire-, water-, or stain-resistant. All fabrics, regardless of fiber content, should be washed prior to use to remove any of these potentially harmful sizing or finishing compounds. The use of dyed fabrics is problematic because permanent damage can occur if the dye transfers or bleeds onto an item due to contact with high relative humidity or water. Preferably only undyed fabrics should be used. For more information about fabrics, see chapter 11.

Storage Furniture

WHAT MATERIALS SHOULD BE USED IN THE CONSTRUCTION OF STORAGE FURNITURE?

Many of the currently available furniture choices contain materials that produce by-products that contribute to the deterioration of the items housed in the furniture. Opinion on what constitutes acceptable storage furniture is changing rapidly. If you are considering the purchase of furniture, you may want to consult a preservation professional for the most up-to-date information. Also, appendix 2 provides additional information.

Steel storage furniture with various powder coatings is a safe choice, and many different types of furniture are available in this material. Museums often choose this material. Anodized aluminum storage furniture is another option and is considered by many to be the best choice, especially for highly sensitive items, but this tends to be the most expensive. Open chrome shelving, made of heavy-gauge, chrome-plated steel wire, is another suitable option, but because the wires can leave permanent marks on items that are not protected, boxing is required.

Until recently, furniture with a baked enamel finish was the recommended choice. Lately, however, questions have been raised about the possibility of the baked enamel coating off-gassing (giving off) formaldehyde and other harmful substances if it has not been properly baked. Note 2 in appendix 2 provides information on how to test for off-gassing. If you have this type of shelving, contact a preservation professional to see if this is a problem in your particular situation.

WOOD

One of the most commonly used materials for furniture is wood. Unfortunately, storage of valuable items in direct contact with wooden storage furniture is discouraged because of acids and other harmful substances exuded by wood and some wood sealants. Even though some woods and wood composites are less damaging than others, all are problematic. Also, questions regarding how long various woods and sealants give off harmful substances still need to be answered. One solution to the problem is to coat wooden furniture with safe modern sealants. In addition to coating, shelves and drawers made of wood can be lined with an effective barrier material. See the section on wood display cases in chapter 11, and also appendix 2 for information on wood and the use of sealants and barriers.

The use of laminate and particle wood furniture is tempting because it is readily available and inexpensive. Furniture from these woods, however, is especially problematic because the wood warps under weight and contains many additives that off-gas, and because the brackets and joining hardware are often inadequate to provide sufficient support. Closed storage cabinets made of wood are even more of a problem because the closed environment intensifies the concentration of acidic and other vapors. If this type of cabinet is used, all inner surfaces of the unit should be effectively coated. If possible, the use of wooden furniture should be avoided.

ARE ANY OTHER MATERIALS A CONCERN?

Some storage furniture has gaskets in the doors or drawers to provide an airtight seal. If the gaskets are rubber, damage, such as corrosion or tarnishing, may occur to some items, especially those made of metal, due to sulfur vapors emitted from rubber. The preferred gasket material is silicone, preferably food-grade that has been heat-cured to remove solvent vapors.

WHAT CONSTRUCTION FEATURES ARE IMPORTANT?

Regardless of the construction material chosen, storage furniture should have a smooth, nonabrasive finish. If steel furniture is painted or coated, the finish should be resistant to chipping, for chips will leave steel exposed and susceptible to rust. The furniture should be free of sharp edges and protrusions; exposed nuts and bolts are particularly hazardous. The furniture should be strong enough so that it will not bend or warp when filled. To protect collections from water damage in the event of a flood, the lowest storage area within the furniture should be at least four inches above the floor.

WHAT TYPES OF STORAGE FURNITURE ARE AVAILABLE? HOW DO YOU CHOOSE?

Several types of furniture are available that are suitable for the storage of American Indian items. The most common ones are described below. Specialty furniture, such as racks to hold canoes horizontally or lances vertically, or supports to brace totem poles, are not covered here. A preservation professional should be contacted to deal with the special needs of items such as these, taking into account your particular situation. Choice of furniture is based on the types, sizes, and quantities of items you have. Remember to take into account the size (particularly the thickness) and shape of items *after* they have been fitted with supports and mounts. This may cause them to require greater storage space.

The choice of furniture can be influenced by conditions in your storage space, such as a lack of security or HVAC equipment. Issues of use, access, and staffing levels also are important considerations when selecting furniture. For example, if you have standard museum closed storage, where the space is often kept locked and public access is only by appointment and when accompanied by a staff member, your needs will be different than if you have open storage, especially where visitors are free to walk about, handle items, and study them within the storage area itself. With open storage you should avoid the use of cabinets with doors, and store items on open shelving instead. On the other hand, if you have closed storage and you anticipate having many visitors re-

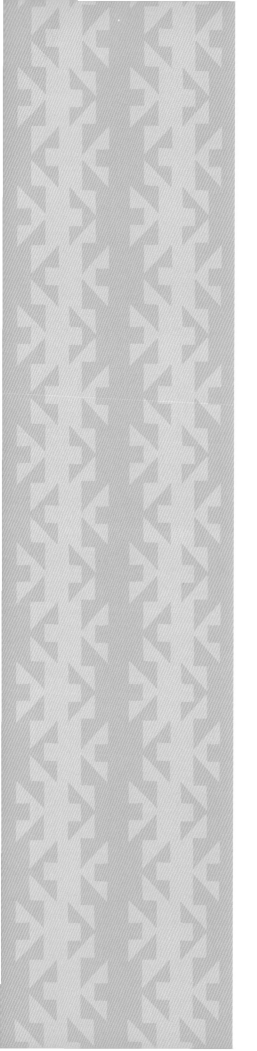

questing to see the smaller items in your cultural center or museum, it may be easier to accommodate them if the items are in a drawer than if they are on a fixed shelf, particularly if you are understaffed. Items can be seen more easily, quickly, and safely when they are in a drawer that can be pulled out for viewing and retrieval than on a fixed shelf, which may require that the items be moved. This facilitates access even when staffing is limited.

In general, the furniture selected should be as flexible and adaptable as possible to accommodate changing needs. Styles that stack or are adjustable are preferable. Nearly any type you need is available commercially from suppliers of museum, library, and office furniture.

Wardrobes

Several wardrobe designs are available. These storage units are useful when only a few items need to be stored and when items are still in sound enough condition to be hung on padded hangers. Some of these units have shelves or drawers built into the lower or upper sections of the wardrobe, which are useful for small items such as moccasins, sashes, or personal bags and pouches.

Cabinets

When security and protection from dust are special concerns, cabinets with doors are often preferred. Cabinets are available in many different sizes and configurations. These are available with shelves or drawers (see below). Other variable features include glass doors for easy visual access, solid metal doors for reduction of light, gasket seals for reducing air flow, and shelves or drawers that are adjustable, sliding, permanent, or removable. The use of piano hinges for the attachment of the doors is advisable if opening them flat will facilitate safe removal of items from the cabinet. If cabinets are made of *uncoated* steel, rusting and mold growth can be a problem in areas with high humidity or fluctuating conditions. Mold growth can also be a problem in cabinets with doors. Unless the cabinets are well ventilated or the relative humidity is closely controlled and monitored, it may be better to avoid using these.

Shelves

Shelving is one of the most frequently used types of storage furniture. It can be open or in cabinets with or without doors. Care should be taken to select shelving that is strong enough that it will not sag from the weight of the items stored on it. It should be easily adjustable so that the distance between shelves can be changed to suit the sizes of a variety of items, making maximum use of storage space.

Open shelving units that fit together so that shelves can be placed side by side or end to end to accommodate oversized items provide the most flexibility. The shelves should fit snugly in place so they do not move when items are placed on or removed from them. Shelving units should be bolted to the floor so they will not wobble or topple, and they may require additional reinforcement by attachment to the walls and ceiling as well. Shelf uprights and supports should never obstruct the removal and replacement of items, and cross-bracing should be kept to a minimum beyond structural requirements to allow easy access to oversized items.

Open steel shelving, frequently used in the restaurant industry, has shelves made of rigid parallel wires or mesh. They allow for maximum air circulation and minimum dust or moisture buildup but also permit light to penetrate. These shelves work well for *boxed* storage of light- to medium-weight items. Solid steel shelving systems have traditional sheet metal shelves. They offer greater support for heavy items and have the advantage of blocking illumination from ceiling fixtures.

Shelves within cabinets can be either fixed or sliding. Sliding shelves are preferred by museum professionals because items on them are easier to see and access. They are particularly well suited to the storage of fragile items such as shields that are usually brittle and have feathers and other attachments that dangle. Sliding shelves enable items such as these to be seen fully without being touched. Sliding shelves, however, are very expensive, and most museums have fixed shelves.

A variation on this is a unit that has large trays, instead of shelves, that slide out easily for viewing or transport. The trays can be constructed of the same material as the cabinet, or they can be made from an aluminum frame that is covered with stretched fabric. The fabric allows for light-weight trays and also increased air flow. This is optimal for hygroscopic material, such as

Left: Sliding and adjustable fixed shelves to hold parfleches of different shapes and sizes. **Below:** Sliding shelves in a powder-coated steel cabinet with doors, demonstrated by Jodell Meyer (Ojibwe), assistant site manager, Mille Lacs Indian Museum, Onamia, Minnesota. Note the polyethylene supports holding the wooden bowl.

Cynthia Hall, museum project specialist at the Minnesota Historical Society, demonstrates a steel rack with locking wheels, an alternative for rolled storage.

buckskin. Large cabinets with shelves can be fitted with brackets for storage of rolled items on tubes. Many sizes of items can be stored rolled in this manner, although flat storage is preferable for most American Indian items.

Shelves are most suitable for the storage of items that are tall and dimensional and need to be viewed that way, such as woven food baskets, ceramic pots, birch-bark wastebaskets, cradle boards, and models or dioramas. They also are suitable for collections of large or heavy items. Examples are snowshoes, antler rakes, scapula hoes, and troughs. A disadvantage of shelving is that it is not as efficient a use of space as drawer storage in most situations. Drawers can be filled more tightly with items than shelves can, because items can be safely removed simply by lifting them. With shelves, on the other hand, items must be widely spaced, or you are forced to reach between items on a shelf and move items around others to remove them. This increases handling and the potential for damage.

Dustcovers for Shelves

When open shelving is used to house uncovered items, hanging dustcovers can be attached to the outside of the shelving unit. Hook and loop fasteners such as Velcro work well for this, as do small magnets and binder clips. Dustcovers can be made from a variety of materials depending on your needs:

- Polyester film or polyethylene sheeting are sometimes preferred because one can see items through these materials, but they have a static charge that attracts dust.
- Muslin provides partial protection from dust and light without static. A low-cost alternative to this is the use of bedsheets. Both should be washed first to remove sizing.
- For optimal protection from dust, muslin covers topped with polyethylene sheeting are recommended.
- For complete protection from light, covers made from opaque blackout cloth are recommended. The cloth should be washed first to remove sizing.

Blackout cloth dustcover attached with hook and loop fasteners

Drawers

In many museums drawers are the preferred type of storage furniture for American Indian items. As already mentioned, this is because access to items in closed storage can be accomplished more quickly, easily, and safely, especially when the museum is understaffed. A disadvantage of drawer storage is that items tend to move as drawers are opened and closed, particularly those that are heavy or rounded. This problem can be solved, however, by the creative use of mounts and supports or the creation of "wells" in drawer linings (see below).

Many types, sizes, and depths of drawers are available. Drawers should be sturdily constructed so they will not buckle from the weight of their contents when full, or otherwise become difficult to open and close. They should be equipped with stops to prevent them from accidentally coming out of the cabinet. They should have ball bearings rather than slide-in grooves because these will allow them to open and close more smoothly, causing less vibration to items and eliminating the risk that the drawers will fall out of the grooves and become stuck. To reduce jarring, vibration, and sliding of items, drawers can be lined with polyethylene foam in roll form for cushioning. Smooth items, however, will slide, even on the polyethylene. This can sometimes be avoided by using two or more layers of polyethylene and cutting out an area from the lower layer(s) that is the shape of the item. This allows the item to sink down into a "well" and prevents it from sliding. This can be abrasive to some items such as those with loosely bound paints. In these situations, lining the well with an appropriate smooth material may be desirable. Depending on what is stored in the drawers, dustcovers or rear hoods may be advisable to prevent items from being damaged at the back of the drawer.

Drawers come in cabinets of various heights, which can be stacked. When security and protection from dust are special concerns, cabinets with doors are often preferred. Drawers work for the storage of a wide variety of items. They are particularly suitable for the storage of items that need to be stored flat, such as sashes, jewelry, beaded panels, beaded bands, bandolier bags, loin cloths, leggings, and vests, shirts, and dresses that are too heavy or deteriorated to be hung. Drawers also work well for such items as moccasins, arrows, quivers, personal bags and pouches of many types, wall pockets, small toys such as dolls and miniature cradle boards, war clubs, and projectile points.

Sioux painted buffalo robe stored on a removable tray that can be used for transporting the item

Oversized Flat Storage

Selecting drawers for oversized items requires special attention to the functioning of the drawers. They should be lightweight and should open and close easily and smoothly without binding. They should also be suitable for the viewing of items within them if the items are too large and cumbersome to be removed for a brief examination. Drawers for extra-oversized cabinets can be specially made of lightweight honeycomb aluminum panels if a particularly large size is required. The flat tray storage mentioned earlier works well for oversized items; the trays slide in and out of a cabinet so the item can be transported as well as stored and examined on the tray. For the best strength to weight ratio, the frame of the tray is made of aluminum, and the bottom of stretched fabric or Coroplast. Examples of items that one museum has stored

in such a cabinet are a shoulder blanket and a buffalo hide. All these cabinets for oversized items are available commercially in standard or custom sizes and tend to be very expensive.

High-Density Storage Systems

Many museums with space limitations and large collections use high-density storage systems, often referred to as compact or movable shelving. These systems minimize the amount of space needed by compacting ranges of open shelves and cabinets tightly together. The ranges slide along tracks so they can be moved apart to retrieve items on a particular range, and then moved back together again. By eliminating most of the distance between the ranges, more ranges can fit into a given area, and overall spatial requirements are reduced substantially.

Bridget White, photo lab clerk, Minnesota Historical Society, demonstrates hand-operated movable shelving holding the audiotape collection.

These storage systems can be operated automatically by pushing a button to separate the ranges, or manually by using a hand crank to separate them. Manual systems are usually preferred because it is assumed they can be operated more smoothly, avoiding jolts that jar items, they require relatively little maintenance, and they can be used during power outages. Note, however, that moving systems, even the hand-operated ones, can be damaging to some items because of the vibrations to which they subject them. Furthermore, items can be jostled off shelves, causing additional damage. Items that hang or are suspended in storage, such as garments, probably should not be stored in a movable system. If a high-density storage system must be used, a design should be chosen that minimizes these hazards for the types of items you need to store in it.

Things to Remember

Several suppliers of preservation-quality storage materials and furniture are available. It is best to obtain catalogs from a number of suppliers so you can make comparisons of cost and assess the full range of available products. If you have questions about the composition of a product, ask the supplier for details. This information should be readily available. Also, call places that have installed the type of wardrobes, cabinets, or shelves in which you are interested and ask how they like them. If you require further assistance, contact a preservation professional.

8

Handling Suggestions

SHERELYN OGDEN

When working with cultural objects, the number one thing is to have respect. I was told by my elders that all ceremonial objects are just like us (humans). They need water for cleansing, air to breath, light (sun) to live, and ceremonies for balance (harmony). Therefore, the handling and care of objects should take into consideration the above statements.

CHAR TULLIE *(DINÉ/NAVAJO)*

The following suggestions for the safe handling of items reflect the standard museum preservation practice followed in non-Indian museums. These museums have long been aware that handling increases the possibility of damage to objects. The use of gloves, supports, and carts decreases the risk of accidental damage. Museums have learned through experience that the use of gloves during handling is especially important in protecting both people and objects. It is up to you to decide when these preservation guidelines are appropriate and to incorporate them into tribal care practices in a way that makes sense in your situation.

Clean Hands Are a Must

Anyone who handles an item should first wash his or her hands. Body oils leave disfiguring fingerprints on items that are difficult to remove and can lead to discoloration or corrosion. The grime transferred from hands to an item mars it visually, causing abrasion to its surface or damage to its decoration. Also, the use of hand lotions should be avoided because the oils and other substances in these can be transferred to items and cause damage.

Gloves

Gloves should be worn when handling most items, even if hands are clean, to protect items from the damage caused by body oils and perspiration. Wearing gloves, however, may not show proper respect for items, and the advice of appropriate members of the American Indian community should be sought.

In general, clean white cotton gloves work well for handling most items. These gloves must be changed as soon as they become soiled so that the dirt is not transferred from the gloves to items. Be aware that the gloves may catch on rough surfaces of such materials as beads, basketry fibers, and skin and must be used with care. If items are too smooth, heavy, or slippery to grip securely with cotton gloves, or if surfaces snag severely on the gloves, clean hands without gloves are safer. Bare hands may also be better when handling items that have oily or tacky surfaces that hold cotton fibers. Two alternatives for these situations are white cotton sure-grip gloves, which have gripping dots or nodules on the palm and fingers that stick to surfaces, and non-powdered nitrile or latex surgical gloves. Be sure to use only non-powdered gloves. The powder can fall out of the gloves, get on the items, and lead to harm. Nitrile gloves are preferred over latex because many people have severe allergic reactions to latex. Some preservation professionals say that gloves with dots should not be used when handling metals because these dots can corrode metals. Also, the dots have been observed to leave patterns on glass, ceramics, and polished wood.

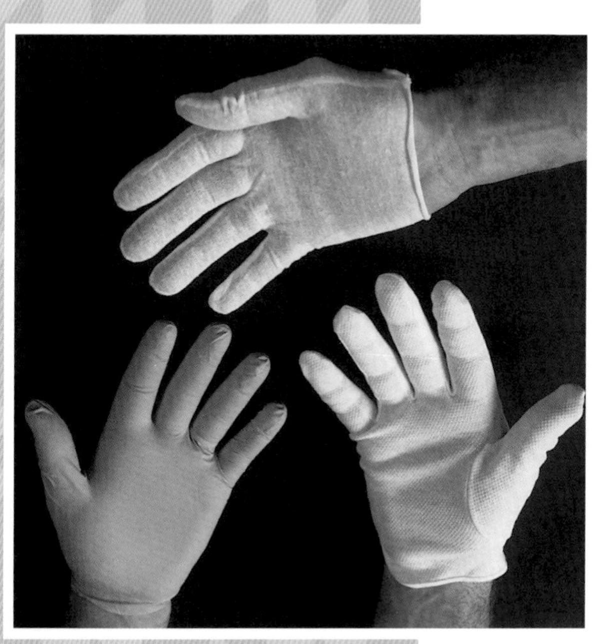

Types of gloves. *Clockwise from top:* cotton, sure-grip, nitrile.

All gloves should be changed frequently, as soon as they become soiled, to prevent dirt from being transferred to items. Even when wearing gloves, wash hands first. No matter what type of gloves you choose, they should fit snugly enough and be thin enough so that the wearer can feel through them and securely grip the item.

You will probably come into contact with items that have been treated with pesticides. Pesticide contamination is a very real possibility. Always be prepared to protect yourself. Pesticide contamination and handling precautions are discussed in chapter 10. Be sure to consult this chapter.

How Should an Item Be Handled?

When you handle an item, lift it from its base or strongest point. Do not pick it up by the handle, rim, or other projection. Use two hands. If an item is heavy, oversized, or otherwise difficult to maneuver, it should be handled by two people. Do not push or drag it. Before you pick up an item, examine it for previous repairs, new cracks, missing pieces, or other weak points. Remove detachable parts, and move them separately. Never rush. Move slowly, avoiding sudden, jerky movements. Handle only one item at a time, no matter how small it is. Never eat, drink, or smoke when handling items; accidents happen, and the resulting damage may be irreparable. Note that dangling jewelry, protruding rings, large belt buckles, hanging eyeglasses, identification badges, breast pocket contents, full loose sleeves, and the like also lead to damage. When taking measurements of an item, use a cloth tape measure rather than a metal one.

How Should an Item Be Moved?

Always plan ahead, even if moving an item only a short distance. Make sure you have the help, equipment, and space you need. Be certain you have a clean, available place to put down the item, and that, if necessary, the surface on which you put the item is padded. Also, know the path you will take when moving the item, and be sure the item will fit through all aisles and doors.

Support nonrigid items, such as bandolier bags or shirts, with rigid supports under them that are larger than the item and made of acid-free corrugated board or similar material. These supports or carrying cards can be cut to the standard sizes of drawers or other storage units. Rigid storage mounts to which items are attached with ties, like the one described in chapter 7 for war clubs, have the advantage of protecting items both in transit and in storage. Padded acid-free boxes work well for some items. An alternative to a rigid support is the use of a muslin sling, which can work especially well for large textiles or hides.

Right: Storage support for bandolier bag. **Below:** Ojibwe floral bandolier bag with glass beads. This custom-made storage support protects the bandolier bag while in storage and when it is being moved.

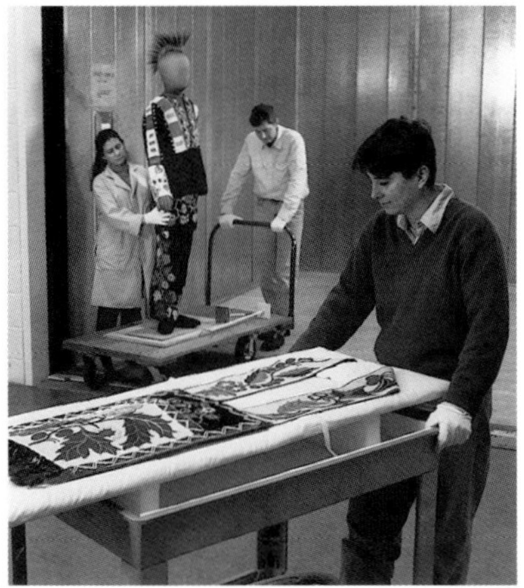

Ann Frisina, textile conservator, and Francis Paraday and Amy Toscani, mount fabricators, Minnesota Historical Society, move items to a display area.

Whenever possible avoid carrying objects, and use carts instead. Carts should be specifically designed for the transport of items: easy to maneuver, provided with protective rails and bumpers on the corners, and fitted with large wheels that minimize vibration. The center of gravity of the loaded cart should be low to help stabilize it. Carts for transporting loose items should contain shelves with a rim around their edge to prevent items from sliding off. Objects should be placed on padded surfaces. For transporting boxed items, carts with rimless shelves may be preferable. For large items, a low, flat, open cart, without a rim or walls, works well. Some museums have carts custom built to accommodate the standard sizes used in the building or to fit into special conveyances, such as dumbwaiters. Ideally, items being moved should not extend beyond the edges of the cart, and all walkways should be clear to prevent collisions. Remember to take into account aisle, hallway, and door widths.

Handling Procedure Book

Faith Bad Bear (Crow/Sioux), Assistant Curator of Ethnology and NAGPRA Project Manager, Science Museum of Minnesota, points out that some museums find it helpful to have a handbook that describes handling procedures. The handbook should have photographs or drawings of the appropriate ways to handle certain items and of ways to *not* handle them. All types of items in your collection should be covered. Bad Bear suggests that in the handbook you stress the importance of using two hands to handle items, no matter what size the items are, and of asking for help if you need it. She also points out the importance of remembering to consider every aspect of an item before moving it—its frailties, age, size, weight, even the environment from which it came originally—and to illustrate this in the handbook. For an example of one type of handbook, see *A Guide to Handling Anthropological Museum Collections*, by Nancy Odegaard, listed in the bibliography.

What If an Accident Occurs?

If an item is damaged in handling, document in writing and photographs the nature of the damage and how, when, and where it occurred. Notify the appropriate curators and conservators on staff. If there is not a curator who is responsible for the damaged item, notify your supervisor. If your museum carries insurance, the insurance company should also be notified.

Visitors

Objects are particularly vulnerable to damage when they are being used by visitors who may not have experience in handling procedures. Such visitors can include distinguished community members and students. Standard museum practice is to establish procedural guidelines for all visitors. Sometimes a written copy of these guidelines is given to visitors, and they are asked to sign an agreement to abide by them. The guidelines are often posted in the study area as a constant reminder to visitors and staff alike of the importance of careful handling.

Coats, briefcases, book bags, backpacks, umbrellas, and other extraneous articles should be checked at the front door of the museum or cultural center and never brought into the study area. Lockers or other secure storage can be provided for these articles. Ideally only research materials should be allowed in the study area, and these should be limited in quantity. Only pencils should be used; pens and other types of writing or sketching materials should not be allowed. Food, beverages, chewing gum, and candy should not be permitted.

In museums, visitors are often asked to sign a logbook upon arrival in the study area and to wash their hands prior to handling items. They are instructed in the best way to view and handle items, and a staff member demonstrates. Visitors always should work at a clean, uncluttered table. They should avoid pointing toward an object with a pencil, and they should be alerted to the hazard of standing over an object and looking directly down on it, inadvertently causing damage with hanging jewelry or eyeglasses. At no time should items protrude over the edge of the table. Oversized items should be handled by a staff member.

Fragile drawings on paper and brittle documents present special handling problems. Drawings should not be touched but should be handled by their storage container instead, such as a mat or folder. If the drawing does not have its own container, a folder should be provided. The same is true for documents. In the case of brittle documents, they can be placed in sleeves of polyester film. The document can be viewed through the polyester and handled without risk of being torn. It should be noted that polyester film has a static charge. Documents with media such as pencil that may be smeared or lifted by the static charge should not be placed in polyester film.

Things to Remember

Safe handling of cultural items is a relatively inexpensive preventive care measure; most of the procedures described in this chapter cost little or nothing. In addition, safe handling can lead to further savings by minimizing the need for repair of items. When in keeping with cultural guidelines and practice, following these guidelines is a practical, cost-effective way to extend the useful life of items.

9

Housekeeping

MARJORIE WAHENEKA ***(CONFEDERATED UMATILLA TRIBES)***
AND SHERELYN OGDEN

Good housekeeping may not seem important when compared to other pressing needs, but it is. The items you want to preserve should be kept clean. This will extend their useful life significantly. Keeping storage and display areas clean will contribute to this. Dust, dirt, and grime disfigure and abrade the surfaces of items, support mold growth, and contribute to the deterioration caused by pollutants. Clutter and trash encourage insects and rodents. Detailed information about how to clean specific items is provided in part 3 of this book. What follows here is a *general* discussion of some of the procedures, equipment, and supplies you will use most often for cleaning storage and display spaces and the items kept in them.

Clean Regularly

Cleaning should be done on a regular basis, with the frequency of cleaning determined by how rapidly dust and dirt accumulate. When deciding how often to clean, observe how quickly dirt gathers on items and surfaces, and record this information. Make note of any periods when dirt seems to accumulate more quickly, such as times when more visitors than usual come through, or during dry, windy seasons. This information will enable you to prepare a written schedule to follow for regular cleaning. Once cleaning is complete, record what you did and the date in a notebook so you know when to do it again. Ideally this "housekeeping notebook" should also contain a list of the procedures that are followed for cleaning various storage and display areas, the cleaning schedule, and a list of cleaning supplies, with brand names, and the equipment that is suitable to use.

Tamástslikt Cultural Institute in Pendleton, Oregon, has been open five years, and during this time our collections and display staff have functioned by developing our own guidelines and procedures. Good common sense with a combination of sound housekeeping techniques has been our foundation. A few of our staff traveled to other museums, either for training internships or for workshops, and had the opportunity to view different storage areas and talk with staff of those museums about their daily routines. From that experience, we discussed in our staff meetings what we observed and developed procedures that would meet our needs.

Establishing rules and posting them in plain view will assist staff in maintaining a professional atmosphere. It is important that all staff who handle the collections know and practice the rules. Randall J. Melton (Creek/Seminole), Registrar at Tamástslikt Cultural Institute, points out that "Tamástslikt has a strict policy of no food or beverages of any kind allowed in our vaulted storage areas or in our storage/exhibit preparation room. While increasing our credibility as a professionally and responsibly operated facility, this policy alleviates the possibility of an accidental spill or of food and drinks being left in these areas and attracting pests. We also encourage anyone who enters the room to wash their hands before and after handling any of the objects in the collection. As a visual reminder, we have put signs up throughout our restricted areas stating the no food or drink policy and to wash hands and take off jewelry. This is just another way to ensure that everyone knows the rules and to show any potential donors or benefactors we are responsibly housing and caring for objects in our custody."

Keeping a notebook will produce a paper trail for others to follow and is a good record of what staff do while they are in the collections area. This notebook will assist the staff in becoming more conscious of their environment and their purpose in the collections area. A special concern with cleaning is the rotation or turnover of staff—summer, seasonal, or maintenance. Their training should include the cleaning routine for the collections area. Permanent staff should develop the notebook that lists the cleaning procedures and where cleaning supplies are kept that the temporary staff can follow. Everyone who has any business in the collections area should be involved with the cleaning routine. It doesn't have to be just one person or group.

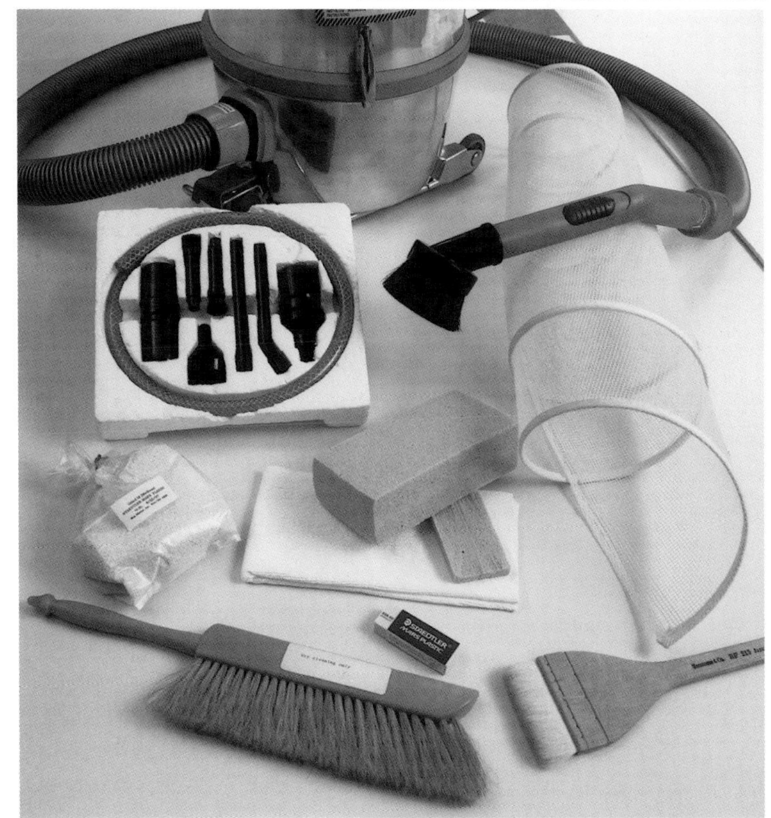

Cleaning equipment and supplies. *Clockwise from top:* vacuum cleaner, screen for vacuuming, brushes, block eraser, magnetic wiping cloth, vulcanized rubber sponge, dry cleaning granules, microsuction attachments for vacuum cleaner.

Keeping the maintenance staff informed of the routines is important. When I worked at Whitman Mission National Historic Site in Walla Walla, Washington, and now at Tamástslikt Cultural Institute, it has always been the maintenance staff who notice first any problems within the permanent exhibits or the building in general. They are the first ones on site in the early mornings and see routinely everyday what is where and how things are operating. In each location the maintenance staff has been very good about notifying the management staff of any problems or concerns.

Clean Storage and Display Areas

The best way to keep items clean is to keep storage and display areas clean. Trash should be emptied daily, especially that which contains food. If possible, keep windows closed, and put filters on air registers and ventilation ducts to help reduce infiltration of dust and dirt. Air registers and ducts can be especially problematic since great amounts of dust and dirt can enter collections and display areas through them. In geographic areas that are especially windy and dusty, having two doors through which to enter a building, an outer and an inner one, with a vestibule between them is advisable. The use of doormats at each door will also help reduce the amount of dirt that enters. Keeping collections in closed containers and using dustcovers on shelves are also important. Floors, shelves, and other surfaces should be cleaned as needed so that dust does not accumulate. In general, clean from the top to the bottom. The most important thing to remember is to take your time and move carefully.

The Tamástslikt Cultural Institute is built on what used to be a wheat field. Our first year we had to contain our rodent problem. Then we worked on our landscape around the building to prevent the dust from coming in. We have made progress, but the dust will never go away. Our building sits on an open plain area, and the wind blows very hard at times. Our building is still settling, and no matter how much we caulk our windows and put door sweeps on the doors, the dust still finds its way inside. Dust is our biggest challenge here, and we have to dust on a daily basis everywhere. The whole building is built on cement with a rock and wood exterior. In our collection vault, we had the cement floors sealed to prevent the dust. We're about to take measures to control the dust on our shelves. The storage shelves are the space-saver type and open shelving. The shelves are being measured to have flexible plastic sheeting covers added from top to bottom to completely enclose the shelves. The sheeting will be held closed by magnets. It is hoped that this will have the added benefit of helping protect against condensation. We have to closely monitor the items in case our HVAC system goes down due to the many lightning storms we have in our area. The whole system is operated by computers, and many times, due to the lightning storms, we have power surges that can result in condensation on items. Again a notebook within the collections area would help all staff to monitor the cleaning process (and other situations) and make sure it gets routinely completed in a timely manner.

How Do You Clean Floors?

One of the most important pieces of equipment to have is a vacuum cleaner. To reduce the amount of dust and dirt that accumulates, floors should be kept as clean as possible. This is best done by vacuuming. Sweeping is discouraged because it tends to stir up and scatter dust.

Many different types of vacuum cleaners are available. When selecting one, consider how you will use it. Because you will be moving the vacuum from one location to another, be sure to consider its portability. Often one vacuum must serve the dual purpose of general building housekeeping as well as cleaning the items in the collections. A vacuum with a HEPA (high-efficiency particulate air) filtration system is best because it prevents dust from blowing through the exhaust back into the air. Keep disposable bags on hand, and replace full bags with empty ones promptly, making sure that they never become overfilled. If the vacuum will be used for cleaning items as well as floors, it is important to be able to vary the suction strength with a variable speed motor, an attached rheostat, or, at the very least, a hole in the hose or wand. Rheostats can be purchased in most hardware stores.

Many different kinds of hoses and attachments are available. Hoses need to be long and flexible enough to reach out-of-the-way places. Be sure to get a variety of nozzles, including ones that go down to a small size, and micro-suction attachments for cleaning items. Such attachments are available from fabric and computer stores.

Vacuums are available from local vacuum cleaner specialty stores, department stores, hardware stores, and directly from some of the manufacturers. For more detailed information on vacuum cleaners, consult the sources listed in the bibliography (National Park Service, *Conserve-O-Gram Series*) or online at http://www.cr.nps.gov/museum/publications/conserveogram/01-01.pdf.

Floors should be washed when needed. Careful consideration, however, should be given to bringing water into storage areas because of the risk of spillage and of raising the relative humidity in a confined area, especially if large areas are cleaned at once. Damp mopping is preferred, using no more water than is necessary. As a rule, avoid the use of commercial products, and use only water. If floors are badly soiled, add one-quarter to one cup of ammonia or white distilled vinegar to a pail of water, or use a mild soap such as Murphy Oil Liquid Soap and follow the manufacturer's directions. These supplies are readily available at local grocery or hardware stores. Note that vinegar can react with metals with which it comes in contact.

It is essential that precautions be taken to prevent items stored close to the floor from being splashed with any cleaning agent, even plain water. If unsealed cement floors need to be washed, make sure that they are thoroughly dry before storing items near them or before closing the area. If these unsealed floors generate a lot of dust, consider having them sealed. This will make maintenance easier. They should be sealed with an acrylic-based low-odor sealant. Contact a local contractor who specializes in sealing floors, and ask what products are available. Then contact a preservation professional for advice on these specific products.

Shelves and Other Surfaces

Shelves and other surfaces are best cleaned with a magnetic wiping cloth, which attracts and holds dust with an electrostatic charge. These are marketed as dust-alls or dust-swipes and go by such brand names as the Dust Bunny, the Dust

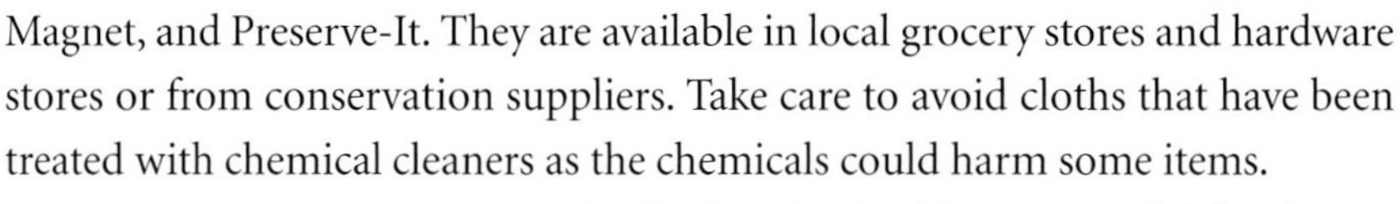

Magnet, and Preserve-It. They are available in local grocery stores and hardware stores or from conservation suppliers. Take care to avoid cloths that have been treated with chemical cleaners as the chemicals could harm some items.

Dry cleaning sponges made of vulcanized rubber are useful for the removal of sooty dirt. They degrade upon exposure to light and with age, so they need to be stored in an airtight container in the dark. As the surface of the sponge becomes dirty with use, it can be sliced off and discarded. Also, these sponges can be cut or sculpted to any shape to fit into places that are hard to clean. They are available from several of the conservation suppliers listed in appendix 4.

Plain, clean, soft rags or cotton diapers also work for dusting. Local diaper services may have inexpensive diapers available. Avoid cloths with raw edges and dangling threads. Do not apply chemical sprays that are intended to attract dust to these cloths. The chemicals may be harmful. Remember to wash the cloths regularly. Feather dusters should never be used because they redistribute the dust rather than collect it.

Heavy dust should be removed with a vacuum. Thick accumulations of dust and dirt may require that surfaces be wiped with a damp cloth. As mentioned earlier, careful consideration should be given to bringing water into storage areas because of the risk of spillage and of raising the relative humidity in a confined area, especially if large areas are cleaned at once. Shelves and other surfaces must be completely dry before items are placed back on them.

How Do You Clean Items?

It is important to remember that the items for which you are caring were made by another person for someone special in her or his life. Many times we do not know who made the items, but they were carefully constructed. I was brought up in a very traditional manner and was instructed by my Grandparents to be very careful how I handled items I did not make. A generation or two back, there were very powerful medicine people, and I was taught that you didn't know what these people thought as they were making these items. I was taught to wash with water to cleanse myself after handling items or to follow other traditional practices. I was also taught how to be very careful when I handle items and how to keep them clean when I use or wear them. "Be gentle and careful with them," my Grandmother used to tell me. "Someone's good eyes and love made that item."

Additionally, the handling required for cleaning may damage fragile items, or parts of them, such as quivers made of dried, brittle leather. Judgment needs to be used when deciding when and how often to clean. Cleaning entails cultural as well as preservation considerations. The decision of when and how much to clean should be made by the appropriate Indian community members. Some tribal care practices indicate that dirt, soot, and grime should not be removed.

When cleaning items, remember to proceed slowly and gently. Remove jewelry and any clothing that could catch on items. Remove street shoes if you need to walk on diorama platforms or other display areas. Make sure your hands are washed and dry, and wear gloves if appropriate. For your own welfare, wear hearing protection when vacuuming.

The supplies you will need most often for cleaning items include gloves, cloths, brushes, and screens. If you are going to clean the items where they are stored or displayed, you will need a cart or some type of carrying basket to transport your supplies. If you are going to transport items to a cleaning area, follow the handling guidelines for moving items that are provided in the previous chapter.

As mentioned earlier, detailed instructions for cleaning specific items are provided in part 3, which should be consulted before any cleaning is undertaken. In general, dust can be removed from items with a cloth, a soft-bristled brush, or a vacuum. As discussed above, clean, soft, cotton cloths, such as diapers or magnetic wiping cloths, work well. If a cloth is inappropriate for the item you are cleaning, a brush may work. Keep on hand several soft-bristled brushes in a variety of sizes and shapes. Natural bristles work best. These are available from grocery, hardware, artist supply, and craft supply stores. Brushes must be used only for cleaning and should be labeled to indicate this. Never allow a dusting brush to be used for painting, cleaning metals, or any other activity no matter how clean it appears to be afterward. If a lot of dust needs to be removed by brushing, brush it into the nozzle of a vacuum to prevent it from scattering.

Sometimes items can be vacuumed directly. If you are concerned about lifting a loose fragment from an item, such as a flat textile, tape flexible fiberglass screening, like the kind used on windows, over the nozzle of the vacuum. Alternatively, the screen can be placed over delicate items, and the vacuuming can take place through it. Wrapping the edges of a piece of screen with masking or cotton twill tape prevents the cut edges from snagging items. Screening is available by the roll from hardware stores.

Feather dusters should never be used to clean items. They may get caught on items and damage them, they may contaminate items by spreading dirt and other contaminates from one item to another, and they scatter the dust. Sooty dirt can be removed from certain types of items with the vulcanized rubber sponges mentioned above. Heavily soiled but sturdy paper is one example.

Tamástslikt Cultural Institute staff attended a curatorial workshop in 2000 offered by the University of Washington/Burke museum staff. Dr. James Nason was the coordinator of this workshop, and from this course, we were introduced to the harmful effects pesticides can have on items. Pesticides like mercury, arsenic, and lead were used on items to prevent bug infestation. In the early 1920s, a handbook was distributed by the Smithsonian Institution to museums and private collectors on how to manage their collections, which suggested using pesticides. Randall Melton points out that "we have always asked for histories on objects as we received them, but it became apparent to us the importance of this policy when we

HOUSEKEEPING EQUIPMENT AND SUPPLIES

- Housekeeping notebook
- Vacuum cleaner, replacement bags, and a variety of hoses, nozzles, and micro-suction attachments
- Mop
- Magnetic wiping cloths or other dusting cloths
- Vulcanized rubber dry cleaning sponges
- Gloves (rubber, cotton, latex)
- Brushes
- Screens
- Cart and/or carrying basket

learned about pesticide residues. We now know to ask directly if the person who owned the object knew if any pesticides were ever used on the object we are receiving. It is also important to the Institute to know who made the object, how it was used, who the previous owners were, what the cultural significance of the object is, and any other provenance available. Adding pesticide histories to the questions asked of an object's owner ensures the best possible preventive measures, without testing the object for pesticides, to keep facility staff, future researchers, and community members safe."

Since our class was conducted, there have been other national conferences focusing on the dangers of pesticide poisoning within museum collections and the Indian communities. This is a nationwide safety concern, and everyone should be aware of it.

See chapter 10 for more information on pesticides and how to handle items that may be contaminated.

A Final Thought

The Minnesota Historical Society has produced the *Historic Housekeeping Manual,* which covers housekeeping guidelines, practices, and resources. Although it is intended for use in the Society's historic sites, you may find much of the information applicable to your situation. It is available online at http://www.mnhs.org/preserve/conservation/reports/manual-0102.pdf.

Because cleaning is such a basic and time-consuming task, it is often overlooked or postponed. But by eliminating the dust and dirt that disfigure and abrade items, support mold growth, and attract insects, you are slowing the deterioration of items so they can continue to be used. Although good housekeeping is a basic task, it is one of the most important for preservation of your cultural items.

The Issue of Pesticide Contamination

NANCY ODEGAARD

For more than a century, chemical poisons have been applied to museum collections to prevent them from being damaged by insects, rodents, and other pests. These poisons, known as pesticides, include herbicides, which kill plants, fungicides, which kill molds, and various other substances. They have been used to prevent, destroy, repel, or mitigate pests. Under the Native American Graves Protection and Repatriation Act (NAGPRA), federally recognized American Indian tribes can take back certain items from museums and federal agencies. Many of these cultural items have been contaminated with pesticides. Because these items are being handled and used in traditional ways, pesticide contamination is an especially urgent and serious concern. In addition, pesticide contamination can be an influential factor for tribes when deciding whether to repatriate certain items through NAGPRA. Also, pesticides have been routinely used in game mounts. Many tribal museums have, for example, mounted deer, elk, or buffalo on display that may have been contaminated with arsenic or other pesticides harmful to people.

What Are Pesticides?

Pesticides are chemicals used to kill organisms that are considered pests. Pesticides enter an organism's body through the skin (dermal), mouth (oral), or lungs (inhalation). Repeated applications are often considered necessary because the effects of many chemical pesticides are temporary. On the other hand, some chemicals referred to as *residuals* remain active, and applications made many years ago are still effective today.

HOW PESTICIDES WORK

Modes of Action

- Stomach poisons: applied to item surfaces to kill insects with chewing mouthparts as they attempt to eat the item.
- Contact insecticides: applied to item surfaces where there will be direct contact with insects; they penetrate the cuticle and body wall of the insects, usually serving as a quick control for crawling or flying insects.
- Residual insecticides: applied to item surfaces so that the poisons contact the insect repeatedly during and after application; these require a long period for poisoning insects.
- Desiccant insecticides: applied to item surfaces so that a powder containing silica and other salts is absorbed by part of the outer protective wax coating of the insect, thereby causing dehydration and eventual death.
- Insect growth regulators: applied to item surfaces where there will be direct contact with insects; they enable the introduction of juvenile hormones that work to restrain the insect's maturation and reproduction.
- Fumigants: applied around an infested item so that the vapors or gases they give off replace oxygen and enter the insect through the body wall or respiratory opening, causing suffocation.

Why Were Pesticides Used on American Indian Cultural Items in Museums?

As noted in chapter 6, the damage caused to items by insects and other pests can be devastating. Many American Indian items are especially vulnerable because they are made of materials that are rich in protein from which these pests derive nourishment. Pests, particularly insects, tend to eat skin, feathers, textiles, fibers, paper, and wood. In the past, museums did not know about the nonpoisonous preventive methods that are practiced today. American Indian items were important to museums, and poisons were the best way that museum staff then knew to protect and preserve these items. American Indian items were not the only ones treated with pesticides. Many natural history, botanical, and other types of collections were treated with these poisons as well. The early use of poisons to control pests is well documented. In fact, during the late-nineteenth and early-twentieth centuries both field anthropologists and museum professionals applied chemical preparations following instructions published by the staff of the larger museums, including the American Museum of Natural History and the Smithsonian Institution.

Were Pesticides Used Only in Museums?

No, private collectors and dealers of American Indian items also used poisons in an effort to preserve collections during transport, storage, and display. Thus, items that were never housed in a museum may still be contaminated with pesticides. It seems that no one (museum board members, scholars, staff, donors, or collectors) ever considered the possibility of repatriation or the return to tribal use or disposal for these items.

What Pesticides Have Been Used over the Years?

Presently we know of more than ninety chemicals that have been used as pesticides within museums. Specific information regarding when they were developed, where they were distributed, and when they were banned may help to determine whether they are likely contaminants for a particular item or in a particular museum collection. Collecting a history of a museum's pesticide use from records and staff interviews is the first step.

As pesticide histories in museums are collected, we see general trends, which suggest the types of pesticides that may have been used during specific periods of time. Botanical (plant) repellents have long been used, but this use depended on custom and availability of the plants. For example tobacco, sage, creosote, cedar wood, lavender leaves, and various seeds were known to be thrown among items, burned to fumigate, or constructed into containers to serve as insect repellents. Metal residuals, such as arsenic and mercuric compounds, were applied to item surfaces throughout the nineteenth century and well into the twentieth century. They were commonly applied to taxidermy and herbarium specimens to prevent insect attack. Other metals, including lead, chromium, cadmium, and zinc, were known for their use as pigments, but like arsenic and mercuric compounds, some of them were also formulated specifically for use in fungicides and mothproofers. Persistent pesticides (chemicals that remain potent and do not degrade or change over time) have always been popular for items that were used for display or stored in open-air conditions.

As collections in museums grew and storage cabinetry became more common, the use of volatile chemicals to treat all items within a space became desirable. Mothballs or fungicidal crystals such as thymol, camphor, naphthalene, and paradichlorobenzene (PDB) came into use. Museum workers could take nuggets, cakes, flakes, cones, crystals, or balls made of these and sprinkle them among items or place them in storage cabinets. As the solid chemical turned into a gas and entered the air (sublimated), insects were killed and effectively repelled because of the chemical absorbed by the cabinetry or items.

As chemical pesticides were developed for agricultural applications, a wider range of domestic and museum pesticides became available. Chlorinated hydrocarbons (including recently banned products such as Chlordane, Lindane, carbon tetrachloride, and Dowfume) were used as fumigants to treat large areas. Organic phosphates (including products such as Dichlorvos, Vapona, Malathion, and Dursban) were introduced as replacements for many of the banned chlorinated hydrocarbons and have been widely used as fogs and sprays and in resin-impregnated strips.

Advances leading to more effective and efficient fumigation treatments introduced the use of sealed vacuum chambers to museums. Volatile fumigants, including methyl bromide, ethylene oxide, and sulfuryl fluoride, were used to treat items. Preventive pesticide treatments were extended to museum grounds and buildings in addition to items. Carbamate powders were often prepared in solutions for poison applications as "crack and crevice" sprays.

Is There a Way to Know If a Pesticide Has Been Used on an Item?

At present we do not have any easy, conclusive, and affordable way to tell if a pesticide has been used. As a rule, traces of pesticides are not easily seen on American Indian items because pesticides that leave visible stains or films were considered disfiguring and unacceptable and were not used. Usually only those that did not leave visible marks were used, making it difficult for us to know if an item has been contaminated.

One way to determine if pesticides were used is to ask a museum what its policy regarding pesticide use has been over the years. Unfortunately, museums cannot often provide this information. The chemical preparations and the methods of application that were used on individual items were rarely recorded, since use of pesticides was thought to be a normal part of general

HOW PESTICIDES ARE USED

Methods of Application

- Spraying or brushing: usually includes a water-based, solvent-based, or emulsified carrier for distributing the pesticide poison.
- Dusting: usually includes a powder, clay, or dustlike carrier for applying the pesticide in a dry state.
- Fogging: usually includes a volatile oil carrier for distributing the pesticide in larger spaces.
- Baiting: usually includes a food that will attract the pest.
- Using a resin or pest strip: usually includes a polymer that can be impregnated with insecticide for a slow volatilization.
- Using an aerosol bomb: usually includes an oil-based carrier for distributing the pesticide in smaller spaces.
- Fumigating: usually includes chemicals that are dispersed as a gas at room temperature.

collections care (much like regular housekeeping). Clarifying a museum's history of pesticide use involves time-consuming and difficult research. Further, many museums contracted the services of a Pest Control Operator (PCO) for the regular application of pesticides to the museum building and the collections. Before the 1972 Federal Insecticide, Fungicide and Rodenticide Act, special training was not required for the use of many chemicals and is still not required for off-the-shelf varieties of pesticides. This has made it even more difficult to know the exact methods, amounts, and types of pesticides that may have been used on museum collections.

Are There Scientific Tests for the Presence of Pesticides on Items?

The development of testing methods for pesticides on museum objects is relatively new, so only a few tests are available, and these are limited in value. The simplest and most economical tests are known as *swipe* or *spot tests.* These determine the presence of a chemical substance that may be a component in a pesticide product. For example, tests exist for determining the presence of arsenic, mercury, lead, zinc, chromium, and other metals that have been used in pesticides. Tests for boric acid and carbamates also have worked in some cases. In general, these tests provide an inexpensive but vague indication of the possible presence of pesticides and are probably most useful for screening or indicating a need for further testing.

More conclusive testing is available, but it requires the use of sophisticated analytical equipment, advanced scientific techniques, and highly trained people to carry it out. As a result, these tests are expensive. Also, multiple tests are usually necessary if multiple pesticides are suspected.

What Are the Signs of Pesticide Contamination?

There are a few indications that an item has probably been treated with pesticides. Look for the following:

- Immediately suspect an item of contamination if it is in markedly better condition than other similar items of the same materials, age, and storage conditions.
- Sometimes items that have been treated have a poison tag attached to them.
- Be suspicious of any fine white dust you see on an item even though this could be just dirt.
- Beware of crystals or colored efflorescence on an item.
- Suspect anything you cannot identify.

What Is a Pesticide Residue?

The term *residue* refers to what remains. In the case of pesticides, it refers to the chemicals that remain on the item after the application process and after any volatile propellants, such as water or solvents, that were used to distribute the chemicals have evaporated.

How Do You Know If a Pesticide Residue Is Toxic?

Determining if a pesticide residue is toxic is not easy. It requires the interpretation of toxicological information by medical doctors. *Toxicity* refers to the killing ability of a poison. Specialized doctors, known as medical toxicologists, consider the chemical composition, chemical form, and chemical quantities within a pesticide along with the known human symptoms (descriptions of condition), physical signs (visible descriptions of condition), and case histories (of past exposures on similar human populations) in order to evaluate the potential toxicity of a pesticide exposure. Special populations including children, the elderly, or the ill are usually considered to be at greater risk from pesticide exposures. The different modes of action used by different pesticide formulations produce different degrees of toxicity. For example, tobacco smoke is toxic, but eaten tobacco can be lethal. Also the form of the chemicals used in pesticides can have a significant effect on toxicity. An example is mercury. Liquid mercury is technically not toxic, but mercury fumes and mercuric compounds are extremely toxic.

Pesticide poisoning may be described as chronic or acute. Chronic poisoning occurs through a buildup of many small doses over a period of time. There is no particular lethal dose (LD). Acute poisoning requires a larger dose that is measured as LD 50 (a lethal dosage for 50 percent of the animals tested) and has immediate symptoms. If a pesticide poisoning is suspected, an exposure history is taken, and medical testing and treatment follow. Limited information regarding health effects and necessary precautions may be found on Material Safety Data Sheets (MSDS) as required by the Occupational Safety and Health Administration (OSHA) Hazard Communications Standard (29 CFR 1910.1200) and on pesticide labels as required by the Environmental Protection Agency (EPA).

Are Different Levels of Exposure Significant?

Yes. For example, handling an item while wearing gloves and a HEPA respirator is less risky than wearing a ceremonial mask or a skin shirt that may touch your mouth and skin. The level of exposure depends on how the pesticide poison enters the body: by eating it, breathing it, or absorbing it through the skin.

It also depends on whether it is in a solid, liquid, or gas form and on its chemical properties. The means of exposure, as for example, from an open container, a spill, or residues of a pesticide, also affects the level of exposure. A person's age and overall health, and the strength of his or her body's defense mechanisms will affect exposure symptoms. When exposed to poison, children and the elderly are more likely to experience symptoms of toxicity than healthy middle-age adults.

Have Museum Workers Been Poisoned by Pesticides?

There is no doubt that pesticides have affected many museum workers. These effects generally occurred during the days of unprotected and unregulated pesticide applications when exposures to large concentrated amounts of chemicals were possible. Since the introduction of professional conservation and collections care practices, there has been an increase in the use of personal protective equipment (gloves, smocks or lab coats, and particle masks), restrictions regarding the use of pesticides, and regulations affecting the application of pesticides. Also, because museum workers do not return items to cultural use (traditional handling or wearing or ceremonial interactions), the points of entry (mouth, skin, nose) on their bodies have not had prolonged or repeated exposure to pesticide residues. Various studies done on agricultural workers and more recently on museum workers illustrate the value of personal protective equipment.

Are There Specific Symptoms of Poisoning?

No specific symptoms or signs are always present in poisonings by particular pesticides. For this reason and because awareness of exposures to pesticide residues in museum objects is relatively new, the information we have is limited. We simply do not have case study information about the risks in a particular situation. Information about this type of exposure is based on interpretation. Begin by talking with a medical doctor or consultant at a poison control center for specific information. Be aware of an employee's pre-existing health problems so these do not intensify or are not mistaken for pesticide poisoning.

Reference material about pesticide dosage, signs and symptoms, and other medical information related to pesticide products can be found in *Recognition and Management of Pesticide Poisonings* (1999), which is also located in electronic format at http://www.epa.gov/oppfead1/safety/healthcare/handbook/handbook.htm.

Can Pesticide Residues Be Removed from Items?

We do not know yet. Currently available methods are still in early stages of testing, and all have disadvantages. Researchers believe, however, that because toxicity is based on the form of the toxin and the exposure, detoxification may not necessarily require complete removal of all pesticide residues present. Environmental efforts to remove pesticides from the water and soil suggest that treatments involving temperature, ultraviolet light, and the use of chemical additives show promise for the future.

What Can You Do?

Consider the following procedures for pesticide-contaminated items. Preservation professionals may be able to help you with these procedures.

- Replacement: removal of the entire item and replacement of it with a duplicate, reproduction, or alternate item.
- Containment: application of covers or coatings that isolate the hazardous material from human exposure.
- Washing: removal of contaminants by water, laundering, or solvent wiping.
- Physical removal: removal by manual scraping, vacuum suction, laser blast, or exposure to high heat or ultraviolet light.
- Chemical removal: removal by the application of chemical processes.
- Biological removal: removal by the application of specialized microorganisms.

How Should Items Be Handled If You Are Not Sure about the Presence of Pesticides?

Unless you can confirm that an item is safe, handle all items as though they were treated with a toxic compound. This means that it is *not advisable* to

- place items in open or nonenclosed exhibit cases,
- handle items in interpretation programs,
- wear or use items, or
- place items near food or other consumables.

In addition, the following precautions should be taken.

- Examine potentially contaminated items in a well-ventilated area. It may be advisable to use a fume hood or fan and to avoid extensive examinations in small rooms or closets that are not ventilated.
- Handle potentially contaminated items as little as possible.
- Try to handle items by their stands, mounts, or storage containers.
- If you must handle the items themselves, never touch them with bare skin. Wear
  - latex, rubber, vinyl, nitrile, or other surgical style gloves;
  - a particle dust mask or a respirator fitted with a HEPA filter;
  - a protective apron, smock, or lab coat.
- Do not clean items that are highly suspected of being contaminated with pesticides. Call a conservator for advice.
- Always dispose of and care for protective equipment properly after working with items. Disposable equipment (masks and gloves) should not be reused.
- While wearing gloves, discard disposable particle masks by crumpling them prior to placing in the trash.
- Discard gloves by turning them inside out as they are removed, and wash hands.
- Wash aprons, smocks, and lab coats separately from other clothing.
- Always wash hands after handling items, especially before eating and drinking.
- Document any health irregularities that occur after examining, handling, or using contaminated items. Depending on where the handling is occurring, report these symptoms to museum staff, a cultural preservation officer, or a tribal health officer.

How Should Items That Have Been Treated with Pesticides Be Stored?

- Label items with a warning. Indicate the name of the toxin if you know it.
- Put items into storage containers such as polyethylene bags or archival boxes and envelopes to isolate them from other items and to facilitate handling.
- Place items in storage cabinets that lock and seal. Post a sign that reads, for example, "Pesticide contaminated materials are stored here. Keep Out."

- Use only a HEPA-filtered vacuum cleaner for housekeeping activities in collections work areas that contain contaminated items. This will prevent toxic particles from passing through the exhaust of a standard vacuum cleaner.

Can Items That Have Been Treated with Pesticides Be Used in Traditional Ways?

Alyce Sadongei (Kiowa/Tohono O'Odham), Assistant Curator for Native American Relations, Arizona State Museum, University of Arizona, has explained traditional use as physical use, symbolic use, and life-ending use. The risks to human health during the physical use of pesticide-treated items is greatest because practitioners of traditional use physically come into contact with, or physically use, the item. This use is usually by individuals who have special cultural knowledge of needs and concerns related to an item. The level of health risk is dependent on the health of the individuals, the nature of the physical contact, the type and quantity of the pesticide poison, and the environment where the use takes place. It would be unwise to place contaminated items near food or to use them for food-related activities.

Items undergoing symbolic use will generally not require physical contact as this type of use is similar to that of researchers in a museum. Because only the presence of an item rather than its handling may be important to symbolic use, health precautions such as packaging and the wearing of gloves when moving the item can be considered sufficient.

Items undergoing life-ending use may involve practitioners engaging in the act of ritual disposal of an item. Depending on the nature of this process, the potential for transfer of contamination to the air, ground, or a water source should be considered when determining if precautions should be taken in handling the item.

Are Museums Still Using Pesticides?

Today museums use pesticides only when nonchemical alternatives prove inadequate. Most museums have adopted the methods of integrated pest management (IPM) to cope with the need to preserve collections and protect them from pests (see chapter 6). The techniques associated with IPM were introduced to museum use in the early 1980s when conservators began to question the widespread use of pesticides on items. Conservators who adopted the IPM approach became more knowledgeable about pesticide products, the chemical reactions they could cause on various materials, and the potential human health hazards they might present. Also, during recent decades various environmental, occupational, and medical studies regarding acceptable levels of human exposure to chemicals have led to the steady removal of many pesticide products from the marketplace. IPM emphasizes the prevention of pest dam-

age by combining monitoring and eradication methods with the least possible hazard to people, property, and the environment. Monitoring collection areas with sticky traps and nonchemical techniques such as freezing, heating, and using modified atmospheres have become popular nonchemical alternatives to the use of pesticides.

Does NAGPRA Address the Issue of Toxic Pesticide Residues?

When NAGPRA was signed into law, the degree of potential health hazard due to pesticide residues remaining in an item was apparently not fully recognized. A reference to pesticides occurs only once in the regulations implementing the statute. The NAGPRA regulations (43 CFR 10.10(e)) say that "the museum official or Federal agency official must inform the recipients of repatriations of any presently known treatment of human remains, funerary objects, sacred objects or objects of cultural patrimony with pesticides, preservatives, or other substances that represent a potential hazard to the objects or to persons handling objects."

Informing tribal recipients of *any* known treatments that may have occurred during an item's museum history is a difficult task for most museums. It will probably involve a thorough review of many museum documents, archives, conservation correspondence, reports, and letters. If a museum is unable to find evidence of pesticide use, you can ask a number of questions that may aid the museum in providing the information you need:

- Is there evidence of prior infestation on the item claimed for repatriation?
- Are residual pesticides indicated?
- Is there evidence of museum repairs, restorations, and alterations? This indicates museum intervention practices.
- Are there any written records that would suggest the use of pesticides?
- Based on past storage locations, what pesticides might typically have been used on or near this item?

In Closing

Pesticide residues on items raise important concerns for tribal communities. Because of the range of tribal diversity, it is not possible to suggest solutions that are suited to everyone. Also, each item presents many variables that must be interpreted. Tribal protocols for use must be considered case by case along with scientific testing and medical counsel in order to formulate appropriate solutions.

Resources

The NAGPRA regulations mention the topic of pesticides under repatriation 10.10 part (e):

> The museum official or Federal agency official must inform the recipients of repatriations of any presently known treatment of human remains, funerary objects, sacred objects, or objects of cultural patrimony with pesticides, preservatives, or other substances that represent a potential hazard to the objects or to persons handling objects.

The following Web sites provide helpful information about pesticides.

Association of American Pesticide Control Officials
http://aapco.ceris.purdue.edu

This site is the homepage of the AAPCO, whose primary goal is to encourage uniformity among the states in their pesticide regulatory programs. The organization provides a directory of pest control officials by state, detailed minutes from their biannual meetings, and links to other helpful pesticide sites.

Beyond Pesticides
http://www.beyondpesticides.org/

This site provides useful information on pesticides and alternatives to their use. The organization also publishes a wide variety of materials, including a Chemwatch series, which tracks chemical effects and alternatives.

California Environmental Protection Agency, Department of Pesticide Regulation
http://www.cdpr.ca.gov/

This site offers several useful searchable databases on chemical ingredients, products/labels, and chemical companies. It also provides downloadable literature for consumers about pesticides and pesticide safety information.

ChemFinder.Com
http://www.chemfinder.com/

This site provides a searchable database on specific chemicals including many of those used in pesticide formulations. Most search results provide links to other sites with health, safety, and regulatory information.

Environmental Defense Fund, Scorecard
http://www.scorecard.org/

This site provides information on a variety of pollution-related issues. It also has a search engine, which offers chemical profiles on specific chemicals as well as on many pesticide formulations. These profiles also provide links to other data sources on these chemicals.

Environmental Protection Agency, Office of Poison Programs
http://www.epa.gov/oppfead1/safety/healthcare/handbook/handbook.htm

This site provides a complete online version of the EPA's handbook *Recognition and Management of Pesticide Poisons,* which covers a variety of pesticide products and discusses toxicology, signs and symptoms of poisoning, and treatment.

Extension Toxicology Network "Extoxnet"
http://ace.orst.edu/info/extoxnet/ghindex/html/

This site offers a search engine and extensive literature on pesticides. The literature includes "Pesticide Information Profiles," "Toxicology Information Briefs," "Factsheets," and toxicology related newsletters.

National Pesticide Telecommunications Network
http://ace.ace.orst.edu/info/nptn/

This site provides information on pesticide products, toxicology, and environmental chemistry. The search engine gives access to toxicology and active ingredient fact sheets, a health information database, product label and MSDS database, and an environmental and chemical properties database.

Pesticide Action Network
http://www.panna.org/

This site has a useful searchable pesticides database, and it offers the latest about pesticides in the news. PANNA (Pesticide Action Network North America) is an advocacy group that has campaigned to replace pesticides with ecologically sound alternatives.

Pesticide.Net
http://www.pesticide.net/

This site provides access to several databases, but its most useful resource is its extensive review of pesticides-related legislation and current events. For full use of the site, one must subscribe, but many resources are available for free.

Society for the Preservation of Natural History Collections
http://www.spnhc.org/

This site offers full text of conference proceedings. Pertaining specifically to the pesticide issue are volume 16, *The Contamination of Museum Materials and the Repatriation Process for Native California;* and volume 17, *Preservation of Native American and Historical Natural History Collections Contaminated with Pesticide Residues.*

University of Nebraska, Pesticide Education Resources
http://pested.unl.edu

This site offers general pesticide-oriented literature, plus links to numerous other sites under several topic headings, which include pesticides and protection of the environment; health protection and pesticide safety; pesticide properties, labels, and MSDS; integrated pest management; and laws and regulations for pesticide use.

U.S. Department of Agriculture, Agricultural Research Service,
The ARS Pesticides Properties Database.
http://wizard.arsusda.gov/acsl/ppdb.html/

This Web site provides access to a database that describes the chemical and physical properties of many pesticides with focus on properties that affect transport and degradation, such as soil sorption and field dissipation rates, half-life in soil, and solubility characteristics.

U.S. Environmental Protection Agency, Office of Pesticide Programs
http://epa.gov/pesticides/

This site offers an immense amount of information related to pesticides. Of particular use are the reports of the Pesticide Reregistration Eligibility Decisions (REDS), the *Rainbow Report,* the Pesticides Products database, and the Pesticide Product Information System. There are links to sites on pesticides legislation. There are also several guides and publications available on numerous other pesticides-related topics.

SOME COMMON MUSEUM PESTICIDES

Pesticide	Approximate dates of use	Persistence
EPA Category I (highly toxic)		
arsenic compounds	1700s–1977	high
carbon tetrachloride	1927–86	low
Dichlorvos (DDVP)	1960–95	low
ethylene oxide	1960–84	high
mercuric compounds	1830s–1976	high
methyl bromide	1938–99	low-moderate
sulfuryl fluoride	1959–98	low-moderate
Vapona (TEPP)	1947–88	moderate
EPA Category II (moderately toxic)		
camphor	1830s–continued use	moderate
carbaryl carbamate powder	1959–continued use	low-moderate
Chlordane	1952–94	high
dichloro-diphenyl-trichlorethane (DDT)	1944–52	high
Dursban (chlorpyrifos)	1964–97	low-moderate
Lindane (benzene hexachlorocyclohexan)	1940–78	high
paradichlorobenzene (PDB)	1912–continued use	low-moderate
EPA Category III (slightly toxic)		
Dowfume (ethylene dichloride)	1918–86	low
malathion	1951–continued use	low-moderate
naphthalene	1887–continued use	low-moderate
thymol	1958–continued use	low-moderate

11

How Should Cultural Items Be Used for Display?

SHERELYN OGDEN

I was raised the old, traditional way, I have insight from both sides. Our cultural items from the past are important. They tell us why things were done back then. It's important that the children of the Tribes understand this. It is important for the children to learn from us. These items shouldn't be in museums. Respectfully, I know our items shouldn't be in museums because they have gotten there as a result of unscrupulous acts. But we can't do anything about that. As of late a new law has set into motion a movement, which has everyone paying attention once again to us as American Indian People and to our ancestors and our lives and how we lived.

Some items are meant to deteriorate and should be left to deteriorate naturally. Some are not. Those that are not should be used to educate our children. Some of our Tribe's traditions are dying out. Items from the past can be used to educate children about aspects of our lives in the past. Some items need to be preserved to display as a teaching tool. But museums should know that there are aspects of our lives that we want to keep to ourselves and not put on display. They should respect that.

Everything about us—how we were raised, how we were talked to, how we were taught—everything revolves around respect. We seek that from everybody but, because of racism and ignorance, it's hardly ever seen. It's important that we teach the children about the past, a past that we don't want to revisit because of the atrocities back then, but, nonetheless, a past that is full of history. Someone said, "if you forget your past you're doomed to repeat it." So the past is important, and that's what preservation is all about.

FAITH BAD BEAR ***(CROW/SIOUX)***

Using cultural items for display is one of the most effective ways to teach, inform, and enrich people. It is, however, somewhat damaging to the items being displayed no matter how carefully it is done. This is because it exposes cultural items to conditions that accelerate their deterioration, such as harmful levels of light, temperature, relative humidity, and pollution. Ideally, items should be displayed in ways that minimize these hazards and protect them as much as possible. The purpose of this chapter is to provide you with the information that will help you accomplish this. The information is based on standard museum preservation practice, and it is intended for the display of items in areas designated for this purpose alone, such as galleries. Issues related to items that are still in traditional use and are displayed in this way are not considered here. At times the information is technical. I suggest that you take what you need from the various sections of this chapter, focusing on the information that is useful in your situation, and not dwell on information you do not need at this time.

For more information on displaying specific types of materials or items, refer to the section on display issues in chapters 13 through 27. Also, the National Park Service (NPS) has produced guidelines in CD-ROM format to assist in preparing displays that meet preservation needs (see the bibliography); *Exhibit Conservation Guidelines,* by Toby Raphael, a conservator at the NPS, is a useful resource. The text is divided into four sections: Exhibit Planning, General Exhibit Design, Exhibit Case Design, and Exhibit Fabrication and Installation. It is available upon request for $49.95 plus shipping from the Harper's Ferry Historical Association, PO Box 197, Harper's Ferry, WV 25425; telephone: 800-821-5206; e-mail: hfha@intrepid.net; Web site: www.nps.gov/hafe/bookshop/catalog.htm. It is also available from several conservation suppliers.

The National Information Standards Organization (NISO) developed guidelines for minimizing harmful environmental conditions when displaying library and archival materials. These guidelines are ANSI/NISO Standard Z 39.79-2001. The standard can be purchased from the NISO Press, Bethesda, MD. Although this standard was developed for library and archival materials, most of the information in it is applicable to all American Indian cultural items.

Light

WHAT ARE THE CONCERNS REGARDING LIGHT?

Of all the hazards to which items on display are subjected, exposure to light is probably the most serious in the majority of situations. Fortunately, this is a problem that you can control, often with little effort and no money. For example, turning the lights off when no one is in the display area is easy to do, costs nothing, and actually saves money.

As discussed in chapter 6, light damages most of the materials from which cultural items are made. The most obvious damage is the fading of dyes, pigments, and manuscript inks. Less noticeable but equally serious is the degradation of materials, especially textiles, paper, fibers, and feathers, which is greatly accelerated by light exposure.

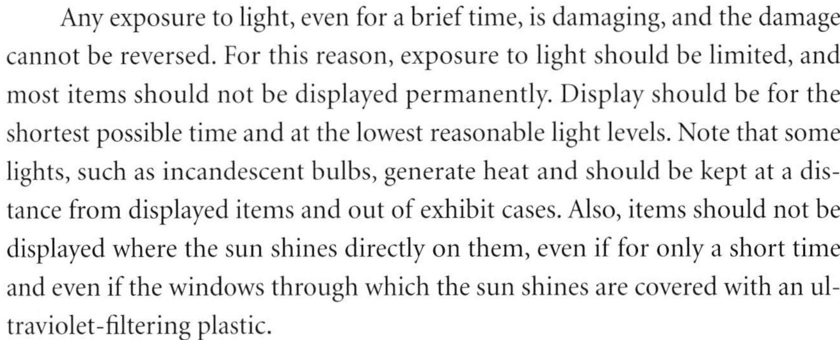

Any exposure to light, even for a brief time, is damaging, and the damage cannot be reversed. For this reason, exposure to light should be limited, and most items should not be displayed permanently. Display should be for the shortest possible time and at the lowest reasonable light levels. Note that some lights, such as incandescent bulbs, generate heat and should be kept at a distance from displayed items and out of exhibit cases. Also, items should not be displayed where the sun shines directly on them, even if for only a short time and even if the windows through which the sun shines are covered with an ultraviolet-filtering plastic.

WHAT ARE ACCEPTABLE LIGHT LEVELS?

Light levels are measured in two different types of units: *lux* and *footcandles* (one footcandle equals approximately 11 lux). For many years, generally accepted recommendations limited light levels for very sensitive materials to no more than 50 lux, and for moderately sensitive materials to 150 to 250 lux, although opinions on these levels varied. In recent years these recommendations have been debated, taking into consideration aesthetic concerns and varying rates of light fading for different materials. Also, it has been recognized that older viewers need higher light levels to discern details than do younger viewers. Ultraviolet (UV) light causes damage more quickly, and all light sources should be filtered to remove UV. This light is measured in units called *microwatts per lumen*. In general, if a light source emits more than 10 microwatts per lumen, it requires a filter.

FOR HOW LONG SHOULD ITEMS BE DISPLAYED?

Even if items are displayed at acceptable light levels, fading, embrittlement, and deterioration will eventually occur if items are displayed for too long. How do you know when this will happen? This is difficult, if not impossible, to determine in advance, so you will need to consider all the relevant factors and make a judgment. Every museum and cultural center must decide for itself what the maximum display times and total light exposure limits should be for its items based on several factors.

HOW DO YOU DECIDE ON LIMITS?

Factors to consider include the amount of time that lights are turned on in the display area, the light levels in the display area, the light sensitivity of the materials in the item used for display (calculations should be based on the most sensitive material in an item, not the least), the physical condition of the item, an item's history of prior display, the desired lifespan of the item, the significance of aesthetic concerns (the importance of seeing details, which requires higher light levels), and the audience (an older audience requires higher light levels to see items well). Begin your consideration by looking at the items you have on display at present. See if you can identify any fading that may already

SUGGESTED LIGHT LEVELS

The following guidelines serve as a general rule for items that are on display. There are, however, exceptions. Also, opinion varies regarding appropriate light levels for different materials. Consult a preservation professional if you have any questions.

- Materials that are *very sensitive* to light include textiles, paper, dyed quills, fibers, feathers, fur, and most dyes, pigments, and manuscript inks.
  - Suggested maximum light level for these materials is 50 lux.
  - These materials are found in such items as garments, baskets, drawings, documents, bags, headdresses, and most everything that has color applied to it.
- Materials that are *moderately sensitive* to light include wood, parchment, rawhide, bone, ivory, horn, and oil paintings.
  - Suggested maximum light level for these materials is 150–250 lux.
  - These materials are found in such items as utensils, drums, decorations, shields, and some weapons.
- Materials that are *generally nonsensitive* to light include unpainted ceramics, glass, metal, and stone.
  - Usually these materials do not have a suggested maximum light level unless they have a light-sensitive material added to them.
  - These materials are found in such items as utensils, bowls, vessels, weapons, spear points, ammunition, and uncolored decorations.
- Suggested maximum ultraviolet (UV) light level for all materials is 10 microwatts per lumen.

Remember, all exposure to light is damaging for most materials. Staying within these light levels will slow the damage but will not prevent it.

have occurred by turning them over to determine if they are darker or brighter where not exposed to light. Note that the amount of light shining on one item in a display area will not necessarily be the same for other items in the display area. The amount of light on each item should be measured, and the position of the items on display adjusted accordingly.

WHAT ARE LUX HOURS?

Some museums track total light exposure in terms of lux hours, which take into account both the intensity of exposure and the number of hours of exposure. The number of lux hours is obtained by multiplying the light levels (in lux) of the light shining on an item by the number of hours the item is exposed to this level of light.

The more intense or bright the light, the shorter the display times should be. Limited exposure to a high-intensity light will produce the same amount of damage as long exposure to a low-intensity light. For example, if the exposure time is kept the same but the intensity of illumination—the light level—is halved, the resulting damage will be halved (100 lux x 50 hours = 5000 lux hours, whereas 50 lux x 50 hours = 2500 lux hours). This relationship, referred to as the *law of reciprocity,* is helpful in deciding on light levels and the length of display time. Some museums have settled on annual light exposures ranging from 150,000 lux hours for very sensitive materials to 450,000 lux hours. These limits, however, will probably change in the future.

HOW DO YOU MEASURE LIGHT LEVELS?

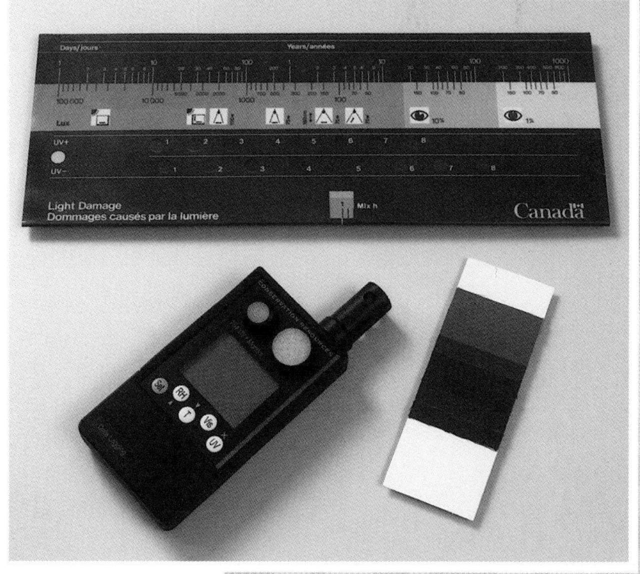

Tools for evaluating the effect of light. *Clockwise from top:* light-damage slide rule, Blue Wool card, light meter.

The easiest and most accurate way to measure light levels is with a light meter. Note that not all meters measure UV, and you will want to obtain one that does if possible. Light meters are expensive, ranging from several hundred to several thousand dollars, and not many museums have them. The ones that do will sometimes loan them by mail. Also, some regional conservation centers have light meters available for loan by mail. See the list of resources in appendix 5 for places to contact. If you cannot obtain a light meter, you can measure non-UV light using a 35mm single-lens reflex camera with a built-in light meter. Several of the sources listed in the bibliography (Canadian Conservation Institute, *CCI Notes;* Ogden, *Preservation*) have information on how to use a camera light meter, or look online at http://www.nedcc.org/plam3/tleaf24.htm. You also can contact a preservation professional for this information.

Two inexpensive tools are available that will enable you to *estimate* the possible damage that could occur in your display area. One is a Blue Wool standards card available from conservation suppliers (see appendix 4). These cards can be cut into vertical strips to increase the number of them for use.

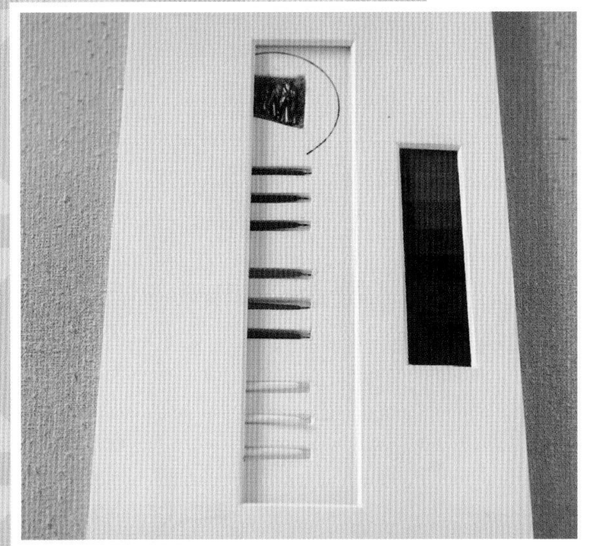

A light fading test being conducted by the Minnesota Historical Society and the Science Museum of Minnesota on dyed quills in a display case. Halves of a Blue Wool card and of dyed quills are exposed to light for later comparison with the halves that were not exposed to light.

Cover half of the card lengthwise with a light-blocking material, and then place it in a display case or in the display area. Periodically remove the light-blocking material and compare the two halves of the card to see the amount of fading that has resulted from the light. This will give you a general indication of how serious your light exposure problem is. The Canadian Conservation Institute has produced a light-damage slide rule that helps derive additional estimated information from the Blue Wool card to help with informed decision making regarding display of items (see appendix 5).

HOW CAN YOU MINIMIZE LIGHT DAMAGE TO AN ITEM?

Decide on an acceptable exposure time and light level for an item, and do not exceed them. If you have reached the limits for a particular item, one solution practiced in many museums is to take that one item off display and replace it with another. This practice of *rotation* is a commonly employed strategy for limiting the damage to an item while maintaining the integrity of the display. It requires, however, that other similar items suitable for the display are available and that staff have the time to carry out the rotation (selection and preparation of the replacement item, modification of display label text, removal and cleaning of the rotated item, record keeping to track this change). Rotation works best when exposure histories in lux hours are kept for each item so you know when to rotate one item on display with another. These histories are referred to as lux logs by some museums.

Another method of minimizing light damage is to illuminate an item on display only when a visitor comes to see it. Lights can be controlled by motion sensors to go on when the visitor's presence triggers the sensors. Alternatively, the visitor can push a button to activate a light when he or she wants to see the item. The simplest and least expensive way to minimize light damage is to cover display cases with a light-blocking cloth that the visitor lifts when he or she wants to view items in the case.

Finally, camera flashes are no longer considered a light problem unless you expect specific items on display to be photographed frequently, in which case you may want to prohibit flash photography. Extended use of photographic or video lighting can cause damage, so you may want to restrict this, explaining to visitors that this restriction is due to the light sensitivity of the items.

Temperature and Relative Humidity

Maintaining acceptable levels of temperature and relative humidity is also important. This will help slow the rate of deterioration for the items on display just as it does for those in storage. The guidelines provided in chapter 6 should be followed in determining acceptable levels.

WHAT ARE MACRO- AND MICROENVIRONMENTS?

Acceptable levels of temperature and relative humidity are controlled within a macroenvironment, a microenvironment, or a combination of both. The definitions of these terms seem to vary within standard museum preservation practice. In general in this book, the term *macroenvironment* refers to the conditions within a large space, such as the entire display area, whereas *microenvironment* refers to the isolated conditions within a smaller enclosed space, such as a display case.

WHAT ARE ACTIVE AND PASSIVE SYSTEMS?

The conditions in the macro- or microenvironment can be achieved by what preservation professionals refer to as an active or a passive system. These definitions also vary in the preservation field. As the terms are used in this book, active systems usually employ equipment such as furnaces, boilers, air conditioners, dehumidifiers, and humidifiers. Passive systems, on the other hand, usually rely on the natural buffering capacity of materials such as paper, cloth, wood, and silica gel.

HOW ARE CONDITIONS MAINTAINED?

In practice, a combination of macro- and microenvironments and active and passive systems is often utilized to maintain acceptable conditions. The temperature and relative humidity of the entire display area—the macroenvironment—are maintained by the buildingwide heating and air conditioning equipment—an active system. For highly sensitive materials, such as metals that corrode in high humidity or wood that shrinks in low humidity, a humidity-buffering material such as silica gel—a passive system—is used in a display case—a microenvironment—to adjust conditions and maintain them at the special levels needed by especially sensitive materials.

If you expect to loan items to a museum or cultural center in another geographic area where the conditions are very different from those to which your items are acclimated, you may need to use a microenvironment with a passive system. The same is true when borrowing items that you need to protect while they are in your care. Do not hesitate to consult a preservation professional for guidance in this.

MONITORING

The temperature and relative humidity in the display area should be monitored just as in the storage area. The instruments described in chapter 6 can be used. Some of these are available in small sizes that work well in display cases.

Air Pollution

Pollutants contribute to the deterioration of items on display just as they do to those in storage, resulting in corrosion and structural breakdown. Pollutants can originate from the environment or from the materials from which display cases are constructed. Environmental air pollutants were discussed in chapter 6, and the information provided there applies here. Pollution deriving from display cases is discussed below.

HOW DO YOU CONTROL POLLUTION IN THE DISPLAY AREA?

Pollution can be controlled in the entire display area (the macroenvironment) by the use of a buildingwide air filtration system to remove gases and particulates. Some systems of this sort use activated charcoal and potassium permanganate chemical filtration. These systems require regular maintenance and replacement of chemicals. If you do not have a system like this (and even if you do), be sure to keep your heating and cooling systems as clean as possible and operating efficiently. Be sure to have all air intakes and duct work checked annually. These measures will help control particulates.

If you do not have a filtration system for your display area, conditions inside display cases (the microenvironment) can be controlled to help protect sensitive items from gaseous pollutants. Cases can be sealed with gasketing to minimize the amount of air exchange between the outside and the inside of the cases (see below), and scavengers can be used in them. Scavengers attract and hold specific environmental substances, such as sulfur, through chemical and physical means. In fact, museums that have a buildingwide system will often still use scavengers in display cases to provide added protection for highly sensitive items, such as metals. Silver and all polished metals are particularly sensitive to atmospheric pollutants, and an anti-tarnish cloth or other sulfur scavenger is often included in cases with items that contain these materials. Both activated charcoal and alumina impregnated with potassium permanganate are frequently included in cases to protect against pollutants. Several of the conservation suppliers listed in appendix 4 sell these scavengers. The suppliers can provide information about the amount of a particular scavenger needed for cases of a given size, the various forms in which the different scavengers are available, and how to install or use them.

A relatively new product on the market, mentioned in chapter 6, incorporates activated carbon and zeolites to capture and retain pollutants. This product, marketed under the trade name MicroChamber, comes both as paper and board and can be included in cases to help control pollution. Because this product is relatively new, little is known about its effectiveness as a display case scavenger.

MONITORING

Scientific tests are available that determine the presence of various pollutants. Most of these require familiarity with testing procedures. Probably the most practical way of monitoring for pollution is to make frequent routine visual checks. If you see color shifts or any other changes, particularly excessive tarnishing or the formation of corrosion, such as a white, green, or rust-colored powder on metal objects, call a preservation professional for advice.

Display Cases

As mentioned earlier, pollutants often originate from the materials from which display cases are made. Woods, wood sealants, paints, adhesives, gasketing materials, and display fabrics are all potential sources of harmful gaseous pollutants. These can build up in sealed cases, intensifying the damage they cause.

SHOULD CASES BE VENTILATED OR SEALED?

Some cases have openings for ventilation, allowing for free exchange of air inside the case with that in the display area. This helps avoid a buildup of pollutants and stagnant air inside the case. These cases work well if dust and gaseous pollutants are at a minimum in the display area and if the temperature and relative humidity are at acceptable levels. Sealed cases, on the other hand, are preferable when items on display require conditions considerably different from those in the display area. It is especially important, however, that these cases be made out of materials that do not emit harmful gases that will build up inside them.

GLAZING, GASKETING, AND ADHESIVES

Glazing materials that are generally considered safe to use include safety glass, acrylic (such as Plexiglas or Lucite), and polycarbonate (such as Lexan). The materials used for gaskets vary widely. A safe material to use is polyethylene backer rod or cord, which is available from larger hardware stores and home improvement stores. Be sure the backer rod is made of polyethylene, as it is available in other materials that are not as stable. Safe adhesives include 3M double-sided tape #415 available in different widths from conservation suppliers, and ethylene vinyl acetate (clear) glue sticks for use in a glue gun, available from hardware and craft stores.

Ojibwe or Métis man's shirt, leggings, and sash displayed on a slant board in a display case with acrylic glazing

WOOD CASES

Wood has traditionally been popular for display cases because it is attractive, easy to use for construction, and economical. Harmful acids and other substances, however, are emitted by wood, wood composites, and some sealants and adhesives. Although emissions are highest initially, in most instances volatiles are present for the life of these materials. To avoid potential damage, avoid the use of wood for display cases. If this is not possible, sometimes you can avoid the use of wood on the case interior, making that part of the case out of acrylic (such as Plexiglas or Lucite), and having it supported by wood. If this is not possible, other measures can be taken to minimize potential problems from the wood.

Certain woods and wood composites off-gas less than others. If you must use wood, select one of the less damaging ones, such as aspen or poplar. Oak, one of the most popular woods for cases, is also one of the most hazardous and should be avoided if possible. Sheet products are commonly used for case construction. These are a combination of woods and adhesives, and both of these components need to be identified to determine if the resulting product is safe for display use. For example, particleboard and interior plywood have been known to incorporate a problematic urea-formaldehyde adhesive. Phenol-formaldehyde adhesive is much more stable. Plywood and other sheet woods that are stamped by the American Plywood Association (APA) to be Exterior Grade Oriented Strand Board (OSB) and Medium Density Fiberboard (MDF) sheet products should be free of harmful adhesives. At present, acceptable sheet products to use include Medex, Medite II, Danoka Featherboard, Wheatboard, Iso-Bord, and Bellcomb. If you are planning on ordering a large amount of sheet board, it is possible to specify both the wood and the adhesive used in manufacture. Aspen is the wood of choice for MDF and OSB. The adhesive should be either phenol-formaldehyde or isocyanate. Follow the manufacturer's safety instructions for personal protection when cutting or machining these products to avoid health risks.

Product formulations change frequently. Obtain current information on available products from a preservation professional before selecting a wood product so the least damaging materials are chosen. When possible, all woods and wood composites should be tested to determine their safety for use (see appendix 2).

SEALANTS FOR WOOD

New cases made from wood should be coated. If you already have display cases made of wood, the wood may need to be coated. Contact a preservation professional for advice. Note, though, that no sealant will completely block the emission of harmful volatiles. Also, some sealants are better than others at blocking damaging substances. Care must be taken to chose a sealant that forms the most effective barrier possible and does not itself emit harmful substances. The most readily available sealant recommended at this time is a waterborne polyurethane. Many kinds of polyurethane are available. Be sure to select one that is waterborne rather than solvent-borne. Contact a preservation professional for the brand names of waterborne polyurethanes that are currently being recommended. Paints can also be used to coat wood if the natural appearance of the wood does not need to be retained. Two-part epoxy paints are best, but these are difficult to use. Again, contact a preservation professional for advice on current products. *Be sure to avoid the use of oil-based sealants of any kind.*

ARE THERE OTHER BARRIERS?

Items should never be placed directly on a wood surface in a case. A barrier should be placed between the items and the wood to prevent them from coming into direct contact with damaging substances given off by the wood, even a coated one. Barriers to use include polyester film, products made from polyethylene or polypropylene, and 100 percent cotton or linen rag board or an otherwise lignin-free, chemically purified conservation mounting board. One material that forms an especially good barrier between items and wood is a laminate of aluminized polyethylene and polypropylene, sold under the trade name of Marvelseal. This product is even capable of serving as a sealant if it can be applied to all wood surfaces in such a way as to completely isolate them from the interior of the case. It is heat sensitive on one side and can be ironed onto wood surfaces.

Display Fabrics

WHAT TYPES OF FABRICS ARE SAFE TO USE?

Several factors determine a fabric's acceptability for use in a display case. One is the fiber from which the fabric is made. Certain fibers, such as silk, are by nature acidic and should not come in direct contact with items that are vulnerable to acid, such as those made of cotton, linen, or paper. Other fibers emit harmful substances, such as sulfur compounds, which can lead to the formation of corrosion on metals. Wool fabrics and felts are an example. Wool is also a food source for some museum pests. These fabrics should be avoided. In most instances the safest fiber choice is cotton or linen because these fibers are chemically stable. If these are not available, an alternative is polyester.

Knit fabrics are found by some museum staff to be easier to shape neatly when covering the base of display cases because they can be stretched. Fabrics that have a nap or "tooth" (small raised lintlike fibers) help hold flat items in place on a slanted board.

WHAT TYPES OF FABRIC FINISHES AND SIZINGS SHOULD YOU BE CONCERNED ABOUT?

Commercially available fabrics may be treated with finishes to make them suitable for a specific end use. Finishes can make fabrics flame retardant, soil/stain

resistant, and water repellent. Because these finishes can give off gasses or cause fading, fabrics with finishes should be avoided if possible. In addition, an unsized fabric is preferred. Sizing is a substance often applied to textiles in the factory while the fabric is being processed. Typically a sizing is composed of starch or a similar compound that stiffens the fabric and allows it to run more easily through the milling machines. All fabrics should be washed before use to remove any of these potentially harmful substances.

DYED FABRICS

The use of dyed fabrics for lining a case is problematic because of the concern that colors may bleed or transfer to items if accidentally exposed to high relative humidity or water. Ideally, only undyed fabrics should be used in the enclosed environment of a display case, Undyed linen or cotton fabrics work well because they come in a variety of natural shades that range from light to dark and may provide the appearance required. Colors range from beige to brown to green. Also, linen can be woven in a variety of weaves from fine to heavily textured that look well with different types of items, and jersey knits are available as well. These linens and cottons are available through commercial suppliers.

HOW DO YOU TEST FOR COLOR FASTNESS?

If a dyed fabric must be used, the fabric needs to be tested carefully. Color fastness is a concern because, as noted above, permanent damage can occur if the dye transfers or bleeds onto an item due to contact with high relative humidity or water. There are two easy tests for color fastness. First, wash a sample of the fabric repeatedly until no color appears in the rinse. Do not add bleach, and add only a small amount of soap to the wash water. When the sample is dry, test the fastness of the dye by spraying the fabric with water and weighting it against a clean white blotter or similar material. If no color is transferred to the blotter, the fabric is probably safe to use. To further check color fastness, wrap the washed fabric around your finger, and rub it back and forth across a piece of white muslin. If no color transfers, then it is safe. As an added precaution, an item on display should not be placed in direct contact with the fabric. Place a barrier material, such as polyester, polyethylene, polypropylene or conservation mounting board, beneath the item.

ARE THERE OTHER CONCERNS WITH DYES?

An additional concern is that dyes may emit chemical substances harmful to items in a closed case, particularly a tightly sealed one. The fabric should be tested with metal coupons to determine if volatiles are being emitted. See appendix 2 for information on this topic, or talk with a preservation professional to set up a test procedure.

LIGHT FASTNESS

Light fastness can also be an issue with some fabrics. There are no simple and quick tests for this that are accurate. To get a rough indication of light fastness, some preservation professionals suggest covering half of a piece of the fabric with a light-blocking material and exposing it to light in a north-facing window for five days. If a color difference is seen, the fabric is not light fast.

WHAT IS THE BEST WAY TO ATTACH FABRIC TO THE EXHIBIT CASE?

The method used to attach the fabric to the case should be carefully considered. Although sewing is usually the safest option, rustproof staples, such as stainless steel or Monel, or rustproof nails or tacks can be employed. The use of adhesives should be avoided if possible. If you must use adhesives, 3M double-sided tape #415 and ethylene vinyl acetate (clear) glue sticks in a glue gun are two choices.

SUPPORTS AND MOUNTS

Supports and mounts are used in displays to protect items. They provide a structure for inherently weak or deteriorated items and allow them to be displayed to best advantage. The information on supports and mounts for storage in chapter 7 is equally applicable to display. The bibliography lists excellent books that provide instructions for making these (Barclay, Bergeron, and Dignard 2002; Rose and de Torres 1992).

Ojibwe dance outfit possibly owned by Kay-zhe-baush-kung. Note the special mount constructed to hold the bandolier bag in its display position.

Dakota pipe bag on a slant board, and mounts custom-molded out of acrylic to exactly fit the shape of these Dakota/Sioux moccasins

Ideally, a support or mount should be custom-made to fully support the item in its display position. Some standard-sized supports and mounts available from conservation suppliers work well, but these can be expensive. Another alternative is to improvise by adapting relatively low-cost commercially available products to meet some of your display needs. For example, acrylic mounts and book, document, and photograph holders or stands can be used in creative ways to hold items. Some museums use these upside down or on their side, or even cut them up to create a support that will provide the protection necessary for an item on display. Photo holders work well for display labels too. Inexpensive glass clip frames can be used with an acid-free window mat for the display of flat items. These frames can also be used for signage in display areas. If you prefer to make your own clip frames, you can buy the clips separately. All of these mounts, holders, stands, frames, and clips are readily available at large art and office supply stores and at large discount stores.

Remember, it is essential that items on display be fully supported in a nondamaging way at all times. For more information on displaying specific types of materials or items, refer to the section on display issues in chapters 13 through 27.

Display without Cases

Many museums use dioramas to realistically depict scenes from day-to-day life or from nature. Often these dioramas are not in a case or behind glass but are in an open space in the display area. The same is true for large or irregularly shaped items that will not fit into a case. In these situations, security should be carefully considered (see facing page). Housekeeping is another concern, and items in an open display should be monitored for dirt and cleaned as often as needed.

Oil paintings and art on paper are usually displayed in frames, as are some other flat items. The framing should be done to preservation standards. These standards vary depending on the type of item being framed. See chapter 27, and contact a preservation professional for further guidance if needed.

Oversized items, such as blankets and decorated skins, are sometimes hung on walls for display. Such items have special needs. It is best to contact a preservation professional for guidance regarding these. Also, see chapter 18.

If possible, avoid hanging items on an outside wall, which may be damp or experience significant shifts in relative humidity. If you must use an outside wall that may pose a problem, insert a moisture barrier, such as polyester film or Marvelseal, between the wall and the back of the item. Also, when possible, be sure the item is held away from the wall slightly so that air can circulate between the item and the wall. For example, small plastic or felt bumpers or pushpins can be attached to the back of a frame to accomplish this.

Security

Items are often most vulnerable to theft and vandalism when they are on display, and precautions should be taken to protect them. Refer to the discussion of security in chapter 6. The building in general and the display area in particular should be made as secure as possible. The extent of the measures you take will depend on what you perceive the level of risk to be in your display area and how much security you think is needed. The minimum is to have display cases that lock with tamper-resistant fasteners. See the sources in the bibliography (National Park Service, *Conserve-O-Gram Series,* and *Exhibit Conservation Guidelines*) and online at http://www.cr.nps.gov/museum/publications/conserveogram/02-09.pdf. In addition, display cases can be attached to their bases and the floor with security screws. For framed items, security devices can be attached to the frames and then screwed to the wall, again using security screws. Oversized items, such as blankets or decorated skins, that are hung on the wall, can have a protective barrier, such as acrylic sheeting, screwed over them if vandalism or theft are serious concerns. Stanchions and other types of barriers can be used to keep visitors a safe distance away from open displays. Motion-detecting alarms also work well for this. Security cameras can serve as a deterrent as well as provide a record of people in the display area. Security personnel who are a visible presence are also a good deterrent. Whenever a single item is removed from display, a sign indicating its removal should be put in place of the item so it is clear that it was removed for a specific purpose and not stolen. Finally, when displaying collections it is also important to be aware of safety considerations for those viewing the items. The placement of display cases and items hanging on the walls should be such that safe viewing and traffic flow will not endanger them or the viewer.

Acrylic barrier topped with birch-bark branches lashed together. Branches make the barrier seem like part of the outdoor scene depicted in the open display.

Use of Substitutes

Everyone enjoys having the opportunity to see cultural items used for display. As noted earlier, though, the display of items is a preservation compromise no matter how carefully it is done and how well protected the items on display are. An effective way to have a meaningful display while at the same time protecting especially light-sensitive items is to use nonoriginal items. For example, displaying a substitute of a color photograph will protect the original from fading. Sometimes it is possible to produce newly made examples of items that are similar to the originals. These new items may have less significance than the originals; they are created for the purpose of being a substitute, so they are not the same as the original. Displaying a substitute instead of the original is becoming an increasingly accepted strategy in museums. Using substitutes for display may not seem as dramatic as using the original, but if done with care, displaying substitutes can be nearly as satisfying and can offer many preservation advantages over displaying the originals.

Substitution works especially well for paper items. While all materials are susceptible to the environmental and security hazards presented by display, paper is particularly vulnerable. Many items made of paper are easy to copy, and thanks to new technologies, the copies look similar to the original. Some examples follow:

A substitute of a traditional Métis man's capote with an original nineteenth-century Red River Métis sash and an original ear pouch that is probably Dakota/Sioux

- High-quality laser color copiers produce excellent substitutes of documents, newspapers, book pages, and some art on paper. If the substitute is made on a sheet of paper that is similar in texture to the original, it is even more convincing. Check your telephone directory for a copy service in your area.
- A substitute of a photograph can be made from the original negative, if it is available and in acceptable condition, or from a copy negative, if that is available. If not, it can be made from the original print. This latter alternative will give you a copy negative to keep for future use. Often a local photographer can do this.
- Digital scanning technology also can be used to produce substitutes of documents, newspapers, book pages, photographs, and some art on paper. This technology allows the image to be manipulated in a variety of ways so that blemishes and evidence of physical damage can be lessened if this is deemed appropriate.

Note that the item you want to use for display may itself be a substitute. Many important documents held by tribes are actually copies of the original document. For example, many tribes have been given copies of important treaties, and these substitutes are themselves important documents. In this instance, you will be making a substitute of a copy.

While it may be easiest to produce substitutes of two-dimensional paper items, it often is possible to make substitutes of other types of items as well. Perhaps the person who made the original item is still available and is able to make another for use in a display so the original can be preserved, particularly if it is in fragile condition. Or perhaps another member of the tribe has the necessary skills to make a substitute of an original item for display, if this is acceptable. Note, however, that although this option may be effective aesthetically, it may be too expensive or take too long, or it may not be acceptable within American Indian practice. Another alternative is to ask a commercial manufacturer to reproduce an item. The Pendleton Woolen Mills in Portland, Oregon, and the Faribault Woolen Mills in Faribault, Minnesota, have reproduced American Indian blankets. Such manufacturers, however, usually prefer to reproduce items in large quantities rather than single items, which is much more costly. Whatever the item, be sure to permanently mark it as a substitute so it will never be mistaken for the original. And, in all instances, seek the guidance of the appropriate American Indian community.

Loans

Lending items is standard practice in many museums, as is borrowing. There are specific procedures to follow when lending and borrowing. These procedures are intended to protect the items while on display or in transit. One important example is the generation of loan documents. Char Tullie (Navajo), Museum Registrar at the Navajo Nation Museum, says, "the importance of always using loan documents when you loan an item to another museum should be stressed. If for some unusual reason you have a difficult time getting an item back, it is helpful to have documentation that you loaned it. Standard museum loan documents—incoming and outgoing—not only say that an item is/has been on loan, but they also contain additional useful information, including a description of the item, its dimensions, the purpose of the loan, and how it was received and sent." Faith Bad Bear (Crow/Sioux), Assistant Curator of Ethnology and NAGPRA Project Manager, Science Museum of Minnesota, adds that "a description of the condition of an item should be prepared before an item is loaned and again when it is returned, to document any damage that may have occurred."

Another document with which you should be familiar is the *American Association of Museums (AAM)–Standard Facilities Report.* This document provides detailed information about the borrower's building and procedures related to security, object handling, and environmental controls. If you ask to borrow items from another museum, you will probably be asked to complete this document. All these procedures and more are explained in chapter 12.

Finally and Most Important

Always remember to show respect for the items being used for display. Handle and display them with great care. Do not hesitate to seek the guidance of members of the appropriate American Indian community when preparing a display. They will assist you in presenting items in a proper and respectful way. Also, ask for advice and assistance from preservation professionals. They can help you select materials and methods that are nondamaging to items so that these items will be available for future use for as long as is desired.

The biggest issue for my tribe is the care of and representation of cultural objects by non-Indian or non-Mohave Indian peoples. Handling and care of sensitive or sacred objects should be dictated by the Tribe and the Tribe's cultural leaders. We already have our laws about sensitive or NAGPRA-related objects, which is religion. This has been continuous since the beginning of time—we know how to represent and deal with religious issues and we see sacred objects as religious objects. Tribes should be consulted any time sensitive objects are being handled.

We have seen a problem with museums "consulting." Frequently we will get a telephone call from a museum—whether we agree or disagree with what the museum is doing, they consider this as a "consultation." People should get written permission from the Tribe before moving or dealing with anything that is sacred or potentially sacred.

Museums should invite Native people to visit their institution when they are installing a show that represents their Tribal group. This would be the best way to get the "Native voice" and to be sure you have accurate representation of their people. NAGPRA has taken us to new places, but museums still have a long way to go.

FELTON BRICKER SR. *(MOHAVE)*

BASIC DISPLAY CHECKLIST

1. Has the proposed display been approved as "proper" by the Indian community of origin?
2. Have all items been displayed in a proper and respectful way?
3. Are substitutes acceptable for use instead of the original item?
4. Does the item's condition permit display? Is the item sound enough?
5. Do the display criteria, especially light levels and duration, meet the needs of the most sensitive item on display?
6. Have light levels and exposure times been determined? What are they?
7. Can appropriate levels of temperature and relative humidity be maintained for all items on display?
8. Heating and cooling sources should be considered. Are any items placed near radiators, heat vents, or air conditioners?
9. Pollution from the air as well as from all display cases, supports, and mounts should be minimized. Are all materials in the construction of cases, supports, and mounts chemically stable? Are you sure they pose no threat to items on display?
10. All supports and mounts should provide total support for the item and avoid the concentration of stress on any one area. Have the effects of gravity been considered when constructing supports and mounts?
11. If security is an issue, have all possible precautions been taken?

Registration Methods and Everyday Business

FAITH BAD BEAR *(CROW/SIOUX)* **AND BRIAN M. KRAFT**

Registration methods are an important aspect of conducting everyday business within a museum or cultural center setting. Whether receiving, loaning, or borrowing a single item or an entire collection, there is a string of do's and don'ts that you must follow to protect yourself legally and ethically as well as to ensure the security of the collection. This task, though daunting, must be done when moving items in your collection. The following information applies primarily to museum collections. If you have library or archival collections in your care, you may want to follow procedures designed specifically for them. For information on this, contact the American Library Association or the Society of American Archivists (see appendix 5).

Why Are Standard Museum Registration Practices Useful to Tribal Museums?

An increasing number of tribal museums are being established. Older members of the tribes are giving items they have had over the years to these museums and cultural centers. Also, as Kathryn (Jody) Beaulieu notes, "non-Indians are donating items to tribal museums, preferring to give items to the community of origin." At the same time, items are being returned to tribes through repatriation. All this is happening more often than in the past, and it is expected to occur even more often in the future. As tribal museums become established and the collections they contain become more widely known, loaning and borrowing items may take place more frequently. Documentation of these transactions is very important. In the past acquiring, loaning, and borrowing, when done at all, could be done informally. But as the number of items and transactions increases, this informality may be less workable. Standard museum registration methods help keep track of items. Since you are ac-

ACQUISITION AND OWNERSHIP

Acquisition is the process by which a museum obtains title, or ownership, of an item. Title is transferred from a donor or selling agent to the museum. Establishing proof of ownership for an item at the time it is brought into the collection is important because proof of ownership gives you legal right to possess the item and allows you to do with it as you wish. Note, however, that even though someone gives you the title to an item, he or she may not have the right to give you copyright permission. This issue may need to be resolved by contacting the living artist or his or her studio or estate to get permission.

An item can be acquired by different methods, and each method has unique rules as to how the museum can prove ownership of the item.

- *Purchase.* Purchases are just that. Money is used to buy an item from a dealer, auction house, or individual for the museum's collection. When purchasing an item, be sure to obtain a bill of sale from the previous owner as proof of the purchase. If the seller has any documentation or information of previous ownership or provenance, get a copy of this as well. If there is an oral history, write it down, and include the name of the person telling the story, the date, and all other relevant information.
- *Gift.* Gifts to a museum are made by the passing of an item's ownership, or title, from a living donor to the museum. Gifts can be outright, fractional, unrestricted, restricted, and promised, and each type has its own set of rules. A document called a *deed of gift* is usually used to complete the transfer.
- *Bequest.* Bequests are similar to gifts, but the tool used to transfer the title is different. In this case an item's title passes to a museum through a deceased person's will. To prove ownership of a bequest, you need to have a copy of the will's

(continues)

countable to the museum's management for the protection of the collection, these methods protect you legally and ethically and ensure that the items will be available when needed for future use.

In large museums, standard registration methods can be elaborate and complicated. Even in small museums such as tribal ones, legal issues are a serious concern, and you need to be familiar with several federal laws, particularly the Endangered Species Act, the Migratory Bird Treaty Act, and the Eagle Protection Act, all of which can change monthly. Also, you need to be aware of customs regulations if you are moving items from one country to another. When dealing with museums outside the boundary of the reservation, you must adhere to federal law to the letter and prepare the necessary documentation.

In the following pages we will state as simply as we can some of the things you need to do under a standard museum registration process. Refer to *The New Museum Registration Methods* and the other books on registration methods listed at the end of this chapter and in the bibliography if you need more information on the topics introduced here.

What Is the First Step?

First, you need to decide whether to accept an item or collection. Be sure that you review the item or collection and all the information available about it, and make the decision to accept or reject it based on the collecting scope of your museum. You should be sure that the provenance, or history of the origin or source of an item, is well documented so that ownership by the donor or selling agent cannot be questioned. According to standard museum practice, a formal meeting of members of the highest levels of management should be held, and the items must be formally approved for inclusion in the collection. Acceptance should be noted in meeting minutes or other official meeting documents as proof of acceptance.

Upon accepting the item or collection, you need to have proper forms and documentation filled out and signed by all parties involved. Usually purchases require a bill of sale. Gifts require a deed of gift form, which releases the donors of their ownership and gives it to your museum. Bequeaths require other forms, such as loan documents, until the passing of the donor, when a copy of the provisions of the will is needed. After all the pertinent information has been obtained, the forms have been signed and exchanged, and a formal meeting has been held, the item is accessioned into your museum's collection.

Accessioning

Accessioning is the process by which all acquisitions are formally accepted into the museum's permanent collection.

WHAT IS AN ACCESSION NUMBER?

One of the first procedures in the accessioning process is to assign the item a number. Whenever an item enters the building, it should be assigned a unique sequential number, identifying it from all other items in the building. If it has not yet been accepted for accessioning or if it is in the building temporarily, such as on loan for a display, it is given a unique temporary holding number. If, however, the item has been accepted for accessioning into the permanent collection, it is given an accession number. Both numbering systems are used to connect the item to its documentation and should be placed on all documents related to the item. If you keep a running list of accession numbers, this can become your accession list or register (see below).

Once an accession number has been assigned, the temporary holding number should be kept with the item's documentation. It should not be reassigned to another item. Instead, it should be retired. In fact, no number should ever be reused, as this can lead to great confusion. Also, if you skip a number or transpose a number accidentally, record the number as closed, and do not use it.

As mentioned above, every item accepted for accessioning is given a permanent number. There are many different ways to create an accession number. One of the simplest and least confusing is to start with the year the item was acquired, followed by a period, then the next sequential number following the last accession, followed by a period, then starting with one and progressing to the total of items that are together in this one accession, for example, 2002.1.1. Working backwards through the number, it would be the first item of the first accession group for the year 2002. If there were only one item in the group, the number would be 2002.1.

American Indian collections can be further identified or sorted by description or functional categories. These might include categories of use such as Implements, Dress and Adornment, Structures and Furnishings, Transportation, Ritual and Medicines, Food and Recreation. Remember, the numbering system that you choose is very important to your collection, so you must take some time to establish one to fit your scope of collecting.

WHAT IS AN ACCESSION REGISTER?

Many museums keep an accession register. This is a ledger that was created at the museum's inception in which newly accepted items are entered. It is the most important part of the record system. It has three main functions: it records the accession number given to each item, it describes each item in great detail, and it gives whatever history and provenance are known for each item at the time of acceptance. Within your museum this register must be kept in a secure and fireproof place, and for peace of mind, another copy should be kept in a different building as a backup in the event of unforeseen disasters.

provisions on file. It is not necessary to have a deed of gift unless the item is donated by the living relatives who are legal owners of the deceased's property. This would be a gift from the relatives, not a bequest from the estate.

- *Exchange.* Exchange is similar to purchase except that no money changes hands. Payment is in the form of similar goods, also known as trading. This type of transaction seems quick and easy to do. Any exchange agreement, however, should be in writing for later proof of ownership. Similar museums may benefit from exchanges by trading for items they do not have in their collection with items of which they have duplicates. This type of transaction may also be used to obtain items from individuals or dealers, but this tends to be rarer. Exchanges require formal approval from the highest levels of management in your museum. Approval should be noted in meeting minutes or other official meeting documents, as proof of approval.
- *Field collection.* An item or items may be collected or purchased from the people who made or used them. Records of provenance, materials, techniques, and use are important to the acquisition record, and legal title should be checked carefully. Legal restrictions often apply.

WHAT DO YOU DO WITH ALL THE RECORDS RELATED TO AN ITEM?

Every item in your collection should have an accession file, also known as an object file or document file. This is one or more acid-free file folders marked with the item's accession, temporary holding, or other unique identification number and a brief description of the item. All the pertinent information you have about an item from the time it first entered the building, including all information related to the item's shipment to the museum and its acquisition, should be placed in the file.

Gathering information and documentation concerning an item is important. Much information can be found on an invoice or deed of gift. You may find more information in catalogs or magazines in which the item appears. You can also obtain additional information by speaking with the person who wanted the item brought to the organization, if that was not you, or by speaking with the donors, appraisers, or other knowledgeable people. Gather all documents, including shipping instructions, your own notes or those from curators, and every "instrument of transfer." Place all this information in the item's file.

IS A CONDITION REPORT IMPORTANT?

Yes. In keeping with standard museum registration practice, a detailed condition report should be prepared every time an item enters the building. Describe every aspect of the item, including all irregularities and unique marks and characteristics. This is your documentation as to how you received the item. If anything happens to the item after this time, you will be able to reference this condition report and determine whether any new damage or loss has occurred. This condition report should be added to the item's file.

PHOTOGRAPHS

Photograph the item, and put all the photographs in the file. This type of visual record is important for insurance and identification purposes. If your item were stolen, the photographs, along with the other documentation on file, would be your proof of ownership.

IS THERE ANYTHING ELSE?

Once you have completed all these procedures, fill out a worksheet, called either an accession sheet or a catalog sheet, for each item, and put this sheet in the item's file. This worksheet records all available information about an item and its acquisition. Enter the item into the accession register with the date, accession number, and name of the person(s) who accessioned it. Depending on what type of storage units you have, you can place the item into storage by cultural group or geographic area or other means of classification and enter the location into the file and accession register.

What Is the Card Catalog Record?

A catalog record is a complete detailed record of every item in the museum's collection. Information is recorded on catalog cards that are kept in a catalog card file. The cards are filed numerically and kept in order as part of the museum's tracking system (see below). This important record serves as a backup system to protect the information about the collection. The information on a catalog card should include the museum's name, the item accession number, the name of the item, a statement of how the item was acquired (whether it was a donation, gift, bequest, purchase, etc.), the date of accession, and provenance. Any other information that you think is essential to the item should also be on this card. Many larger museums are substituting electronic collection management databases for card catalogs.

How Do You Track Movements of Items?

Every museum must keep good tracking records of the movements of items within and also outside the building. The larger the museum, the more this tracking system is needed to ensure that everything is tracked and its location, no matter for how short a time, is known. The simplest form of tracking is to place a card in an item's place when it is moved for whatever reason. The card should state where the item is going and for how long so that anyone else looking for that item will know where it is. This tracking system is also an essential part of recording incoming and outgoing loans (see pp. 104–108). A computerized system also works well.

Is There a Place in Tribal Museums for Electronic Record Keeping?

Yes. An electronic database containing all your records enables you to access information quickly. If need be, you can go to the accession file to look up more detailed information. Enter all pertinent information that you have compiled into a simple database where you can keep track of all records, movements of items, location, and basic information for the items in your collection. Using a digital camera to produce images for the electronic record is also a good idea.

Where Should Files Be Stored?

Keep all files in a central location so that information can quickly be found for every item in the collection. Staff members of your museum will appreciate the convenience of having all the information on an item located in one place accessible whenever they need it. Ideally this central location should be a fireproof records vault. Having paper copies of all information is also important. Having

electronic and paper copies is the backup plan for any unexpected disasters, and keeping these copies in a fireproof vault provides added protection. In the time it takes you to get out of the building in an emergency, maybe all you can grab will be the disks of the electronic copy of information and nothing else. So be prepared. Plan ahead for circumstances beyond your control.

Marking or Labeling Items

Physically number each item. With a number written on or attached to the item, you will always be able to know what the item's number is and can reference its documentation more quickly. The number is also proof the item belongs to your museum. There are several different ways of marking or labeling your collections. See appendix 1 for instructions on how to do this. You can use labels of cotton twill tape with the numbers written in black ink and sew them to the item. You can mark other items with reversible clear coats of an acrylic on which the numbers are written in black ink. Another way to ensure that items are marked or labeled is to put their respective numbers on the trays, mounts, or sheeting on which they rest. Drawings and documents on paper and ledger books can have their numbers written on them discreetly with pencil. It is sometimes important for American Indian items that the number be easily removable because you do not know how the items will be handled or used in the future. If this is the case, you may want to use acid-free paper tags attached with string or thread or just sitting in or next to the item.

Before you begin, sit down and plan out the places on certain types of items to mark them. You should be consistent throughout those types as to the location of the marking or label so that it is easily accessible without actually handling the item itself. Among American Indian items are war bonnets, roaches, pipe bowls, pipe stems, shirts, leggings, dresses, parfleches, saddles, cruppers, martingales, bridles, baskets, horn spoons, ornaments, tipi liners, tipi doors, and various other things. Nothing in your collection should ever be overhandled. In marking or labeling your items, you should consider the simplest, most secure place on the item to place the number where everyone will know to look for it. For instance, on shirts you may put the number at the bottom right- or left-hand corner in the front (taking into consideration display so that the number does not show). You can do the same for dresses, yokes, and all clothing items. For moccasins you can use pre-existing thread at the back seam and loop through it to attach a tag or label. On anything that has a hard, unforgiving surface, label on the underside on a reversible acrylic base coat, writing the number in black ink and covering it with another coat of clear acrylic, making sure it is legible.

Loaning and Borrowing

Loaning and borrowing items are standard practice for a museum. These transactions happen for a variety of reasons, the most common probably being

for display. Borrowing is a way to enhance or fill a gap in a display. Good record keeping is especially important for loans. If, for some unusual reason, you have difficulty getting back an item you have loaned, documentation to prove that you loaned it is helpful. If you borrow an item, you are responsible for it and will be held accountable if anything happens to it. You need to document where it is and its condition at all times. Every step of the process should always be thoroughly recorded, and sometimes a separate record should be kept. For example, long-term loans can be registered in the same way as normal donations to keep track of the item's movement within the museum and the purpose for this movement, while short-term loans should be registered in a separate loan book to record movements within the museum until the item's exit at the end of its stay. Numerous forms are available to assist with this record keeping. Refer to *The New Museum Registration Methods* and the other books on registration methods listed at the end of this chapter and in the bibliography for samples and in-depth information.

WHAT IS A FACILITIES REPORT?

When you ask to borrow an item from another museum, that museum will expect a Facilities Report from you to determine if you have the ability to safely care for, ship, handle, and install the item. The official title of this document is the *American Association of Museums (AAM)–Standard Facilities Report,* and it is available for purchase from the AAM Bookstore. It is a confidential, highly detailed, extensive chronicle that makes available your policies and procedures related to security, item handling, and environmental controls, as well as providing detailed information about your building. The report also identifies key staff members, giving their position within the museum and contact numbers.

For a Facilities Report to work, the borrower must be completely honest when compiling information for the report. If you provide incorrect information, a loan may be approved when it should not have been. This situation could jeopardize the condition of the loan item. As well, the lender should use common sense when interpreting the report. If you do not properly interpret the information provided, a loan to an important exhibition may not be approved.

When interpreting a Facilities Report, keep in mind the standards for your own museum. What are your standards for environment, security, physical structure, shipping, display, handling, and insurance? In most instances these should be the standards to which you hold museums interested in borrowing from your collection, not standards that are higher than those you have yourself.

It is important to request and review the borrowing museum's Facilities Report before formally agreeing to lend your item. By doing this you will be able to rule out any potential problems and safeguard your item from harm. For example, when sending a large item to another museum, you should determine the largest entry to the building. You may need to reconsider lending

the item if it cannot fit through the door. This consideration may seem elementary, but such problems have been known to arise when the report was not reviewed carefully.

A Facilities Report should be completed by a group of staff members who have a variety of responsibilities at your museum. A museum will typically have someone from registration, security, curatorial, facilities maintenance, upper management, and conservation participate. Identify one person to organize and complete the report using information supplied by the others. This person should also be responsible for the report's safekeeping, distribution, and updating. Note that not all questions in the report will be relevant to every organization.

Make sure you retain a copy of your completed Facilities Report so when asked to provide one again, you will not have to complete it from the beginning. All you will need to do is update it.

CAN ANY ITEM GO ON LOAN?

No. Before agreeing to a loan, examine the item carefully to determine if it has any physical problems. Is it physically sound enough to travel without harm? Even the best packing cannot reduce the risks and protect an item that is not stable enough for travel. Weigh the risks against the benefits of loaning the item, and then decide.

HOW CAN I REDUCE THE RISKS OF A LOAN?

Plan Ahead

Once the loan of the item has been approved, work out the details as far in advance as possible. This will allow time for fine-tuning and last-minute changes as the loan date gets closer. Expect changes. Take each in stride, and work through them one at a time as they arise. Questions to ask include the following:

- Does the item need conservation treatment or framing? If so, who will do the work? Who will pay the expenses?
- Is it necessary to provide a microenvironment to maintain certain environmental conditions (see chapters 6 and 11)?
- Does someone (a staff person or a courier) who knows how to unpack and handle the item need to travel with it?
- How will the item be packed and transported?
- Who is responsible for insuring the item? Do you have the necessary documentation in place?

Maintain Control

Be in control of your item at all times. This does not necessarily mean physical control, but know where your item is and who is responsible for it during each step of the loan process. Some main steps may include the following:

- framing
- conservation
- packing
- shipment
- unpacking
- installation
- display
- de-installation
- repacking
- return shipment
- unpacking
- storage or display at your museum

Know Your Details

Before sending an item out on loan, you should have the following information on hand, in a file for reference:

- borrower's name, address, contact name, and telephone number
- condition report
- loan agreement
- certificate of insurance
- transportation company's name, address, contact person, and telephone number
- pickup date and time
- delivery date and time
- for international shipments, the customs broker's name, address, contact person, and telephone number, both here in the United States and on the receiving end

Prepare Handling Instructions

You may need to request special handling for extremely fragile or large items. Relay any special instructions to your shipping company and borrower when setting up transportation. Doing this in advance of the pickup date will avoid unexpected surprises. Typical requests when dealing with a trucking company may include trucks that have two drivers, air-ride suspension, and climate control.

Get Shipping Receipts

Get a receipt for your crates, boxes, and items from the shipping company before allowing them to take control of your property. Make sure the receipt has a tracking or airway bill number so you will be able to reference it if you try to locate your shipment later. Forward this information to the borrower as well. This will allow the borrower to track the shipment and make sure that what you sent was received.

If you are the borrower, send an incoming receipt to the lender immediately after receiving the item, and call them to let them know it has arrived. The receipt will verify for them that you received their item. Information on the receipt should include the lender's name and address, loan number, who received the item, how it was sent, how many items there were, waybill or airway bill number, date the item was received, complete detailed description of the item, condition report, and item value. Both the recipient of the item and the lender should sign it. Send multiple copies, and sign each so everyone will have an original for their file.

Provide Packing Instructions

Provide unpacking and packing instructions with all of your boxes and crates, especially if they are complex and require multiple steps. Photographs and drawings are especially helpful when trying to remember how an item is oriented when packing. Affix these aids to the interior of your container, and feel free to write on the container and packing material as well. Or send written directions to the borrower in advance. Many crate builders like to use colored rings around any screws that are to be removed. This is a great trick of the trade, especially if there are numerous screws and only a few actually need to be removed, or if there are interior braces holding an item in place.

Prepare Condition Reports

These reports are essential. Every time an item travels outside of your museum, complete a condition report before and after it is transported. Complete the first condition report before packing for travel. Keep one copy in your files, and send another with the item. Upon unpacking at the receiving end, another condition report comparing it to the first should be prepared, and any changes noted. If there *are* any changes or problems, you should be notified immediately. Information should be written down as to what happened and who was involved. Photographs should also be taken for documentation. If the problem is serious enough, the insurance company covering the item should also be notified. These actions are all taken for the protection of the item and yourself. When the item returns, complete a final report, and place all the documentation in the item's permanent file.

Things to Remember

Registration methods differ from museum to museum but the purpose is always the same—to keep good legible records. Having both an electronic and a paper copy of these records is good practice. Legal issues are the most important aspect of keeping good records. These range from loans, to migratory bird concerns, to endangered species acts, to emergency plans, and everything in between. The records you keep will ensure that when questions arise or events happen, you will have within reach all the information needed to answer any questions.

Most museums have registrars to tend to these matters. A registrar is an integral part of a museum or cultural center because the registrar is the one person who knows where everything is and how it is doing, both when it is in-house and out on loan. Traveling displays are an added challenge for registrars because of the additional documents that must be prepared to ensure the safety of the items while on the road and even while going through customs. Whether or not your museum has a registrar, the necessary records must be kept. Although the paperwork may seem tedious and voluminous, it is an essential part of a museum's everyday business.

For Further Information

Books

Buck, Rebecca A., and Jean Allman Gilmore, eds. *The New Museum Registration Methods.* Washington, D.C.: American Association of Museums, 1998.

Malaro, Marie C. *A Legal Primer on Managing Museum Collections.* 2d ed., rev. Washington, D.C.: Smithsonian Institution Press, 1998.

Perry, Kenneth D., ed. *The Museum Forms Book.* 3d ed. Austin: Texas Association of Museums, 1999.

Reibel, Daniel B. *Registration Methods for the Small Museum.* 3d ed. Walnut Creek, Calif.: AltaMira Press, American Association for State and Local History, 1997.

Web Sites

The American Association of Museums (AAM)
http://www.aam-us.org

The Registrars Committee of the American Association of Museums (RCAAM)
http://www.rcaam.org

The Rights and Reproduction Information Network (R.A.R.I.N.)
http://www.panix.com/~squigle/rarin/01rcsite

PART III

SPECIFIC PRESERVATION CONSIDERATIONS

The first two parts of this book provide the general information you can use to preserve the American Indian cultural objects in your care. They deal, for the most part, with issues and procedures that contribute to the preservation of all items regardless of the materials from which they are made. The information provided in this part of the book is more specific. Each chapter deals with one of the following materials or group of similar materials:

- skin and skin products
- quills, horn, antler, hair, feathers, claws, and baleen
- shell
- bone, ivory, and teeth
- glass beads
- textiles
- metals and alloys
- wood and birch bark
- ceramics
- stone
- plastics and modern materials
- paper
- plant materials
- audiotapes and videotapes
- framed items

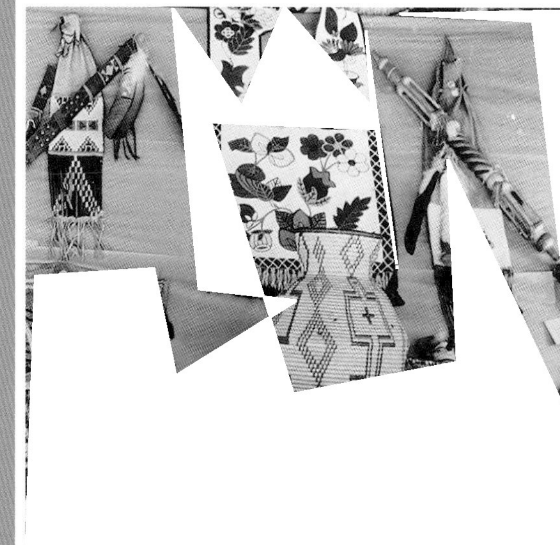

Indian crafts at Mille Lacs Indian Trading Post, Onamia, Minnesota, ca. 1935

Each chapter is sub-divided into sections that provide the specific information you will need to care for these materials. The sections are:

- identification and general information
- basic care and storage
- special pest concerns
- routine handling
- display issues
- mounts and supports
- cleaning and minor repairs

Most, but not all, of the materials from which Indian items are made are discussed. Indian cultural objects have been made from materials from all over the world, obtained either locally or through trade. Because of the wide variety of materials used, a few have been left out of this discussion. On the other hand, a few present-day materials, such as plastics, audiotapes, and videotapes, have been included because they are important in preserving the lifeways of American Indians and in recording the traditions of the culture. Also, several of the American Indians consulted (see preface) requested that these materials be included.

Archaeological materials are not addressed as a separate topic in this book. Most materials found in American Indian archaeological contexts are either discussed in a general way in the chapters on specific materials or are addressed by NAGPRA guidelines or state or provincial laws, or in archaeological field and laboratory manuals. See the bibliography at the back of the book and online at http://www.cr.nps.gov/aad/collections/. Identification and handling are important issues when dealing with these materials. The fragmentary state in which they are often found is another issue. Reconstruction of cultural items can be problematic or undesirable, even when all the pieces are available.

You may notice that the first paragraph is repeated in each chapter, along with some other information. This repetition is intentional. The assumption is that these chapters will be used for reference and read selectively rather than in their entirety from beginning to end.

These chapters were written by conservators. The information provided and the terminology used reflects their approach to preservation. We hope that the chapters will enable you to communicate more easily with conservators and will help bridge the gap between their standard museum understanding of materials and your tribal-based understanding. The writers frequently suggest that you contact a conservator if you have questions about how to implement their suggestions in your situation. This is because what may appear to be a straightforward procedure often is not, and their recommending it without an understanding of the details of your situation may lead to problems for you. Do not hesitate to seek guidance.

One way to locate a conservator is to contact the museums in your area and ask if they know of someone. If they do not, or if there are no museums in your area, another way is to contact the American Institute for Conservation (AIC), listed under "Organizations and Professional Associations" in appendix 5. If you have Internet access, http://aic.stanford.edu/select/select.html will take you directly to information on selecting a conservator. AIC provides a *Guide to Conservation Services* that will help you locate the conservator nearest you and assist you in making informed decisions when selecting a conservator. AIC provides a list of conservators around the country and provides information on what questions to ask and what to expect when dealing with a conservator. For information on conservators in Canada, contact the Canadian Association of Professional Conservators (CAPC), which is also listed under "Organizations and Professional Associations" in appendix 5. Finally, feel free to contact any of the conservators listed as contributors at the back of this book. All have indicated a willingness to provide assistance.

13

Skin and Skin Products

Found in such items as drumheads, quivers, clothing, shields and shield covers, moccasins, and saddles

PAUL S. STORCH

Indian people have used tribal methods and techniques to care for their cultural items for generations. These caregivers are highly skilled and knowledgeable individuals in possession of sound information. They have developed excellent methods that have been proven by the test of time. The purpose of this chapter is not to replace any of this knowledge or information. Instead, we are offering additional methods that American Indian people can use for the cultural items in their care.

Identification and General Information

Of all the American Indian items made from natural materials, those derived from animal skins are some of the most versatile and durable found in collections. Processing animal skins and skin products into clothing, cooking vessels, storage containers, and many other items is considered one of the first industries in human history. Membranes from bladders, stomachs, tendons, and other animal parts are also used to make clothing, bags, and threads and to decorate items.

Skins are found in items in all shapes, sizes, and colors and come from many different animals, including mammals, birds, and fish. Each American Indian culture used the animals in its region, with some overlap between regions and cultures. Identifying the animal origin of a skin can be easy or difficult, depending on how it was processed and used. Frequently, the pelt has been minimally processed, and the fur or feathers have been left on, making the identification easier. More commonly, however, the hair has been removed by chemical and physical processing. The skin has been turned into a durable material by means that are explained below. Most skins are smooth, at least on one side, which is called the hair or grain side. The other, rough, felted surface

Skin: (1) the outer covering of a vertebrate animal; the main constituent consists of collagen, which is a type of protein; (2) the finished product from a smaller animal.

Hide: the skin of larger animals, such as elk, moose, or bison.

Sinew: the connective tissue of larger mammals, such as deer; it is generally used for sewing threads.

Gut: the tissue found in stomachs and intestines; it is usually processed into a type of rawhide and used for clothing, fishing floats, and other items.

Rawhide: skin that has been scraped and stretch dried; it is generally used for fasteners, food containers, shields, and body armor.

is called the flesh side. Skins used as drumheads or for documents like treaties have been scraped very thin on both sides and stretched and dried, producing a smooth, almost shiny material. To identify these highly processed skins, you have to look closely at the grain pattern, which is formed by hair follicles (holes) where the hair grew.

The skin is the largest organ found in most animal bodies. It is made up of natural chemical building blocks called polymers. Polymers are very long chains that give the material certain properties, such as elasticity. Skin is made up of a protein polymer called collagen.

Creating a usable item from a raw skin requires processing by both chemical and physical means. To make a durable, waterproof material for clothing and footwear, most Native American cultures used a mixture containing animal brains to chemically stabilize the skin. This process is known as *brain tanning* or *semi-tanning. Leather tanning* is done with vegetable or mineral tannages, or a combination of both. Vegetable and mineral tanning were introduced to North American native cultures by the Europeans.

In general, the conversion of skins and hides into semi-tanned items or leather includes the following essential steps:

1. Cleaning and purification of the fibrous (corium) layer of the skin

2. Chemical stabilization, for example, brain tanning

Left: Zo-zed smoking deer hide to color, Red Lake Reservation, ca. 1910. **Below:** Bull-hide boat, possibly taken at a Mandan Indian village, ca. 1880

3. Lubrication, for example, with marrow or fat, and coloring, such as with clay to make white buckskin
4. Drying and stretching and surface treatments, for example, smoking, to produce a dark-colored, waterproof material

The deterioration of skin products is caused by

- excess heat, which leads to shrinkage of the fibers, tears, and stiffness;
- excess moisture, which leads to swelling, distortion, stiffening, or putrefaction, and which also promotes mold growth and further deterioration;
- combination of high heat and moisture, which causes the collagen to break down;
- insect attack, especially on skins with fur and feathers, which causes loss, weakness, and disfigurement;
- acids or alkalies (bases), which break down the skin fibers;
- exposure to light, which causes fading and chemical deterioration.

Basic Care and Storage

Consistent temperature and humidity conditions are important. Follow the recommendations in chapter 6. Stable, cool, and dry conditions are best except for items that may have acclimated to conditions that are different from these (see chapter 6).

Avoid storing items near sources of heat that could cause excessive drying and shrinkage. Shrinking skins places stress on the structural framework of some items, such as wooden drums, boats, and snowshoes, causing strain that can lead to warping or cracking, and the skins may tear.

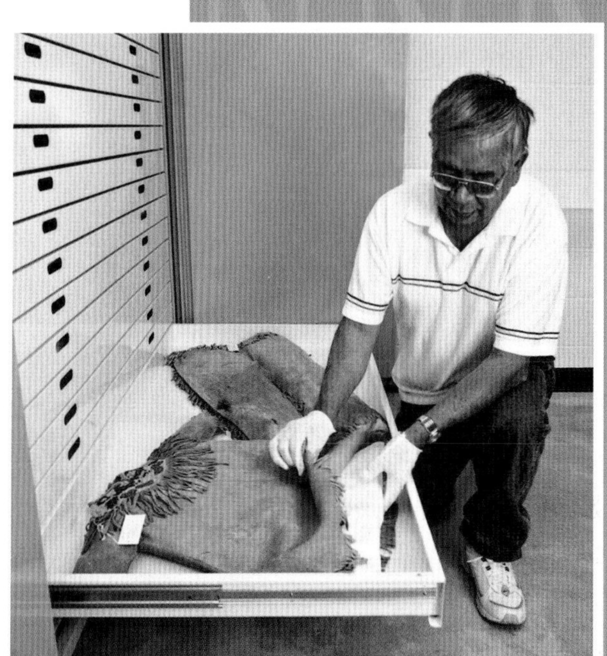

Ojibwe man's fringe skin leggings and shirt, handled by Kenneth Weyaus Sr. (Ojibwe), site technician, Mille Lacs Indian Museum, Onamia, Minnesota. The leggings and shirt are stuffed with acid-free tissue for support and stored flat in a drawer in a powder-coated steel storage cabinet.

Three-dimensional skin or leather items that still have some flexibility may be stuffed with unbuffered, acid-free tissue paper in order to retain their shape. Some items may need external supports for proper storage and display so that the pressure of the item's weight does not distort its shape (see chapter 7).

Skin garments and hides can be stored on flat mounts. A flat mount acts like a supportive inflexible tray for an item in storage or used for display. Flat mounts serve two purposes: to support an item when it is in storage, and to provide a support to facilitate moving it without undue flexing and handling. Garments can be stored on this type of mount if, when lying flat, they are not distorted. Some may need to be stuffed with unbuffered acid-free tissue. Flat mounts are commonly stored within a box or drawer or on a shelf covered with muslin fabric.

Use acid-free corrugated board for flat mounts. If an item is heavy, it may be necessary to use a thicker board that will not flex. Another material for support is called Coroplast, a polypropylene and polyethylene corrugated board. Coroplast is used by sign makers and may be available locally. However, if acid-free board or Coroplast is not available, then corrugated cardboard with a barrier of Marvelseal or polyester film is another option.

Items with straps, handles, or other attachments must never be hung or supported by those attachments. A support can be provided at the base of the item, and the handle or strap can be supported in a natural position.

Special Pest Concerns

Skin items are highly susceptible to mold growth, so high levels of relative humidity in combination with still air are a problem. If, however, you keep the relative humidity below 60 percent and maintain good air circulation, you probably will not have a problem with mold.

Insects are another concern. Several species attack skin items and can destroy them. Dermestids, especially hide and larder beetles and carpet beetles, are common threats. Maintaining acceptable levels of relative humidity and implementing a program of integrated pest management will discourage insects.

Rodents and other small mammals may attack skin items as a food source. As with insect control, good housekeeping and maintenance of the building in which items are kept are important. Glue boards are a useful rodent monitoring and trapping device if used properly and checked regularly. Live traps are also a useful and humane control method. Consult your licensed pest control operator as to which method best suits your situation.

Routine Handling

The general methods and techniques for handling all items apply to skin and leather items (see chapter 8). Skin items can be handled with bare hands as long as the hands are clean and dry. Be sure to wash your hands before handling skin items so that you do not leave dirty or oily fingerprints behind. Body oils can stain skin items, especially those that are light colored and have a sueded surface texture. Use your judgment on whether to wear gloves. If the gloves do not fit snugly, they may catch on the edge of some skin items and tear them. Also, if you choose to wear gloves, be sure to change them as soon as they become soiled.

When lifting and moving a skin item, make certain that it is supported well and that no stress is put on weak seams or attachment points. Use a tray or other support if necessary. Large, complex, and heavy skin and leather items, such as saddles and shields, should always be moved and handled using their storage supports.

If skin and leather items are suspected of having been treated with pesticides, see chapter 10 for specific ways to handle the items.

Display Issues

The temperature and relative humidity ranges mentioned above in the Basic Care and Storage section also apply to display conditions. In particular, skin and leather items used for display should be supported fully to prevent stress to attachments and seams and inspected regularly for rodent, insect, and mold infestation and damage.

Plan to rotate skin and leather objects during displays of long duration. Items that are dyed or have light-sensitive components should not be left on permanent display as irreparable fading and physical damage of the skin will occur. The length of time that an item should be used for display depends on the particular item and the amount of light to which it will be exposed.

Mounts and Supports

As mentioned above, internal supports for leather and skin items that have some flexibility can be made of unbuffered, acid-free tissue paper. Internal supports for footwear and containers, for example, can be easily constructed from polyester thermal-bonded batting or crumpled, unbuffered, acid-free tissue paper. Paper or batting are inexpensive, easily obtained, and easily shaped to conform to the object.

External supports can be fabricated from acrylic plastic sheeting, such as Plexiglas, and shaped with heat to conform to an item's surface shape (see Barclay, Bergeron, and Dignard 2002). Avoid the use of unpadded metal wires, and do not attach skin objects through existing holes with fasteners such as metal screws. These methods can cause staining and tearing at the attachment points. Adhesive mounts also should be avoided. These can cause irreversible damage to the skin and leather such as staining, loss of surface texture, and stiffening, and if the adhesive bond fails, the item can fall from its mount. Stitching skin and leather items, such as buffalo robes, to backings for vertical display is discouraged. These items can be very heavy, and stitching thread can cause tearing of the skin around the holes from the item's weight over time. An alternative is to support large, flat skins and hides on tilted boards (slant boards) that are covered with a coarse textile to help grip the item. It is better to attach items to mounts with padded wires or flat acrylic plastic clips rather than to pierce the skin with a needle and thread. Stapling a skin item to a backing will also cause permanent damage from the pressure of the staples and the size of the holes, and possibly staining from rust. Avoid using copper or brass attachments or supports in direct contact with skin or leather. The oils in the skin and leather can react with the metals and permanently stain the items.

Cleaning and Minor Repairs

Periodic inspection and maintenance are the best way to assure the long-term preservation of skin and leather items. Surface dust can be removed with a

variable speed vacuum, brushes, and micro-attachments (see chapter 9). Carefully inspect the item before cleaning for loose parts, weak seams, and fragile decorations such as flaking paint layers.

Undecorated skin surfaces that have greasy dirt can be cleaned with vulcanized rubber sponges after the surface has been vacuumed to remove extraneous dust. Gently move the sponge across the surface in one direction. Cut away the dirty part of the sponge when it becomes soiled. Avoid using liquid cleaners or detergents on skin and leather items. Saddle soap should also be avoided as it can never be completely removed from skin and leather and can cause stiffening and discoloration over time. If a greater level of cleaning is required, contact a conservator for further advice.

Skin and leather items do not need to be lubricated or fed on a regular basis with moisturizers, oils, waxes, or lubricants. Excess use of these, especially on gut and rawhide, will soften and stain the items permanently. This will change the appearance and nature of the items, lessening their historical and cultural value. Semi-tanned skins should never be treated with any oils or waxes, as these will change the surface coloration and texture. Sometimes a wax coating is applied to certain leathers after surface cleaning. A museum-quality microcrystalline wax can be used for this.

Skin and leather items are often stiff and distorted. Humidification in a controlled manner can be used to reshape an item and restore its original appearance. Steaming or spraying water directly on skin and leather to humidify it for reshaping can be dangerous. These treatments may cause staining and in the case of colored items may cause the color to dissolve and to bleed. Consult a conservator for more details about treatment if you have stiff or distorted items.

As mentioned in the section on mounts and supports, sewing should not be used to reattach loose parts unless the original stitching holes are present and are strong enough to withstand the stress. Using adhesives and backing fabrics to repair tears and holes is also discouraged, as these repair methods are difficult to do and may result in stiffening and staining of the skin. Tears and holes can be evidence of use and may provide information about an item's history. If an item is not required for use, standard museum practice would leave it unrepaired.

Metal attachments, such as tinkler cones and buckles, should be cleaned as recommended in chapter 19, on metals. Protect the skin or leather surfaces below the metal with plastic to avoid staining. The stabilization and repair of other attachments, such as beadwork, quillwork, and feathers, are addressed in the chapters on those materials.

14

Quills, Horn, Hair, Feathers, Claws, and Baleen

Found in such items as clothing ornaments, headdresses, necklaces, and containers

PAUL S. STORCH

Indian people have used tribal methods and techniques to care for their cultural items for generations. These caregivers are highly skilled and knowledgeable individuals in possession of sound information. They have developed excellent methods that have been proven by the test of time. The purpose of this chapter is not to replace any of this knowledge or information. Instead, we are offering additional methods that American Indian people can use for the cultural items in their care.

Identification and General Information

This chapter discusses a group of animal products that have been widely used by American Indian cultures throughout time. All these products are specialized forms of hair.

These materials come from a variety of birds and mammals, including large sea mammals. Generally, these materials have been used as decorative elements in various items rather than as structural parts or as tools. Although these materials are similar in composition, they are quite visually distinct from each other and from other materials, which aids in identification.

Quills, such as those taken from porcupines and birds, have usually been processed for use as decorations on garments, bags, and woven and birch-bark containers. They are split into strips and then colored with various pigments and vegetable dyes. The quill strips are arranged in patterns and sewn onto the item. The surface of a quill is compact and smooth. Where decorative quills have come loose from an item's surface, the ends may be slightly fibrous and can split lengthwise. Care must be taken to avoid further damage.

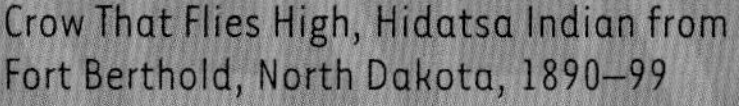
Crow That Flies High, Hidatsa Indian from Fort Berthold, North Dakota, 1890–99

Horn is the outer covering of a bony outgrowth on an animal's skull. Horns are composed of very compact hair fibers that grow out of the skulls of large mammals. Unlike antlers, horns are permanent and are not seasonally shed. Horns have been used in many different ways, including being left attached to hides in headdresses, and as carved and formed utensils, such as spoons or containers. Horn has a smooth and somewhat shiny outer surface and a rough inner surface. It can be formed by heating or steaming and, once shaped, becomes rigid. Both surfaces can then be compacted and polished with an abrasive. When used in utensils, the horn has usually been prepared in that way.

Hair is found on virtually all mammals and is a specialized outgrowth of the skin. Most mammals that were used by American Indians have an undercoat of soft, fine hairs and an outer coat of coarse, larger hairs called guard hairs. While the hairs of various animals differ greatly in size, color, and appearance, their basic structure is similar. Hairs are hollow tubes with scales on the exterior surface. The interior of the tubes may be filled with colored pigments or may be hollow. Moose and horse hair were often used as a decorative material. Unlike other materials discussed in this chapter, the microscopic identification of animals by their hair is relatively easy since the patterns of the scales and the interior pigments vary with the type of animal and species. When hair was used as ornamentation on American Indian items, it was often dyed various colors.

Feathers are widely used in the construction and ornamentation of American Indian items. They consist of a central shaft called a rachis, out of which extend the vane structures. The vanes are made up of thin barbs and barbules. These function like the hooks and loops on Velcro products and are what form the light, yet strong feather vane. When stripped of the vanes and split, the feather shaft can look similar to quills. The vanes in feathers were sometimes dyed when used in headdresses and other articles of clothing. Feathers can vary in appearance, depending on the type of bird that they come from, and where they grew on the bird. Tail and wing feathers, often call flight feathers, tend to be large relative to the size of the bird. Contour feathers are smaller vaned feathers that form the outline for the bird's body. The softer underfeathers, called downy feathers, are much smaller and more loosely structured and help insulate the bird. The color of feathers is generally due to a combination of natural dyes and the internal structure of the barbs and barbules. This will be explained in more detail when cleaning is discussed near the end of this chapter.

Claws and talons are used in various items by many American Indian cultures. These parts are hard and compact outgrowths of the skin at the end of paws and feet. Claws are found on predatory mammals and birds, such as bears, wolves, eagles, and hawks. Generally, the claws are separated from the bones and are used whole. Often holes have been drilled in one end of the claw to allow for attachment to an item with a fiber, such as sinew. The surface appearance is hard, shiny, and slightly translucent. The color varies with the animal from which it was taken and with the condition of the claw.

Baleen is widely used by American Indian cultures of the Northwest Coast and the Arctic regions. It is extracted from the mouths of humpback whales. Like horns, baleen is fused hair. Baleen objects are processed by soaking in water, splitting, and sanding with an abrasive to a smooth, compact, and shiny surface. The color is usually dark. More recently made baleen objects may be coated with an oil or varnish to impart a more durable shine.

Quills, horn, hair, feathers, claws, and baleen are all composed of a fibrous protein called keratin. Keratin is different in structure from collagen, the protein in hide and skin, and has different properties of rigidity, compactness, and hardness. All of these materials (quills, horn, hair, etc.) are affected by water, which swells and softens them. This property can make these materials easier to work and shape when forming an object, but they should not be allowed to become wet in storage, display, or use, as they will soften, distort, and degrade over time. Excessive heat will speed up the chemical deterioration of these materials. Alkaline storage or display construction materials will cause the chemical deterioration of items made from these animal products, so it is important to use pH-neutral or unbuffered materials. Keratin is broken down over time by alkalies, or bases, such as calcium carbonate. Keratin-based items are also sensitive to chemical breakdown by ethanol and isopropanol, which may be used in cleaning. These chemicals will change the shape of the items by shrinking or swelling them. Since the surfaces of quills, horns, hair, claws, and baleen are hard and smooth, they are also susceptible to damage by abrasion.

In general, the conversion of quills, horn, antler, hair, feathers, claws, and baleen for use in items includes the following essential steps:

1. Separation from the skin or bones of the animal
2. Cleaning: removing the blood and other fluids
3. Washing: soaking in water to soften for shaping and working
4. Drying, done slowly to avoid cracking and splitting
5. Shaping: working quills, horn, claws, or baleen into the desired shape by cutting with stone or metal tools, grinding with stones (compacting), and polishing with abrasives
6. Finishing: decorating with pigments such as ochre or charcoal

The deterioration of these materials is caused by

- insect and rodent attack, especially on quills, horns, hair, and feathers;
- excess moisture, which leads to swelling, distortion, and deterioration of the materials and may promote mold growth;
- excess heat, which leads to destruction of the keratin protein and dehydration, which leads to shrinkage and cracking of the fibers;

Quills: keratin-based specialized hair from porcupines.

Horn: keratin-based growth of compact hair; grows over a bony core on animal skulls.

Hair: keratin-based fiber that grows out of mammal skins; formed as hollow tubes with surface scales.

Feathers: keratin-based outgrowth of the skin of birds; the physical structure allows for both low weight and strength.

Claws: keratin-based outgrowth of skin found on predatory mammals, reptiles, and birds.

Baleen: keratin-based fused hairs found in whales and used for capturing food by straining seawater through its comblike structure.

- combination of excess heat and moisture, which can cause the keratin to be degraded, resulting in warping and cracking;
- acids and alkalies in inappropriate storage and display materials that degrade keratin;
- exposure to high light levels, which causes bleaching of the natural or dyed colors of hair, quill, and feathers and degrades all keratin materials.

Basic Care and Storage

A consistent temperature and humidity are particularly important for the preservation of these materials, as they are especially sensitive to moisture and heat. Follow the recommendations in chapter 6 for guidelines. As with other materials, keep in mind exceptions for items that may have acclimated to conditions that are different from these (see chapter 6).

To minimize temperature fluctuations, avoid storing and displaying items containing these materials in the direct line of a ventilation duct outlet. Storing items near radiators, heat pipes, outside windows, or incandescent lights can cause excessive drying.

Items with holes, straps, appendages, or other attachments must never be hung or supported by those attachments. A support can be provided under the item to hold it, and the handle or strap can be held in a natural position by additional supports.

Special Pest Concerns

Horn, baleen, and claw items are not particularly susceptible to insects. They can, however, be attacked by rodents and other small mammals that cause structural damage by gnawing on the surfaces of these items. Practicing good housekeeping, following an integrated pest management program, and employing pest control services regularly will help prevent infestations. Vacuuming is particularly effective in keeping areas clean. Glue boards are a useful rodent monitoring and trapping device if used properly and checked regularly. Live traps are also a useful and humane control method. Consult your licensed pest control operator as to which methods best suit your situation.

Quills, hair, and feathers are highly susceptible to insect attack and damage. All three materials are food for dermestid beetles, such as hide and carpet beetles. Dermestids are a group of beetles that scavenge and feed primarily on dried animal matter. Hair can also be attacked by clothes moths, which feed on wool and woolen products. Insect attacks on items made from these materials will leave holes, frass, and loose pieces.

Keratin-based items can also become infested with mold, particularly if the relative humidity in storage or display areas is allowed to exceed 60 percent for relatively long periods. Mold infestations can be recognized by white or greenish fuzzy growths on the surface of items. Good ventilation and air circulation in storage and display areas will help to prevent infestations. If mold growth does occur, take measures to reduce the relative humidity. Contact a conservator on how to clean the surfaces safely. Personal safety is the primary concern when dealing with mold infestations, as many types of mold can cause serious and permanent health problems.

Insect damage to quills

Routine Handling

The general methods and techniques for handling all items apply to quills, horn, hair, feathers, claw, and baleen (see chapter 8). These materials can be handled with bare hands as long as the hands are clean and dry. Body oils, however, can stain feathers and quills, especially those that are light colored. Wearing cotton or latex gloves is usually suggested when handling most items that include these materials.

When lifting and moving an item composed of or including these materials, make certain that it is supported well and that no stress is put on weak areas or attachment points. Use a tray or other support if necessary. This can be made from a piece of acid-free corrugated board that is cut to the standard sizes of drawers or other storage units.

Special note: Quill, horn, hair, feathers, claws, and baleen are generally the types of items that may have been treated with pesticides. Latex, nitrile, or vinyl gloves should be used to handle these items. If items are suspected of being treated with pesticides, see chapter 10 for specific procedures before handling the items.

Anecdotal evidence suggests that individuals with allergies or asthma should probably avoid working on items that contain old fur, such as old hides and buffalo robes.

Display Issues

The temperature and relative humidity ranges mentioned above in the Basic Care and Storage section also apply to display conditions. When used for display, items with quill, horn, hair, feather, claw, and baleen should be protected from high light levels, ultraviolet radiation, and heat from incandescent lights; inspected regularly for rodent, insect, and mold infestation and damage; and inspected regularly for changes in overall condition.

If items containing these materials are going to be used for display for an extended period, such as longer than one year, it is best to "rotate" them. Do not leave items colored with light-sensitive components, like natural or artificial dyes, on exhibit indefinitely, or irreparable fading and physical damage will occur. Incandescent floodlights inside cases and dioramas will generate heat and dry out the display items. The length of time that an item should be used for display depends on the particular item itself and the amount of light to which it will be exposed. Never display these items using natural light from windows or skylights. Both the visible and ultraviolet types of light in sunlight will fade and destroy these items in a relatively short time. By the time that you notice that dyes have faded, other more serious invisible damage may have been done. See chapter 11 for other general display concerns.

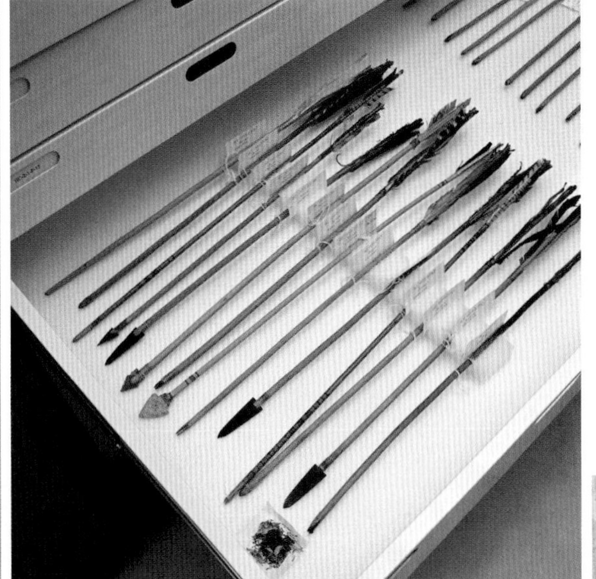

Mounts and Supports

External supports can be fabricated from acrylic plastic sheeting, such as Plexiglas, and shaped with heat to conform to an item's surface shape. Consult the bibliograpy for information that will help you fabricate your own mounts (see Barclay, Bergeron, and Dignard 2002). Avoid the use of unpadded wires and attaching items through existing holes with fasteners such as screws, as these will cause abrasion damage or corrosive stains. Adhesive mounts should also be avoided. These can cause irreversible damage as the adhesive breaks down, and may result in staining and loss of surface texture. In addition, if the adhesive bond fails, the item can fall from its mount. It is best to attach items to mounts with padded wires or flat acrylic plastic clips.

Above: Arrows held above base of storage drawer with polyethylene mounts to protect feathers on shafts. **Right:** Game made of leather, metal thimbles and pin, and deer dewclaws. Note the rigid padded storage mount with ties.

Cleaning and Minor Repairs

Periodic inspection and maintenance is the best way to assure the long-term preservation of quills, horn, hair, feathers, claws, and baleen items.

Surface dust can be removed from quill, horn, claw, and baleen items with a variable speed vacuum, brushes, and micro-attachments (see chapter 9). Distilled or deionized water with two to three drops of mild detergent, such as an unscented dishwashing soap, added to approximately a quart of water, can be used sparingly to remove dirt and finger marks. Follow this with the sparing use of plain water to rinse. Be careful when wet-cleaning materials that are attached to skin, textiles, or basketry, which can stain easily. Care must also be taken to inspect the item before cleaning for loose attachments and fragile decorations such as flaking paint layers. Quills that are attached to an item, such as a hide shirt or woven fiber basket, may be loose at the ends. Do not vacuum quills that are in this condition, as the suction will cause the loose ends to break off. In this case, use a soft natural-bristle brush to remove dust.

Hair can be gently brushed and vacuumed to remove dust. If it is particularly stiff and brittle, do not continue cleaning. To remove surface dirt, some conservators wipe the hair in the direction it grows with water on a soft, lint-free cloth.

Feathers usually need surface cleaning and realignment of the barbules onto the barbs. This can be done by placing the feather on a smooth, hard surface, such as a piece of flat glass. The surfaces of the feather can be cleaned with a low-power vacuum with micro-attachments. The barbules can be reattached to the barbs by gently "preening" the feather with a soft natural-bristle brush or by fingers wearing cotton gloves. Some barbs may be permanently distorted or broken. In these cases, the barbules will not line up completely, and there will still be gaps visible in the feather vanes, which is acceptable. If the feather shaft is broken, consult a conservator for further advice.

Avoid using liquid-based cleaners, detergents, or alcohol on keratin-based items, except as described above. If a greater level of cleaning is required, contact a conservator for further advice.

Using over-the-counter adhesives to repair cracks and breaks is discouraged, as these repairs are difficult to do and may result in staining and further deterioration. In addition, breaks and cracks can be evidence of use and may provide historical information. Unnecessary repair of such damage can obscure historical evidence. Consult a conservator if major repairs are needed or for advice on other alternatives.

15

Shell

Found in such items as beads, bracelets, and vessels

PAUL S. STORCH

Indian people have used tribal methods and techniques to care for their cultural items for generations. These caregivers are highly skilled and knowledgeable individuals in possession of sound information. They have developed excellent methods that have been proven by the test of time. The purpose of this chapter is not to replace any of this knowledge or information. Instead, we are offering additional methods that American Indian people can use for the cultural items in their care.

Identification and General Information

This chapter discusses shell, an animal product widely used by American Indians for at least six thousand years. Shells are the calcium-containing outer protective covering of invertebrate animals known as mollusks. The most commonly used shells are those of snails, clams, oysters, and mussels. Generally, these have been used for decorative purposes more than as structural parts or tools. Although shells from these different kinds of mollusks are identical in composition, they are quite distinct visually from each other and from other materials, which facilitates their identification.

Clams, oysters, and mussels are called *bivalves,* because their shell consists of two halves (or valves) connected by a flexible hinge. The outer surface of bivalve shells can be light or dark colored and is usually slightly porous in texture. The interior surfaces are smooth and shiny and often display colors of pink, green, yellow, and red. These surfaces are often referred to as mother-of-pearl and are widely used in decorative items.

Snails, both land and aquatic types, have a single shell in which the animal lives. The exterior surfaces of most snail shells are compact, shiny, and smooth. They may be one color or have various patterns.

Left: Curley, Crow Indian, ca. 1890. Note the dentalia breastplate. **Right:** Fragment of Ojibwe bead and shell necklace

All shells consist of a matrix of calcium carbonate covered with a noncalcareous membrane called the periostracum, which is similar to the periosteum on the outer surfaces of bones. The protein component of shell is called conchiolin, which is the molluscan equivalent of collagen.

As the periostracum membrane dries and flakes from the shell, it breaks the delicate growing outer edge of the shell. The shell then becomes susceptible to deterioration by acids. Acid can be present in groundwater and cleaning solutions and as vapor from wood and other construction materials used for storage, shelving, and display. Acid vapors in the presence of water vapor can dissolve the carbonate portion of shell and form fuzzy crystals on the surfaces. Conservators refer to the appearance of these crystals as "Byne's Disease." This type of deterioration can destroy or permanently disfigure the surface of finely etched and decorated shell items.

Shell can also be affected by high relative humidity and high temperatures (see below). Being hard and somewhat inflexible, it can break when improperly packed, transported, or dropped.

In general, the conversion of shells for use in items includes the following essential steps:

1. Detaching: separating the shells from the viscera of the animal
2. Cleaning: removing sand and dirt from the interior and exterior surfaces
3. Working: drilling, grinding, incising, and coloring

The deterioration of shell is caused by

- acids and acid vapors, which dissolve calcium carbonate;
- the delicate, brittle nature of shells, which makes breakage a constant problem;

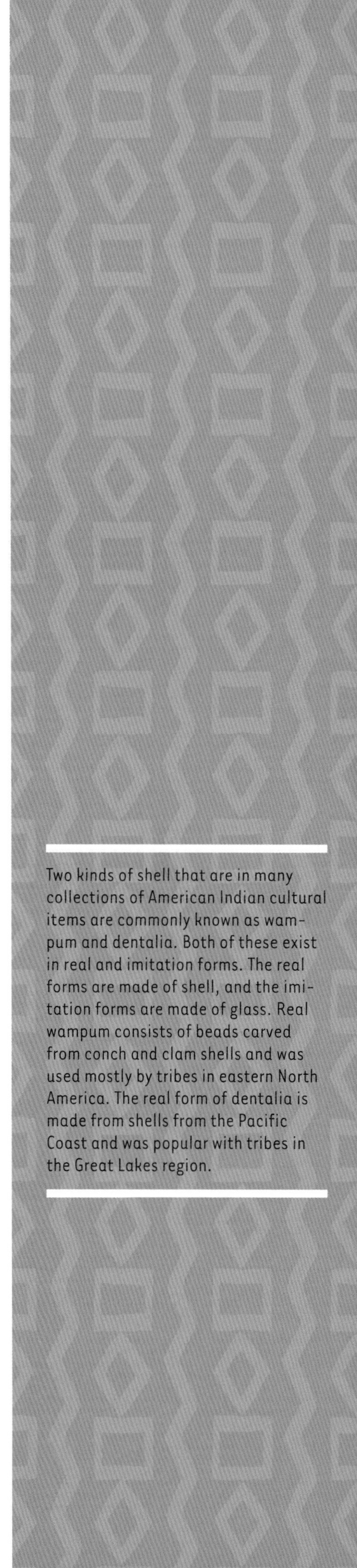

Two kinds of shell that are in many collections of American Indian cultural items are commonly known as wampum and dentalia. Both of these exist in real and imitation forms. The real forms are made of shell, and the imitation forms are made of glass. Real wampum consists of beads carved from conch and clam shells and was used mostly by tribes in eastern North America. The real form of dentalia is made from shells from the Pacific Coast and was popular with tribes in the Great Lakes region.

Shell: the calcium-containing outer protective covering of invertebrate animals known as mollusks.

Periostracum: a noncalcareous membrane covering the exterior surfaces of the shell.

Conchiolin: the protein component of shell, which is the molluscan equivalent of collagen.

- excess heat, which leads to loss of moisture, resulting in shrinkage and cracking;
- excess moisture, which leads to swelling, distortion, and deterioration of the material and which can promote mold growth and further damage.

Basic Care and Storage

Shell items are especially prone to deterioration by acids and acidic materials. Storage or display on corkboards or in wooden cabinets, especially those made of oak, will destroy shell items, turning them into white powder over time. Untreated oak and most other hardwoods give off acetic acid (vinegar), which can dissolve calcium carbonate. Formic and other acids are in certain adhesives used in the manufacture of Masonite, plywood, and particleboards. Consult a conservator for information on safe storage and display materials. Do not glue or attach shells to a support as the adhesive will stain the shells, and breakage may occur during removal.

Buffered rather than unbuffered board and paper materials can be used for storage and packaging of shell items, as the calcium carbonate in the board and paper will help neutralize acid vapors before they can attack the shell surfaces.

A consistent temperature and humidity are particularly important for the preservation of shell items. Keep in mind exceptions for items that may have already acclimated to ambient conditions (see chapter 6). Refer to chapter 7 for general storage information.

Special Pest Concerns

Shell items can become infested with mold, particularly if the relative humidity in the storage or display area is allowed to exceed 60 percent for long periods. Mold infestations can be recognized by a fuzzy growth on the surface of objects that is usually white or greenish. Consistent ventilation and air circulation in storage and display areas will help to prevent mold infestations. If mold growth does occur, take measures to reduce the relative humidity, and contact a conservator for advice on how to clean the affected surfaces safely. Personal safety is the primary concern when dealing with mold infestations, as many types of mold can cause serious and permanent health problems.

Routine Handling

The general methods and techniques for the proper handling of all items apply as well to shell items (see chapter 8). These items can be handled with bare hands as long as the hands are clean and dry. Body oils, however, can stain the porous shell surfaces, especially those that are light colored, so cotton or latex gloves are recommended for handling these items.

When lifting and moving an item composed of or including shell, make certain that it is supported well and that no stress is placed on weak areas. Use a tray or other support if necessary. This tray can be made from a piece of acid-free corrugated board that is cut to the standard sizes of drawers or other storage units.

Display Issues

The temperature and relative humidity ranges mentioned on the facing page in the Basic Care and Storage section also apply to display conditions. Most important, when used for display, shell items must be protected from acidic materials. Refer to the display guidelines in chapter 11 for light levels, handling, and other issues.

Mounts and Supports

Many museum personnel can fabricate external supports from acrylic plastic sheeting, such as Plexiglas, using heat to conform the acrylic to an item's surface shape. This requires only minimal tools and training. Avoid any mount or support that will cause abrasion and breakage, for example, unpadded wires or screws attached through existing holes. All adhesive mounts should be avoided. Adhesives can cause surface damage, resulting in irreversible staining and loss of texture.

Cleaning and Minor Repairs

Periodic inspection and maintenance is the best way to assure the long-term preservation of shell. Surface dust can be removed with a variable speed vacuum, brushes, and micro-attachments (see chapter 9). Before cleaning, carefully inspect the object for loose attachments and fragile decorations such as flaking paint or pigment layers. Consult a conservator for further advice on treatment.

Avoid using liquid-based cleaners and detergents or alcohol-based solvents on calcium carbonate items, except as described in chapter 16, on bone. If after removing surface dust, further cleaning appears to be required, to remove fingerprints, for example, contact a conservator for advice.

Do not use over-the-counter adhesives to repair cracks and breaks, as these repairs are difficult to do and may result in staining and further breakage as the adhesives age. Breaks and cracks can be evidence of use and may provide historical information. In addition, unnecessary repair of such damage can obscure historical evidence. Consult a conservator if major repairs are needed.

Bone, Antler, Ivory, and Teeth

Found in such items as hide scrapers, awls, diggers, games, necklaces, and decorations on bags and outfits

PAUL S. STORCH

Indian people have used tribal methods and techniques to care for their cultural items for generations. These caregivers are highly skilled and knowledgeable individuals in possession of sound information. They have developed excellent methods that have been proven by the test of time. The purpose of this chapter is not to replace any of this knowledge or information. Instead, we are offering additional methods that American Indian people can use for the cultural items in their care.

Identification and General Information

Items derived from skeletal materials are both versatile and durable. Bone, antler, ivory, and teeth have been used for various tools and for ornamentation. Because ivory is easily carved yet durable, it has also long been used by many cultures as a medium for recorded information.

Bones and teeth from many different animals, including mammals, birds, and fish, may be found in items in all shapes and sizes. Each culture uses the indigenous animals in its region. Identifying bones and teeth used in an item can be easy or difficult, depending on how they were processed and used. Frequently, bones and teeth were minimally processed, and the surfaces are still visible, allowing identification by color (off-white to pale yellow), shape, and composition. Bird, fish, and reptile bones are usually lighter in mass and color than mammal bones.

Bone and antler can be used in their natural form, or polished with sand and other abrasives to a very smooth and glossy surface. Bone is sometimes confused with ivory, which is also yellowish and compact. Sea mammal ivory, which is the prevalent source used by American Indians, is distinct in structure. Walrus ivory, the most common sea mammal ivory, has a dense outer layer and a mottled inner core.

Bone and antler in archaeological collections are often burnt and can be blue black to whitish gray. Charred bone or antler can be mistaken for wood. Magnification helps to distinguish bone from similar materials, as it has a thin solid layer surrounding a porous interior structure with a hollow core where the marrow is contained.

Antlers are composed of bone and are shed once a year. They have a soft membrane on the outer surface (velvet) when first grown. Antlers have been used for headdresses, and the tips have been used for projectiles and piercing tools. The internal structure of antler is similar to bone, with a large porous area below the surface. Deteriorated archaeological antler can be confused with wood. The outer surfaces can be distinguished from bone by the fact that the larger sections of antlers generally have raised bumps and protrusions, whereas skeletal bones are smooth except in attachment areas.

Teeth have two major components: the root area, which is similar to bone in composition and appearance, and the upper surface, which consists of compact enamel. The root area is usually a yellowish tan color with a matte surface, and the enamel is shiny and can be white or yellowish white. The enamel layer is generally resistant to decay and breakage. The root section, however, can dry out and split, causing stresses to the enamel layer that may result in further delamination and breakage.

Bone, ivory, and teeth are composed of both mineral and carbon-based materials. The mineral part of bone is made up mostly of calcium, phospho-

Bone: material that makes up the skeleton of vertebrate animals.

Antler: the seasonally shed outgrowth of the skin and skull of various large mammals; similar in composition to bone.

Tooth: a bonelike structure rooted in sockets in the jaws of most vertebrates; teeth are generally composed of a core of soft pulp surrounded by a layer of hard dentine that is coated with enamel at the crown and is used to seize, hold, or chew.

Dentine: the calcareous part of a tooth, beneath the enamel, containing the pulp chambers and root canals.

Ivory: the hard, smooth, yellowish white dentine that forms the main part of the tusks of sea mammals and of living and extinct elephants.

Left: Indian woman and child in elk tooth dresses, ca. 1880. **Above:** Hidatsa Indian woman hoeing squash with a bone hoe, 1912

rus, and fluoride. The carbon-based portion is composed of a protein called ossein. This protein is similar to the collagen found in skin.

In general, the conversion of bone, antler, ivory, and teeth into usable materials for tools and ornaments includes the following essential steps:

1. Detaching: separating the bone, ivory, or teeth from the muscles and connective tissue of the animal
2. Cleaning: removing the blood and marrow from the interior of the bones
3. Drying slowly to avoid cracking and splitting
4. Working the bone, antler, ivory, or teeth into the desired shape by cutting with stone or metal tools, grinding with stones, polishing with abrasives, and decorating incised areas with pigments such as ochre or charcoal

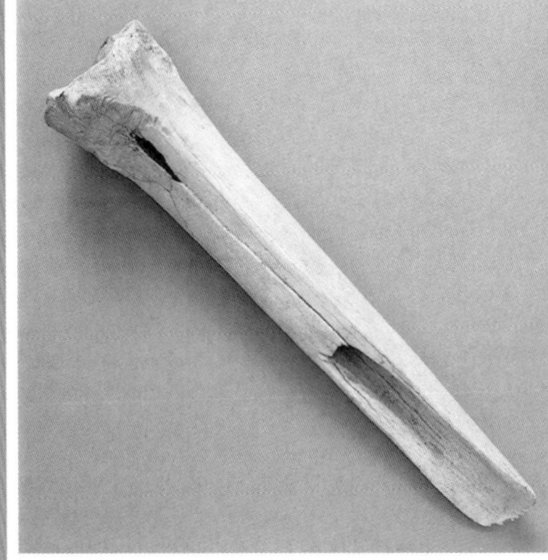

Mandan bone scraper. Cracks are probably caused by loss of moisture due to excessive heat or dryness.

The deterioration of bone, antler, ivory, and teeth is caused by

- extreme dryness;
- excess heat, which leads to destruction of the protein portion and loss of moisture, causing shrinkage and cracking of the surface;
- excess moisture, which leads to swelling of the protein portion and promotes mold growth;
- combination of excess heat and moisture, which destroys the ossein and can cause warping and cracking when the items dry out;
- rodent attack, especially on bones and the dentine of teeth;
- acids;
- exposure to strong visible and ultraviolet light, which causes bleaching of the natural color of ivory.

Basic Care and Storage

A consistent temperature and humidity are important for these materials. Generally a relative humidity level of not less than 30 percent in the winter and not more than 55 percent in the summer is best, with fluctuations of not more than 15 percent during each season. When possible to achieve, the optimum temperature is 68°F with fluctuations of no more than +/- 3° a day. Avoid storing and exhibiting items containing bone, antler, ivory, or teeth near radiators, heat pipes, outside windows, or incandescent lights, which can cause excessive drying and temperature fluctuations.

Items with holes, straps, appendages, or other attachments must never be hung or supported by those attachments. A support can be provided at the base of the item, and the handle or strap can be supported in a natural position.

Special Pest Concerns

Bone, antler, ivory, and teeth items are not particularly susceptible to insects. Rodents and other small mammals can cause structural damage by gnawing on the surfaces of these items. Maintaining good housekeeping, following an integrated pest management program in storage and display areas, and employing regular pest control services will help prevent infestations. Consult your licensed pest control operator as to which methods best suit your situation.

Bone, antler, ivory, and teeth items can become infested with mold, particularly if the relative humidity in the storage or display areas is allowed to exceed 60 percent for long periods of time. Mold infestations can be recognized by a white or greenish fuzzy growth on the surface of items. Good ventilation and air circulation in storage and display areas will help prevent mold. If mold does occur, take measures to reduce the relative humidity around the items, and ask a conservator about how to clean the surfaces safely. Personal safety is the primary concern when dealing with mold infestations, as many types of mold can cause serious and permanent health problems.

Routine Handling

The general methods and techniques for handling all items apply as well to bone, antler, ivory, and teeth (see chapter 8). These items can be handled with bare hands as long as the hands are clean and dry. Body oils, however, can stain bone, antler, dentine, and enamel, especially those that are light colored and have a matte, porous surface texture. For this reason, wearing cotton or latex gloves is suggested for handling most items of bone, antler, ivory, or teeth.

When lifting and moving an item that contains bone, antler, ivory, or teeth, make certain that it is supported well and that no stress is placed on weak areas or attachment points. Use a tray or other support if necessary. This can be made from a piece of acid-free corrugated board that is cut to the standard sizes of drawers or other storage units.

If bone, antler, ivory, or teeth items or the items on which they are found are suspected of having been treated with pesticides, see chapter 10 for specific procedures before handling the items.

Display Issues

The temperature and relative humidity ranges mentioned on the facing page in the Basic Care and Storage section also apply to display conditions. Apply the display guidelines discussed in chapter 11 to items containing bone. Bone items are consistent in their reactions to display conditions.

Rotate bone, antler, ivory, and teeth items that are going to be used for display for an extended period, such as five years. Light exposure will bleach surface color from ivory. Incandescent floodlights inside cases and dioramas

can cause extreme drying, leading to damage, especially of teeth. Consider the particular item itself when determining the length of time it can be used for display and the amount of light to which it should be exposed. Contact a conservator or exhibits lighting specialist for further details.

Mounts and Supports

External supports can be fabricated from acrylic plastic sheeting, such as Plexiglas, and shaped with heat to conform to an item's surface shape. Consult the bibliography for information that will help you fabricate your own mounts (see Barclay, Bergeron, and Dignard 2002). It is best to attach items to mounts with padded wires or flat acrylic plastic clips. Avoid using metals directly in contact with bone, ivory, or teeth. The fats that might remain in those items will react with the metals, forming corrosion products that will permanently stain the items. Also, avoid all adhesive mounts.

Cleaning and Minor Repairs

Periodic inspection and maintenance is the best way to ensure the long-term preservation of bone, antler, ivory, and teeth items. Surface dust can be removed with a variable speed vacuum, brushes, and micro-attachments (see chapter 9). Soft, lint-free cloths can be used to remove minor accumulations of dust. If the soiling is heavier, vinyl eraser crumbs and vulcanized rubber sponges can be used to surface clean stable, compact bone and ivory surfaces. Care must be taken to inspect the item before cleaning for loose attachments and fragile decorations such as friable paint layers.

Avoid using liquid-based cleaners or detergents on bone, ivory, and teeth items. If further cleaning appears to be required after dust and soil has been removed with the methods suggested above, contact a conservator for advice.

Using over-the-counter adhesives to repair cracks and breaks is discouraged, as these repairs are difficult and may result in staining and embrittlement as the adhesives age. Breaks and cracks can be evidence of use and may provide historical information. Unnecessary repair of such damage can obscure historical evidence. Consult a conservator if major repairs are needed.

Avoid wax or other protective coatings as these can obscure surface details and can age over time, resulting in yellowed or darkened surfaces. These coatings can also become difficult or impossible to remove without damage to the item.

17

Glass Beads

Found in such items as moccasins, clothing, bags, blankets, containers, and jewelry

ANN FRISINA

Indian people have used tribal methods and techniques to care for their cultural items for generations. These caregivers are highly skilled and knowledgeable individuals in possession of sound information. They have developed excellent methods that have been proven by the test of time. The purpose of this chapter is not to replace any of this knowledge or information. Instead, we are offering additional methods that American Indian people can use for the cultural items in their care.

Identification and General Information

Beads of all sorts have been used to beautify American Indian cultural items. Often many different types of beads were used on a single item. Beads vary greatly in size, shape, color, and the material from which they were made. The threading materials and the threading methods used to attach them were also varied. This chapter deals primarily with glass beads. For information about beads manufactured from bone, ivory, plastic, fired clay, and metal, refer to the chapters on these materials.

The types of glass beads found on American Indian cultural items were usually obtained by American Indians through trade. Although these beads come from many sources, the majority of those obtained during the trading period were manufactured in Europe.

Glass beads can be strung in single strands, sewn to items with various stitches, or needle woven like a fabric band. Beads strung on a single strand of threading material are often used as necklaces or bracelets; and a single strand can be sewn to an item, creating elaborate designs. Beads can also be sewn to items individually to form complex patterns. In comparison, needle-woven beads require that the beads be strung in strands and then woven together into

Indian woman wearing a beaded outfit, 1901

a band on a loom. The term *backing material* as used in this chapter refers to the materials to which the beads are attached, such as a skin shirt, a cotton dress, or a wool bag. Threading materials commonly include cotton and linen thread as well as sinew. When it comes to beading, variations in techniques and materials vary greatly from region to region.

Indian woman with a child in a beaded cradle board, Glacier National Park, ca. 1912

Glass beads are made of silica and other minerals melted at a high temperature to form a thick, viscous liquid. The liquid is molded into the desired shape and hardens as it cools.

When a colored glass is made, the formula is modified by adding or subtracting minerals or other substances to produce the desired color. Color can also be added in other ways during the manufacturing process, such as by rolling a warm molten bead in crushed colored glass or in minerals or in both.

Indian women from Grand Portage, Minnesota, demonstrate beadwork at "American Hands in Action," National Works Progress Administration exhibition in Duluth, 1939.

Glass beads are made in many sizes and shapes. Commonly, beads are manufactured by winding molten glass around a long iron rod. Different shapes can be created while the bead is still semisoft. For instance, square and oval beads can be manufactured by pressing the bead while it is still hot against a flat surface. More intricate shapes are manufactured with molds.

Seed beads are commonly used on American Indian cultural items. These are made by creating glass tubes or rods. Thin tubes of drawn glass are cut to size, creating very small seed beads. Larger beads, constructed with fatter tubes, are often decorated with chevron linear designs around their sides. Chevron beads are manufactured by applying colored strips of glass to a cone of molten glass. Once the colored strips start to soften, they are combed or dragged through the soft glass and made into a rod, creating a V-shaped chevron design. This rod is then cut into sections to create beads.

Another type of glass beads is mosaic beads, which are constructed with glass rods melted together to create a design. Mosaic beads often look like small clusters of flowers. They are referred to as millefiori, an Italian word meaning "thousands of flowers."

All of the beads mentioned above are manufactured with a glass oven or kiln. Another method of manufacture, however, requires no oven. Melting thin glass canes in a lamp flame and wrapping the softened glass around a copper tube creates lamp beads. With this method, elaborate beads of varying shapes and sizes can be created at a table without the need for an oven or a long iron rod.

The primary concern with glass beads is their fragility. They can crack, break, or be scratched if the items to which they are attached are not handled with care. Most beads are relatively stable chemically. Some older ones, however, may show visible deterioration. This deterioration is usually the result of improper formulation of the glass, fluctuations of heat and humidity, or a combination of these. In some instances the glass from which the beads were made was unstable; when this glass is subjected to unfavorable environmental conditions, it deteriorates. The visible deterioration that results is often referred to as glass disease. This type of deterioration is unusual, however. More commonly, burial soil that obscures the surface of beads will falsely appear to be glass disease. Even so, you should know the signs of glass disease since some of the beads you see, particularly those on older items, may suffer from it.

Conservators commonly cite five signs of glass disease: broken beads, sweating beads, crusty deposits, crizzling, and damage (bleaching or darkening) to the backing material to which the beads are attached. Glass beads can suffer from more than one of these characteristics at the same time. Many properly made glass beads will never succumb to glass disease. Nevertheless, all items that have glass beads should be stored carefully in conditions that will not encourage glass disease.

Ojibwe woman's beaded velvet leggings. Deteriorated beads in the center of the flower are probably suffering from glass disease. Many other beads are missing because the threading material has broken in several places.

Basic Care and Storage

Glass beads are fragile and will fracture and break if handled roughly. Take care when moving items to which beads are attached to prevent striking or scraping of the beads.

The strength and stability of the threading material used to string or attach the beads to an item are extremely important. No matter how the beads are attached, the threading material employed, whether cotton, linen, sinew, or fishing line, acts as the connecting element. If the threading material breaks, the beads are either lost, or the band of beads loses structural stability. Stiff and brittle threading materials will fracture with moderate flexing. Moving fragile beaded items with a supportive board will help to prevent damage due to flexing.

High humidity damages glass beads. It promotes sweaty, crusty beads. Also, the threading used to join the beads, whether it is cotton, linen, or sinew, will readily absorb water. Wet threading will promote glass disease within the holes

SYMPTOMS OF GLASS DISEASE

Broken beads: The fracturing or complete loss of beads can be the result of either rough handling or an inherently unstable form of glass.

Sweating beads: This is the result of storing unstable glass in a humid environment. Atmospheric moisture combines with alkali fluxes used in the manufacture of the glass that have migrated to the surface forming a soapy, sticky alkaline solution. This solution forms abrasive and caustic by-products, which will eventually promote the breakdown of the glass beads as well as of the cotton, wool, silk, skin, or hide threading and backing materials.

Crusty deposits: These are another result of unstable glass and high humidity. Alkaline products that migrate out of the beads turn into alkaline salts, which deposit on the surface of the bead or on the threading material. This hard alkaline coating makes the beads look as if they are dusty.

Crizzling: This is the result of unstable glass. It is characterized by a fine all-over cracking or fracturing of the beads. The fragmenting of the surface renders transparent beads opaque.

Bleaching or darkening: Bleaching and darkening are the result of unstable glass and high humidity in contact with textiles, skin, or hide. Alkaline products from the beads initiate a reaction with the textile, hide, or leather with which they are in direct contact. Wool and silk textiles will often turn white, while tanned skins will darken.

of the beads and cause the breakdown of the threading material. Glass disease will spread in a humid environment through direct contact with other beads.

While glass beads can endure exposure to light, the threading and backing materials cannot. All light will promote a photochemical reaction, breaking down threading and backing materials at the molecular level. Once this photochemical process has started, it cannot be reversed.

Special Pest Concerns

Mold is not a direct threat to glass beads. However, mold will attack the threading materials of cotton, linen, and sinew, causing them to become discolored and fragile. Damage caused by mold cannot be reversed.

The risk is the same for insect and rodent infestation. While the beads are not attractive to these pests, the threading and backing materials are. Breaks and unstable areas begin when insects or rodents eat the threading material. Highly acidic urine and feces can also weaken threading materials. In addition, insect damage may weaken the backing material to which the beads are sewn, leading to an unstable foundation. As always, routine cleaning and inspection will help prevent this damage.

Routine Handling

Wear gloves so that body oils are not deposited on the surface of glass beads. Oils from your hands promote sweaty beads as well as create a tacky surface to which dust and dirt can stick. When transporting beaded items, use a support board or a sling of washed muslin fabric to carry them. Beaded items are often heavy and need extra support to prevent ripping and tearing of the fragile textiles, skins, or hides to which the beads are attached. Support is especially important when moving needle-woven beaded items, where one break in the connecting material can cause many beads to be lost.

Display Issues

It is important to support items on display at all times. A flat or slanted padded board or a mannequin will support most items well enough. However, the mounts must be able to support the weight of the beads. If possible, avoid vertical hanging. If you cannot, seek guidance from a conservator, because the weight of the beads can cause breaking of the threads and backing materials.

Mounts and Supports

Placing items on storage boards in a drawer or box or on a shelf will facilitate handling. Instead of moving and flexing the item, you can lift and move the board. If the items on storage boards in a drawer tend to shift when you open and close it, you can secure them in place with loosely tied undyed cotton twill tape through slits in the storage board.

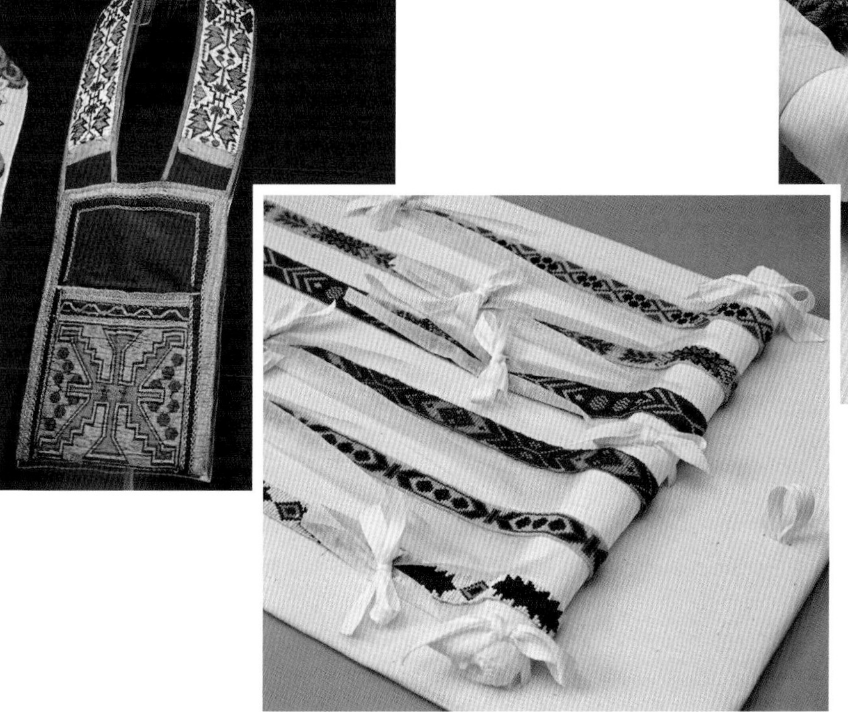

Left: This Ojibwe beaded wool bandolier bag is displayed at too steep an angle vertically. The weight of the beads is causing the bag to sag, which is causing the unbeaded red blanket wool above the pocket of the bag to buckle.
Middle: Ojibwe beaded necklaces rolled over a tube made of acid-free tissue.
Right: A beaded pin cushion on a padded storage board

When storing beaded items, take care to minimize folds with unbuffered acid-free tissue, as described in chapter 18. Take care to pad out folds and arms of more complex items, like beaded shirts or dresses, with rolled tubes of unbuffered acid-free tissue. Avoid hanging a necklace from its support cords, or a bag from handles or straps. In most cases, these items will not be able to support their own weight.

If you have a large, flat item that needs to be rolled, and it is heavily embellished with beads, be sure that rolling it will not break the threading materials. Protect layers of beads from scratching, catching, or otherwise damaging each other. Separate beads with an interleaving sheet of unbuffered tissue when they lie on top of one another. This is usually necessary when a large item needs to be folded or rolled to fit within a storage container.

Using padded hangers is recommended for only the strongest of outfits. When choosing to hang beaded outfits, examine the shoulders carefully for weakness. Gauge the weight of the garment in your hands. If the shoulders are not strong, a heavily beaded outfit will not be able to support its weight and will distort or tear at the shoulders. See chapter 18 for more detailed instructions for hanging storage.

Cleaning and Minor Repairs

Since beads and their threading can be so fragile, prevention is the best solution. Protect items from dust and dirt accumulation by storing and using them

for display in protective boxes and cases. The less accumulation of soil that you have, the less handling and abrasion the beads will receive during surface cleaning. Cleaning any composite item, whether a beaded outfit or a bag, is difficult. Different cleaning agents, such as solvents, can cause dyes in the backing fabric to bleed. Soap and water can also promote dye bleeding. Another problem is that even diluted soap solutions can leave a sticky residue behind on glass beads to which dust, dirt, and sooty particulates will stick like glue.

VACUUMING

Vacuuming with the aid of a soft brush can help remove loose dust and dirt with minimal risk to the item. Prior to any surface cleaning, do a thorough examination for any broken threading material that would allow a bead to fall off during cleaning. To examine the item, it is helpful to place it on a white surface, like a piece of muslin, with a layer of firm padding below. A stark white color will help you see any lost or errant threads or beads. You can then brush the beads gently with a soft brush to help loosen the dirt. This dirt can be picked up with the micro-suction attachment of the vacuum. You do not want to lose a bead into the vacuum. Take care to set the vacuum on a low suction setting. For a delicate or larger item, vacuum through a nonmetal flexible fiberglass screen laid over the item. This screen functions as a protective barrier for beads, threading, and other loose parts of items. Remember to vacuum the surface in a methodical row-by-row manner. This will facilitate cleaning the item overall, so that no one area is cleaner or brighter than another.

SWABBING WITH RUBBING ALCOHOL OR SALIVA

If the beads are still dirty after vacuuming, use a swab dampened slightly with isopropyl (rubbing) alcohol or your own saliva for a more thorough method of surface cleaning. Be sure to choose a rubbing alcohol that does not contain glycerin, as this will be left behind as a sticky water-attracting residue. Conservators within the museum community commonly use saliva to clean beads because of its mild enzymatic cleaning action. Traditional values, however, may not allow this. Check with the appropriate tribal community members for an answer about this. Note that at present opinion varies on what to use for cleaning glass beads that show signs of glass disease. The safest approach is to consult a conservator for advice.

The method of cleaning with saliva is the same as with alcohol. Take care with these treatments to avoid endangering the threading material or the surface of the glass beads themselves. Surface cleaning with a swab is not recommended for beads with glass disease. Consult a conservator for an appropriate method. It is important to perform the following examination prior to surface cleaning with a swab:

- Examine the threading material for fragility. If the threading material is dark and fractures easily with subtle manipulation, then it is probably too risky to perform aggressive surface cleaning with a swab.
- Spot clean a small test area, and examine the threading material. It is important to prevent any moisture soaking into the threading material. Cotton, linen, and sinew threading will expand as it absorbs moisture. If you see the threading material darkening with moisture, then refrain from cleaning.

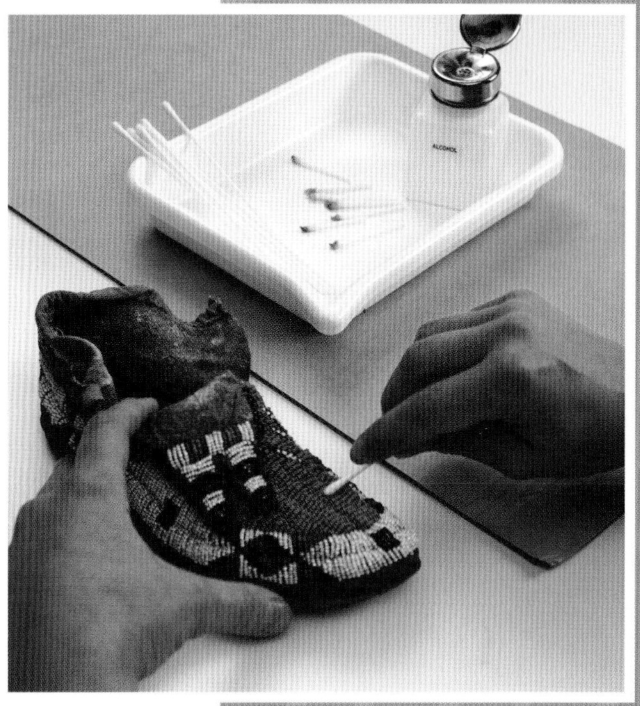

Discard swabs as soon as they become dirty. Place bottles of liquid in a tray to avoid damage if spilled.

Alcohol is good for cleaning glass beads and quickly evaporates. Alcohol is especially helpful with greasy dirt. Before cleaning the beads, moisten a swab with alcohol and then roll the moistened swab on an absorbent piece of washed cotton muslin to remove excess solvent. The swab should feel slightly damp to the touch. Next, take the slightly dampened swab and spin it gently in one direction over each bead. Do not apply heavy pressure as this could break the threading material. Do not rub the swab back and forth over many beads; this will drive the dirt deeper into the spaces in between the rows. Repeat this procedure using one swab per dip of alcohol, working row by row, top to bottom. A thorough overall cleaning will prevent bright, cleaner spots from occurring.

LOOSE OR DISENGAGED BEADS

If you find any disengaged beads, address the problem immediately before any further damage occurs. Store an item with loose beads in a container to prevent further loss of beads. When examining a fragile beaded item, you may want to do the following:

- Stabilize the item overall by supporting it on a board or table. Any flexing of the item may cause more loose beads to fall off.
- Find the area where the bead or beads were attached. Once you have located the area, examine the threading material until you find the broken one. If the area of bead loss cannot be found, then bag, label, and store the errant beads in the item's file for future examination and possible reattachment.

If you can identify the area from where the beads came, choose a thread and needle that can easily pass through the beads without breaking them. Many conservators use a beading needle size 15 or thinner to pass through glass seed beads. Cotton or cotton-wrapped polyester thread should be used to reattach beads to an item. These threading materials are stable, come in many colors, and are readily available. The thread should be thin enough to pass

through without causing stress to the bead or any remaining original threading. Try not to split original threading material. When choosing a thread color, look for something that will be slightly different from the original thread color. This will help to differentiate what is original from what is a later repair. Also, keep a sample of the new thread in your file, and note its maker and color. Finally, identify the stitches and stringing methods originally used to attach the beads, and use the same stitches during repairs. If possible, seek the assistance of members of the appropriate American Indian community in identifying stitches and making repairs.

Careful, methodical organization will help to simplify the process of sewing disengaged beads back onto an item. Some conservators use a piece of corrugated board with one side peeled off to expose the ribs. Using this board as a tray allows them to line up the beads row by row within the exposed ribs and keep them from rolling away. They can then reattach the disengaged beads in their original position with the appropriate stitching and stringing method.

TRADITIONAL REPAIR AND BEAD REPLACEMENT

Sometimes items lose beads. When this happens, stabilize the remaining beads in that area of loss by restitching. This way you will prevent further loss from occurring. Some American Indian people replace the missing beads with recovered old beads and new beads. It is extremely important to document which beads are original and which are replacements when the item repaired is of great historical value to you or your community. This documentation will help those who follow to distinguish the original materials from later repairs. Remember to

- document the area of lost beads with photography, diagrams, or photocopies noting the precise location;
- use easily identifiable thread to secure replacement beads, and record the new bead size, its location, and type of stitching used;
- document the thread used by noting the maker and color number and putting a sample in the item's file;
- seek the guidance of members within the appropriate American Indian community when unsure about adding replacement beads.

18

Textiles

Found in such items as blankets, clothing, and bags

ANN FRISINA

Indian people have used tribal methods and techniques to preserve their cultural items for generations. These caregivers are highly skilled and knowledgeable individuals in possession of sound information. They have developed excellent methods that have been proven by the test of time. The purpose of this chapter is not to replace any of this knowledge or information. Instead, we are offering additional methods that American Indian people can use for the cultural items in their care.

Identification and General Information

Although today many textiles used by American Indians are made of synthetic fibers, until recently they were made of animal and plant fibers. Protein fibers, like wool and silk, and cellulose fibers, like cotton and linen, are commonly found in these textiles. Methods of construction include spinning and weaving, plaiting or braiding strips, and felting through shocking woolen fibers with heat and cold and then agitating the unspun fibers repeatedly. Both hand and machine methods of production are used. Textiles are commonly made into blankets, outfits, and bags as well as many other items. Decorations can include dyeing, surface painting, embroidery, appliqué, quillwork, beads, and tinkler cones. The variety of materials, production techniques, and decorations often results in a composite item.

Basic Care and Storage

In general, textiles are extremely vulnerable to deterioration. The very things that make them pleasant to wear and use close to our bodies, such as flexibility, softness, bright colors, and decorations, also make them fragile. Wear, heat, moisture, and light are the main causes of textile deterioration.

Above: Ojibwe Indian child, ca. 1875. **Right:** Indian women, ca. 1890

Textiles do not support themselves; they are constantly flexing and folding. Flexing and folding of any fiber, whether wool, cotton, or linen, will result in breakage at some point. Breaks of this type are most evident along sharp knife-edge creases where the textile separates with a clean fracture. Abrasions, a type of wear commonly found in the knees of pants, will also result in an area of loss. Repetitive handling will further weaken fragile abraded areas.

Extreme heat is dangerous for textiles. It dries out the naturally existing moisture in fibers that gives flexibility, leaving textiles brittle and fragile. Heat also causes discoloration through the aging of starches and the formation of acidic by-products. For example, white cotton items often turn yellow and brown, sometimes looking like they have been toasted under a broiler. Finally, heat can also cause dyes to bleed faster in a humid environment. This type of damage is not easily reversed.

Textiles readily absorb both high humidity and water, which can cause extensive damage. Types of water damage include tide lines, dye bleeds, shrinkage, distortion, and mold growth. Tide lines form when a textile becomes wet enough to move acidic by-products and dirt by a wicking action through the fibers. A tide line often appears as a wavy, dark, sharp dirt line. Once one has occurred, it is not easily removed. Dye bleeding and fabric shrinking and distortion are also difficult to reverse on all textiles. Finally, humid environments can accelerate and promote mold growth, resulting in serious staining and discoloration. If left unchecked, mold will digest textile fibers as well as other organic embellishments, resulting in discolored, embrittled, and fragile items.

More information on mold and its treatment is available online at http://www.cr.nps.gov/museum/publications/conserveogram/16-01.pdf.

Light accelerates the fading of both vegetable and chemical dyes, as well as other colorants like paints. Light also promotes the embrittlement and weakening of textiles, especially silk. It is important to understand that while the fading of dyes or other colorants may slow with time, actual deterioration of textiles accelerates the longer they are exposed to light. Over time, even if you see no visible change, it is occurring on a molecular level.

When using textiles for display, a common rule of thumb is to expose them to light for no more than four months at a time every four years at the light levels suggested in chapter 11.

Special Pest Concerns

Insects and rodents can decimate any group of textiles. Carpet beetles and clothes moths feed on protein fibers like silk and wool, including sheep, goat, and camel hair, while silverfish feed on cellulose fibers like cotton and linen. Even more damaging is the use of precious textiles by mice, rats, and squirrels as bedding. Constant inspection and routine cleaning are the best ways to prevent infestation, along with implementation of an integrated pest management program.

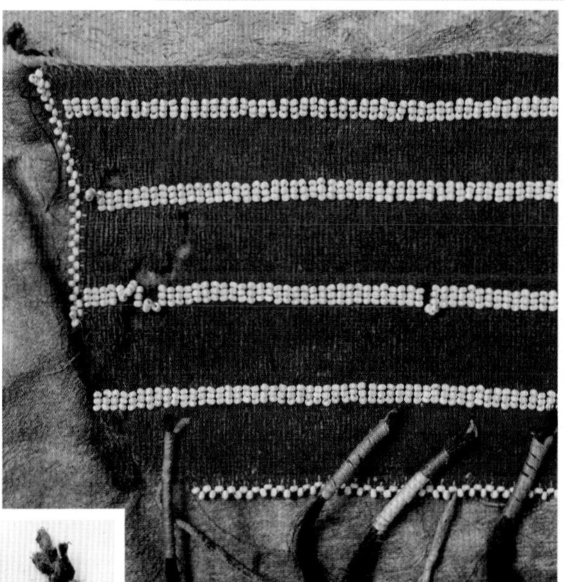

Routine Handling

You should remove any jewelry you are wearing. You do not want to snag a ring or watch on a textile, causing a tear or detaching surface decorations like beads or quillwork. Be sure to wash your hands because textiles can absorb the oils, dirt, and lotions on the surface of your skin. Check the measurements of the textiles. Do you have a big enough space prepared on which to work? Do you need a second set of hands to help you move large or fragile items? Make sure your work surface is clean. Clear off debris, and wipe the work surface with a clean cloth before you lay out the textile.

Above: Insect damage to textile. **Left:** The damage to Ojibwe man's beaded black velvet leggings was probably caused by a rodent.

Once the textile is laid out, be sure to examine it all over. Look for areas of weakness or loss as you unroll or unfold it. Check for active infestation. You can never be too vigilant when

monitoring textiles for insects. Finally, check for areas of dirt, accretions, or stains, as these can indicate areas of damage.

Display Issues

When using textiles for display, standardize the size and color of the mounts. In this way, mounts can be reused within cases, saving dollars and time on future mount preparation.

If possible, always place textiles in cases. If cases are not available, and items need to be in the open, maintain a weekly surface-cleaning schedule. It is important to clean regularly so dirt and dust do not accumulate. Try not to place items directly under or near heating or cooling vents, which may generate dust.

Slanted boards or mounts are frequently used for the display of many different types of textiles. Beaded outfits or fragile blankets too heavy to hang can be placed on slanted mounts. This method of presentation allows you to place an item out for viewing without securing it to the board with tacks or staples or by sewing.

The slanted mount is a board that rests on an incline at no more than 35 degrees. Slanted mounts can be easily made with acid-free double-walled corrugated board. Place thermal-bonded polyester padding on top of the board and wrap a show cover of de-sized washed cotton fabric over it. This creates a soft supportive platform for a textile or outfit to rest on. The show cover fabric can be neatly secured to the back of the board with 3M #415 double-coated transparent tape or white glue. Another option is to fold the material in half and sew up the side with machine stitching. An easy way to measure the right width is to lay the board on top of the material and draw lines, which you will sew through, down the side of the material. Now turn the fabric inside out so that the seam allowance is on the inside. You can then slide the board inside, turn the remaining edges in, and sew up the bottom by hand. Large slanted mount boards will need to be sturdy and may require the extra support of a wooden stretcher frame. Using a wooden stretcher frame will also enable you to secure the fabric show cover to the reverse of the board with staples.

Velcro hook-and-loop strip heading bands are another technique used to display large flat textiles, like rugs and blankets, by hanging. Note that only items with strong weave structures that will not pull or stretch out of shape during hanging may be used for display in this manner. If the item is woven loosely, has unsupported areas of loss, or heavy embellishments like beading or tinkler cones, then a slanted mount may be more appropriate.

To make a Velcro strip heading band, machine stitch a 2-inch-wide strip of loop Velcro to a strip of cotton canvas 3 inches wide. The strip should extend the entire length of the piece to which it will be sewn, without any breaks. Position the Velcro approximately ⅜ to ½ inch from the top of the cotton canvas. Machine stitch the Velcro to the canvas on the top, and herringbone stitch the bottom as well as down the middle. Next, position the prepared Velcro along the top edge of the textile and pin it in place. Hand stitch the canvas to the textile with herringbone stitching. Take care to match the thread with the item so that the stitching will not show on the front of the textile. Place half of the herringbone stitching within the edge of the Velcro. This will help to support the item by joining it and the Velcro closely to one another. Finally, staple the matching strip of hook Velcro to a sealed wooden slat. The wooden slat can be sealed with a waterborne polyurethane that has been allowed to dry for four weeks (see chapter 11 and appendix 2). Once you secure the slat to the wall, roll up the prepared item with the loop Velcro edge exposed. Position the textile, and gently push the Velcro loop strip against the slat-mounted Velcro hook strip to create a secure bond. You can adjust the Velcro strip up and down to improve the flat hanging of the textile. For more information about attaching a Velcro heading band, go to http://www.mnhs.org/about/publications/techtalk/TechTalkSeptember1997.pdf.

Velcro sewn to reverse and attached with a herringbone stitch to a contemporary quilt about John Beargrease

Outfits used for display can be presented on the storage hangers described below under hanging storage. Three-dimensional mounts, such as mannequins, often carved from sheets of Dow 220 Ethafoam, can also be used for display. Mannequins, considered ideal for museum exhibition, are often expensive to buy new and difficult to fabricate. An industrious person may be able to find older mannequins free, or for a small fee, from department stores no longer using them. These can then be retrofitted by museums for historic outfits.

There are several methods of adapting older mannequins for display. One is described here. Conservators often remove the breasts from commercially manufactured mannequins by sawing them off, and expand the stomach, hips, and chest areas to create a more natural form for the outfit. The stomach, or any other area, of a secondhand mannequin can be expanded by stretching two pairs of queen-sized nylon panty hose over the bottom and top of the mannequin. Take the first pair of panty hose and dress the lower half of the mannequin. Fit the head and neck through a slit cut in the crotch of the other panty hose. Pull the waist over the head, and extend it down over the chest to meet the first pair of panty hose in the middle. Once the second pair of panty hose is on the mannequin, sew a twill tape strip or binding edge along the neckline to prevent the panty hose from running and losing structural stability. Extend the waistband down over the chest to meet the first pair at the middle. If necessary, remove the excess panty hose legs by cutting them off. Another option is to feed the arms through the leg holes of the top pair, further securing the panty hose in place at the shoulders, trimming them to rest under the sleeve and out of sight. You can now stuff clean thermal-bonded polyester batting around the torso where the two waistbands meet, expanding midriff, chest, and hips as needed. When the final shape is complete, sew the two waistbands together to seal them. Finally, go back and adjust the twill tape at the neckline so that it is not visible. Though these methods may seem crude, they are used by many professional museums.

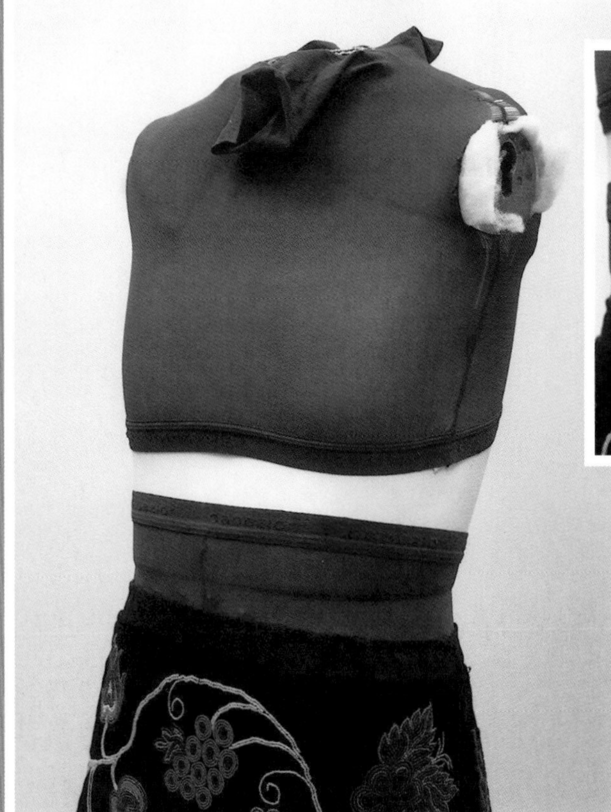

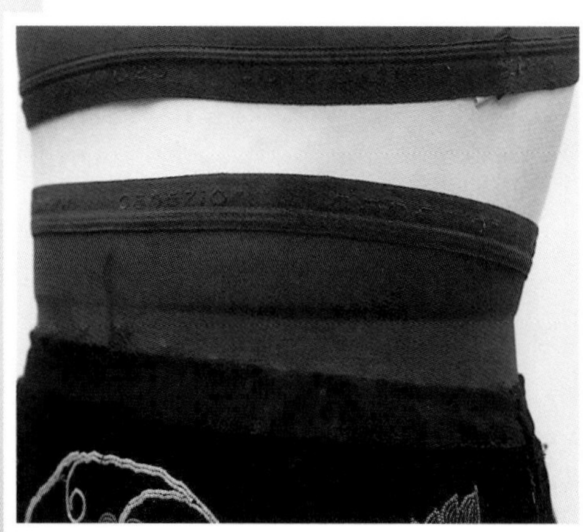

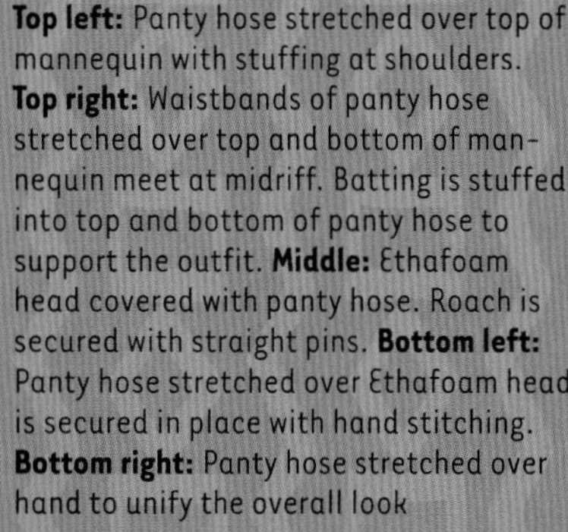

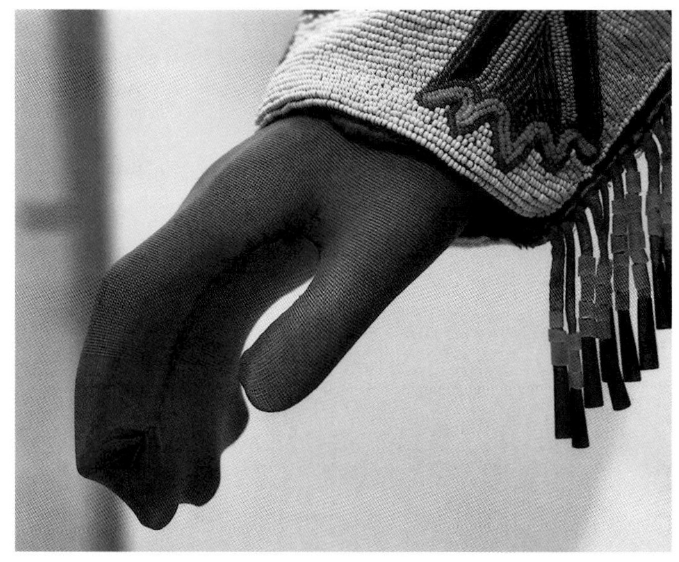

Top left: Panty hose stretched over top of mannequin with stuffing at shoulders. **Top right:** Waistbands of panty hose stretched over top and bottom of mannequin meet at midriff. Batting is stuffed into top and bottom of panty hose to support the outfit. **Middle:** Ethafoam head covered with panty hose. Roach is secured with straight pins. **Bottom left:** Panty hose stretched over Ethafoam head is secured in place with hand stitching. **Bottom right:** Panty hose stretched over hand to unify the overall look

Hand-carved Ethafoam museum mannequins are another option, but the materials are sometimes difficult to obtain as well as to carve. You can order this foam from a conservation supply catalog. If you do decide to use Ethafoam, contact a conservator to help design and guide the construction of mannequin mounts that will fit your needs.

Mounts and Supports

Storing textiles with mounts and supports is necessary for their preservation because textiles do not support themselves. The goal of all mounts and supports is to prevent any further distortion or physical damage. Flat, boxed, hanging, and rolled mounts and supports are commonly used to store textiles.

FLAT MOUNTS

A flat mount acts like a supportive inflexible tray for an item on display or in storage. Flat mounts serve two purposes: to support a textile when it is in storage, and to provide support to facilitate moving an item without undue flexing and handling. Textiles can be stored on this type of mount if when lying flat, they are not distorted. Flat mounts are commonly stored within a box or drawer or on a shelf covered with unbuffered acid-free tissue or a muslin fabric.

Use acid-free corrugated board for flat mounts. If an item is heavy, it may be necessary to use a thicker board that will not flex. Another material for support is Coroplast, a polypropylene and polyethylene corrugated board. Coroplast is used by sign makers and may be available locally. However, if acid-free board or Coroplast is not available, then corrugated cardboard with a barrier of Marvelseal or polyester film is another option.

If the textile needs to be folded, line all folds with soft rolls of crumpled acid-free tissue. Line the sleeves, leggings, and the sides of dresses with tissue when storing flat. This additional support prevents folds from turning into stiff, hard creases that will eventually break or split. You can make a soft roll of crumpled tissue by loosely rolling a length over itself like a tube. A soft roll of crumpled tissue does not need to be perfectly smooth, just supportive for the fold or sleeve.

When placing smaller textiles on a flat mount, keep in mind the following: the opening and closing of drawers will cause smaller textiles to slide and shift. This is especially problematic if you have several small items on one board. To prevent movement, secure smaller items with white cotton twill tape ties anchored through slits in the board. Another option is to line the board with fabric that has enough surface texture to hold an item in place. Suitable fabrics for this are washed and undyed cotton muslin or washed white cotton flannel. Do not use fabric softeners or bleach when washing fabric for use next to an item, and try to use as little soap as possible so that no residue will be left on the fabric. You can secure this fabric to the board with small tabs of 3M #415 double-sided tape laid near the perimeter of the board.

Finally, when planning the size of a flat mount, be sure to leave room for a handling edge around all four sides of the board. You need to allow easy access without touching the textile.

BOXED STORAGE

Indian-made lace for the tourist trade. Lengths of lace are stored on tubes with acid-free tissue in an acid-free storage box.

A box with a lid is a good way to protect textiles on open shelves. Stacking one or two boxes on top of one another will give you more shelf space. Using acid-free materials for boxes is best. However, if acid-free boxes are not available, line corrugated board boxes with a barrier material such as polyester film or Marvelseal. Wrap items in unbuffered acid-free tissue before placing them in the lined acidic boxes. Smaller items can be safely stowed in custom-made trays of acid-free board to fit within the box, preventing shifting or crushing. You can make these trays yourself or purchase them from conservation suppliers. Larger textiles and garments can be folded to fit within a box, freeing valuable shelf space. When folding items, keep the following procedures in mind:

Folded Storage for Flat Textiles in Boxes

- Lay the textile out on a flat surface, and examine it for former fold lines. If a flat textile, like a rug or blanket, has been folded in quarters, fold it in thirds to prevent damage.
- Line all folds with rolls of crumpled unbuffered acid-free tissue. Then fold the item over the rolls. Insert your hand into the folded textile to reposition the tissue rolls if necessary. Make these rolls of crumpled unbuffered acid-free tissue as described on page 149 under flat mounts.

Folded Storage for Garments in Boxes

- Lay the outfit flat, and fill sculpted areas, like the arms, legs, and chest, with crumpled unbuffered acid-free tissue to create a soft, flat pillow. If you are storing a dress or skirt, line folds with soft rolls of crumpled acid-free tissue to prevent creasing.
- If the garment needs to be folded in half or thirds, line each fold with rolls of crumpled acid-free tissue.

HANGING STORAGE

Outfits that are strong and show no weaknesses are candidates for hanging storage. Be sure to carefully inspect the shoulders for weakness since they carry the weight. Do not ever hang heavily decorated outfits, outfits with weak shoulders, outfits that are fragile overall, or knitted outfits.

Plastic molded hangers can be easily padded to properly support hanging outfits. Purchase plastic molded hangers with curves at the shoulders. Pad the hanger with one or more layers of thermal-bonded polyester batting so that the item rests on the hanger and does not slide off. Cover the padded hanger with washed cotton knit fabric, and sew closed by hand. When finished, the hanger should easily fit within the outfit, supporting the shoulders without distorting or stressing them.

If molded hangers are not available, you can use wire ones if they are clean and in good shape. The benefit of a wire hanger is that it can be bent to accommodate small items if necessary. Nevertheless, you must make sure that the hanging hook is strong enough to carry the weight of the outfit and will not bend over time under stress. Be sure to examine the hanger for rust. If any type of corrosion is found, discard it. After examining the wire hanger for rust and hanging strength, cover it with two or more layers of thermal-bonded batting. Once the batting is wrapped around the hanger, to create support for the shoulders, cover it with washed cotton knit fabric. Sew the fabric closed by hand to secure the batting inside the hanger. When completed, the hanger should resemble a semi-flat pillow with a hanging hook. An online pamphlet about padded hangers is at http://www.cr.nps.gov/museum/publications/conserveogram/04-05.pdf.

Once a garment is hung for storage, protect it from dust, dirt, and abrasion with a muslin cotton dustcover. The dustcovers should fit easily over the outfits and not squeeze them in any way. White or off-white cotton or Bemberg rayon fabrics are good for dustcovers because they will show dirt and dust accumulation. Checking for dust accumulation is especially important if garments are stored in an open area. Bemberg rayon is a fabric commonly used to line clothing. Its slippery surface allows a dustcover made from it to glide on and off a garment without abrading the surface. Additional details about dustcovers are available online at http://www.cr.nps.gov/museum/publications/conserveogram/dustcovers4-15.pdf.

ROLLED STORAGE

Rolling a flat textile around a strong tube is a good way to store a large item without creating fold lines. Rolled storage is good for large flat textiles like rugs and blankets. Do not roll items that are heavily decorated with embellishments such as beads, tinkler cones, or shells. Rolling these items will create creases and distortion of the textile as well as place stress on the threading used to secure these embellishments to the textile. Instead, fold heavily decorated items

Rolling a contemporary quilt about John Beargrease on a tube for storage. Note placement of paper around tube and under quilt.

with supportive rolls of crumpled acid-free tissue. When rolling a large textile, try to use a tube with at least a 6-inch diameter. Also, make sure that the tube is longer than the textile. Allowing the textile to hang over the edge of the tube once it is rolled will promote distortion, ripping, and areas of loss. If you do not have access to acid-free tubes, you can substitute a regular 6-inch-wide Sono tube, the kind of tube used on cement footings, providing you cover the tube with a barrier such as Marvelseal or polyester film. This is especially important with Sono tubes because of their oily surface. Finally, cover the tube by rolling on a length of washed muslin or acid-free paper.

Once the tube is prepared, leave a small length of the cover paper or muslin unrolled. Next, place the top edge of the textile on the paper. Align the edge so that the textile is centered and square with the tube. Slowly roll the tube over the textile. Take care to roll the textile onto the tube evenly so that neither side telescopes out. If telescoping occurs, take the time to adjust the tube and start over. After rolling, cover the textile with washed muslin or acid-free paper. Once the textile is rolled, store it on support cradles so it will be suspended from the roll. The rolled textile should never rest upon a shelf or the floor.

This same method of storage can be used for smaller items on thinner cardboard tubes like those used in fabric stores. Sometimes these tubes are available free from fabric and carpet stores.

Cleaning and Minor Repairs

If done with care, surface cleaning can usually be successful. Before surface cleaning, be sure to examine the textile thoroughly for loose beads, open seams, splits, or areas of loss within the fabric. If there are any loose pieces, such as beads, quills, tinkler cones, or bits of the textile, bag them and document their original location with photographs, diagrams, or even photocopies, if this will not harm the item. This documentation will help you return those loose pieces to their original position. If the pieces cannot be returned to the textile, they can be stored in a file with the item.

You can surface clean with a low-suction vacuum cleaner. As stated earlier, vacuum cleaners can be fitted with micro-suction attachments found in fabric and computer stores. When placing the soft brush of the nozzle on the textile, do not drag it back and forth across the surface. Rather, place the head on the textile in a systematic row-by-row manner. Do the same thing on the back of the textile. By methodically moving across the textile, you can be assured of equal cleaning throughout. If the textile is exceedingly fragile, or the suction of the vacuum is very strong, vacuum through a nonabrasive piece of fiberglass window screen, the cut edges of which have been bound with cotton fabric and a seam binding.

A second method of surface cleaning is to use a vulcanized rubber dry cleaning sponge. These sponges were originally used to clean soot in homes after fires and are good for removing greasy, sooty, particulate dirt from surfaces. This sponge will help to remove any buildup of greasy dirt from previous use and handling. First, cut a piece of the sponge to fit comfortably within your hand. Gently place the sponge on the textile, and make a swooping motion with light pressure. As soon as the sponge is black with dirt, cut or shave it down to reveal a clean portion underneath. A soot sponge is not appropriate for a fragile textile or embellishments with fragile threading.

Conservators consider washing an item to be an intrusive and irreversible act. Washing can damage historic items in many ways. Impure water can leave deposits that will become visible at a later date. For instance, water heavy with iron or copper can cause later rust spots or a green overcast. Textiles can shrink or lose their sizing when washed, changing their appearance and feel. Items not properly supported while wet or drying can distort or rip. Dye bleeding is a real threat when washing items that have dyes that are not fast. Navajo blankets are particularly susceptible to dye bleeding. Contact a conservator for advice if you feel an item needs more aggressive cleaning like washing.

19

Metals and Alloys

Found in such items as jewelry, military ornaments, tinkler cones, saddles, and weapons

THOMAS J. BRAUN

Indian people have used tribal methods and techniques to care for their cultural items for generations. These caregivers are highly skilled and knowledgeable individuals in possession of sound information. They have developed excellent methods that have been proven by the test of time. The purpose of this chapter is not to replace any of this knowledge or information. Instead, we are offering additional methods that American Indian people can use for the cultural items in their care.

Sioux Indian wearing metal armbands, ca. 1880

Identification and General Information

Everybody knows what metal is; it is found in thousands of items that surround us every day. When you begin to conserve some of these metal items, however, you find that the substance is more complicated than it seems. Most things we call metals today are more accurately called alloys. True metals are pure elements, while alloys are blends of two or more metals that have been melted together. Metals and alloys are easy to distinguish from nonmetals because they are usually shinier, heavier, and harder than most materials, and they are excellent conductors of heat and electricity. Even so, visually distinguishing various metals, and especially alloys, from one another can be difficult. If you need to identify a metal exactly, contact someone who is skilled in identifying metals, such as a conservator, a jeweler, or a metallurgist. This section will refer to metal in the larger sense of the word, meaning both true metals and alloys.

On the most basic level, conservators describe metals that appear white as *white metal.* Some examples of white metals commonly found in American Indian items are silver, tin, nickel, iron, and lead. The most commonly used term for metals that are not white metal is *copper alloy.* One of the most common alloys of copper is *brass.* Brass is a blend of copper and zinc and usually has a very shiny golden appearance when polished. Brass is commonly found in many American Indian items of daily use.

Identifying metal items is also made difficult when they are plated, since a thin layer of one metal covers another. Common examples of plating include tin cans, which are made of steel plated with tin; silver-plated spoons, which are usually made of a cheap base metal covered with the more expensive silver; eyeglass frames, also made with cheaper metals plated with gold. Identifying the base metal helps you decide how to preserve a plated item. For example, if an item looks like it is made of gold, you might assume that it will not corrode. However, if you observe green corrosion on it, you would suspect that it was gold-plated copper alloy, which requires a drier environment than gold alone.

Indians making maple sugar, Cass Lake, ca. 1905

Many metals will often have a *patina,* or protective finish. A patina is a coating on the outside of a metal object that usually acts as a protective layer and also is intended to make the item more beautiful. A patina can be intentionally applied using chemicals or coatings, or it forms naturally when the metal slowly accumulates a thin film of stable corrosion on the outside. Intentionally applied metal patinas are usually composed of various chemicals, oils, resins, or waxes. Copper and its alloys are the most common metals to have patinas. Items made of silver often have a natural patina of dark tarnished silver in the recesses, while the smooth parts of the metal are brightly polished. This patina makes any engraved areas stand out better, and it often improves the overall appearance of a silver item.

A *stable patina* is simply a very thin layer that is usually darker than the polished metal. In copper alloys, the color may range from tan to brown or black and is usually smooth textured. An *unstable patina* on a metal is usually uncontrolled corrosion. On copper alloys, this patina is usually a powdery or greasy green corrosion product that is typically bumpy or uneven. A significant amount of thought and consultation should take place before any patina, tarnish, or corrosion is removed (see Cleaning and Minor Repairs, pp. 158–159, for more details). A stable patina is highly valued by some people and can form a protective layer over the metal. Stable patinas may take many decades to form, and removing them may damage the item, harm its appearance, or decrease its value.

Basic Care and Storage

Metals have no sensitivity to light and no biological pests. The primary concerns are tarnish and corrosion. Corrosion cannot occur without moisture. For this reason, it is advisable to store metals in dry conditions. One of the best ways to accomplish this is to place the metal item in an enclosed space, such as a resealable polyethylene or polypropylene plastic container intended for food storage, with a drying material such as silica gel. Silica gel can absorb large quantities of moisture and can remove almost all of the moisture in a plastic container. Every few years, the silica gel will need to be dried in an oven to re-

Copper spear point in polypropylene container with silica gel

move all of the accumulated moisture that has penetrated the plastic container from the outside environment. *It is important that the metal not touch the silica gel directly.* Place the silica gel inside a separate open container, such as a cup, in the larger plastic container to avoid contact with the metal. An alternative is to place the metal item in a resealable polyethylene bag, such as a Ziploc, and put the silica gel around it in the plastic container.

Metals are not significantly harmed by everyday variations in temperature unless the melting point is approached. All chemical reactions, however, including corrosion, are accelerated by heat, so metals are best stored at cool temperatures. Note that metals stored in a cool environment should be allowed to slowly adjust to the warmer environment before their storage box is opened. This is because bringing cold metals into a warmer environment will cause water to condense on their surface, which can quickly lead to corrosion.

Left: Corrosion on fur trade kettle, which was found on the Minnesota-Canada border and used in trade with the Indians in that region. **Below:** Metal spangles along the flower stem and beads at the flower center are corroded on this Ojibwe beaded velvet breechcloth.

Many items that contain metal are composite items. Examples are leather garments with metal rivets, bells, or other decorations, guns with wooden stocks, and medals with cloth ribbons. In items such as these, metals can interact with other materials and cause corrosion. These items are particularly difficult to preserve because the different materials from which they are made can have conflicting storage and display needs. An example is a leather outfit with metal tinkler cones sewn onto it. The tinkler cones need a very dry environment, preferably at or below 30 percent relative humidity, while the leather can become dry, inflexible, and even brittle in these conditions. On the other hand, the leather will be more flexible at higher humidity, but the metal tinkler cones will be more likely to corrode. In these cases, it is sometimes advised to coat the metal parts of a composite item so that these parts can better withstand higher humidity. If you think specific items need this type of care, consult a conservator. Another alternative is to choose a relative humidity halfway between the extremes.

Eventually all coatings on metals will get scratched, peel off, or otherwise break down. At this point they should be removed so that another coating can be applied. Varnishes or lacquers are difficult to apply correctly, so if you need this done, you should contact a conservator. A thin coating of wax, however, is easier to apply to most metals and is less difficult to remove than varnish or lacquer. See the section Cleaning and Minor Repairs for more information on coating metals.

Special Pest Concerns

As mentioned above, metals have no natural biological pests. Residues left by insects, however, such as flyspecks, can permanently etch and corrode metals.

Routine Handling

Metals should always be handled with clean gloves made of cotton, nitrile, or latex. Metals that are roughly corroded or that have small details that could easily catch on cotton threads are better handled with nitrile or latex gloves. Also, do not use cotton gloves that have plastic dots on the palms and fingers, because these dots can be made of polyvinyl chloride, a substance that quickly corrodes metal. Do not touch metals with your bare hands because moisture and oils from the skin can corrode, etch, and permanently mark metals.

Display Issues

Compared to nonmetallic materials, metals can be used for display with fewer concerns since they are impervious to low humidity, pests, and light damage. However, they must be used for display in an environment that is not chemically damaging to metal. Ideally, this environment should have a low level of humidity and be free of pollutants. Display materials that release damaging vapors can corrode metals and should be avoided. See chapter 11 for more information. Be aware that any silver kept in a display cabinet with items made of rubber, wool, or any other material containing sulfur can rapidly turn black, because the sulfur reacts with the silver to form silver sulfide.

Since metals have no sensitivity to light, they can be exhibited at high light levels. Materials attached to the metal, however, such as textiles, hides, or stones, may be more sensitive. For example, stones inset in metal jewelry can fade in light (see chapter 22).

Rigid storage mount for Ojibwe jingle leg bands. Note the polyester fabric that folds over the jingles to restrain their movement when the leg bands are transported on the mount.

Mounts and Supports

Even though metals are often stronger than other materials, they must still be supported. Thin metal sheets or heavily corroded metals can be very weak and require significant support. Materials that will release acidic vapors, such as wood and wood products, should be avoided for mounts and supports as they can corrode metal. The stable plastics mentioned in chapter 7, on storage, are often the best materials to use with metals.

Cleaning and Minor Repairs

If an item is composed of only metal, it can usually be cleaned and repaired more easily than if it is a composite. When a composite item needs to be cleaned, it is better to remove the metal parts before cleaning, if this is possible, and then to reattach or reassemble them after cleaning. You should clean different materials separately because many of the compounds used to clean one material will harm other materials.

Carefully study a metal item before cleaning. Examine the stability of the patina (see section on Identification and General Information). If the patina is stable, the best option usually is to simply leave the item as it is. Items with stable patinas have been preserved adequately up to now, and they will probably remain stable if conditions do not change significantly. However, if the metal is undergoing active corrosion and has an unstable patina, then you should change the environment. Corrosion cannot occur without moisture, so make the environment as dry as possible. Only after the environment has been improved should you consider cleaning. This is because cleaning may cause metal in a poor environment to corrode even faster.

Degreasing metal is the most basic cleaning procedure. Degreasing refers to using a solvent to remove oils and other soil that can cause corrosion. Because solvents are a health hazard, careful precautions must be taken to avoid exposing yourself or others to the solvent and its vapors. Acetone is one of the best solvents for degreasing metals. It is, however, highly flammable and can irritate the eyes and skin. When using acetone, follow the precautions provided by the manufacturer or supplier. Alcohol can be used to degrease metals, but it has drawbacks. It usually contains a significant amount of water, which can cause metal to corrode. Acetone, in fact, can also contain water and often will cause water condensation on metal artifacts as it evaporates. To prevent this condensation, thoroughly dry a metal artifact with a soft cloth or tissue after it is degreased to completely dry it. Setting the item in a sunny space for a few minutes will also help to remove any remaining moisture. Some other solvents, such as mineral spirits, are not very pure and may leave oils or other contaminants behind after evaporation and should not be used.

Since metals become oily and soiled from handling without gloves, be sure to handle a metal item with gloves during and after degreasing. Apply the solvent with cotton swabs or a clean paintbrush, and allow the item to dry in a warm place, as described above. Since the metal is now very clean, it may actually corrode faster if it encounters moisture. To keep a clean item from corroding again, you can coat it with a protective wax finish. Conservators sometimes use a paste wax composed of carnauba wax or microcrystalline wax to protect metal. These waxes can be purchased from conservation suppliers and at furniture shops. Two common brands are Butcher's carnauba wax and Renaissance microcrystalline wax. These paste waxes are applied with a soft cloth, allowed to dry for a few minutes, and then buffed with a clean dry cloth. The wax provides a nearly invisible coating that resists moisture but is not so durable that it is difficult to remove should you need to.

Like cleaning, repair of metals should not be done without careful thought. If the item is in pieces, but the pieces are stable while in storage and used for display, the best option may be to do nothing at all. Consult a conservator for advice if you have an item that you think needs repair.

With metal items that are severely corroded, such as items that are weathered from being outdoors, carefully consider all options before removing any thick layers of corrosion. The layers of corrosion often conceal the original surface layer of the metal item. This surface can be destroyed by cleaning, causing the original shape of the item to be lost forever. Sometimes severely weathered metal items will preserve the image and texture of a piece of textile or other perishable material that was next to the metal as it corroded. When the corrosion products contain images or textures, or the original layer of the metal is at risk, it is better not to remove the corrosion.

20

Wood and Birch Bark

Found in such items as totem poles, arrows, bowls, canoes, teepees, containers, pipe stems, and scrolls

THOMAS J. BRAUN

Ojibwe baby in wood cradle board, Mille Lacs Indian Reservation, ca. 1909

Indian people have used tribal methods and techniques to care for their cultural items for generations. These caregivers are highly skilled and knowledgeable individuals in possession of sound information. They have developed excellent methods that have been proven by the test of time. The purpose of this chapter is not to replace any of this knowledge or information. Instead, we are offering additional methods that American Indian people can use for the cultural items in their care.

Identification and General Information

A wide variety of American Indian items are made from wood and tree bark. The types of tree bark commonly used are birch and black ash. Because these are similar, only birch bark will be discussed in this chapter. The suggestions made for birch bark apply to black ash as well. Wood and birch bark are composed primarily of *cellulose* and *lignin,* with minor amounts of waxes and oils. The quantity of lignin, a structural polymer, in both bark and wood, varies widely from one type of tree to another. Typically, lignin is found in higher quantities in the bark of trees than in the wood. For example, birch bark contains higher levels of lignin and waxes than most types of wood.

The way a tree grows creates the patterns that make up the *grain* of the wood. Wood has more strength across the grain. When stress is placed on wooden items parallel to the grain, they are more likely to split.

Recently cut wood is considered "wet" or "green" and usually requires six months to a year before it dries out. As it dries, it shrinks slightly and changes shape. These changes will often cause cracks and splits to form in the wood. After wood ages for several years, this process slows, and new cracks are unlikely to form, unless the wood is exposed to high or low humidity. Even after wood dries, it can still absorb and lose moisture and will expand and contract as the temperature and humidity change.

Items made up of many pieces of wood are particularly prone to damage from expansion and contraction. Within a few years of manufacture, these items usually show distortion unless the construction allows the pieces of wood to move independently.

Birch bark is composed of many thin sheets or layers, which are adhered together. When the layers expand and contract at different rates, they curl. This is a particular problem with birch-bark items, and frequently they are found tightly curled in rolls or damaged because they were prevented from curling and the stress placed on them made them split.

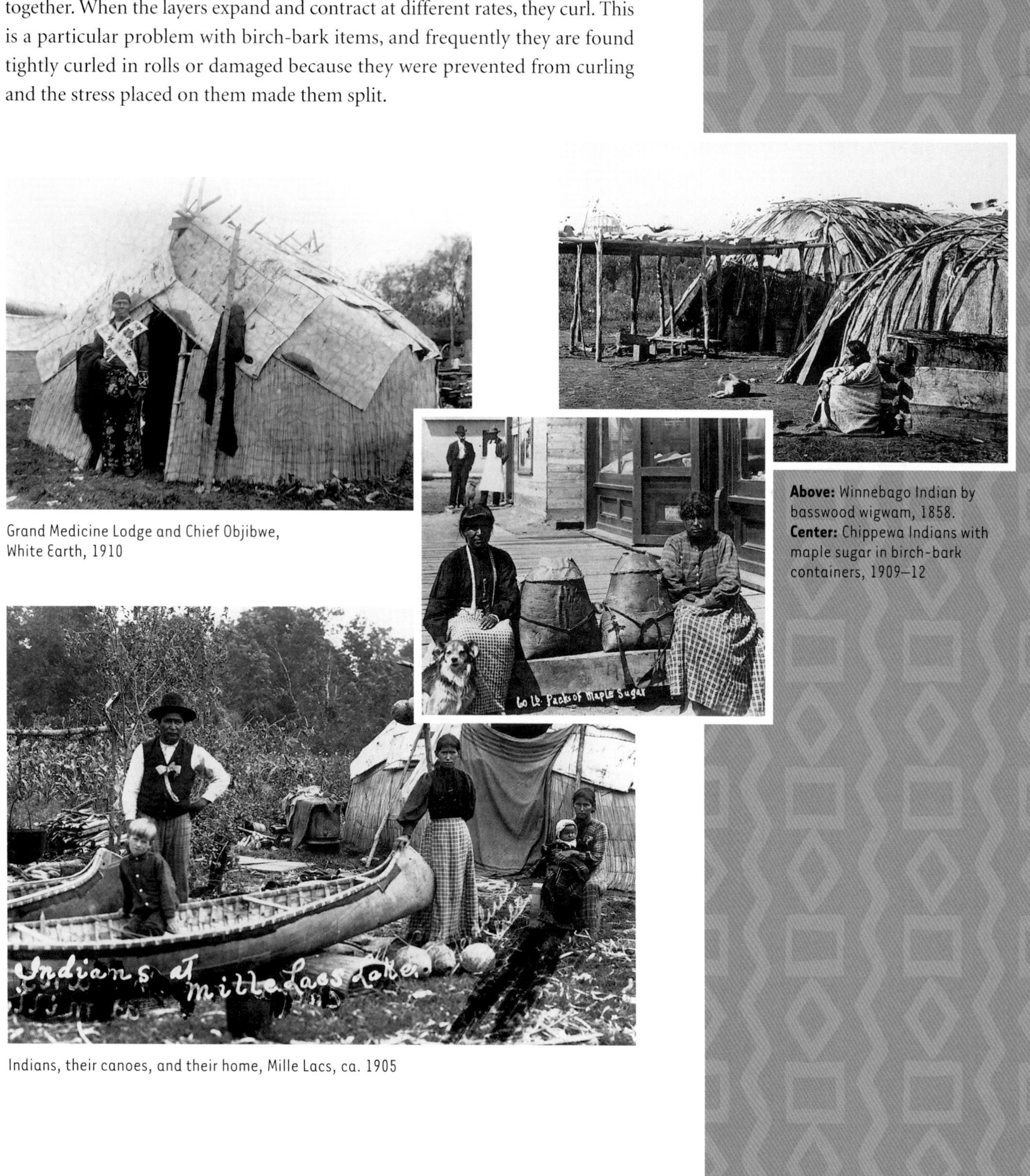

Grand Medicine Lodge and Chief Objibwe, White Earth, 1910

Above: Winnebago Indian by basswood wigwam, 1858.
Center: Chippewa Indians with maple sugar in birch-bark containers, 1909–12

Indians, their canoes, and their home, Mille Lacs, ca. 1905

Basic Care and Storage

Above: A wooden feast bowl, probably cracked from excessive drying. **Right:** The birch bark is split on the cover of this makuk.

Wood and birch bark attract mold, insects, and other pests. To avoid these pests, wood items are best stored in an environment that discourages the pests, that is, cool temperatures and a relative humidity below 60 percent. When stored at a relative humidity below 30 percent, wood can split and crack, and birch bark can curl and may split into many layers. A fluctuating environment harms wood and birch-bark items that are held together with adhesives, stitching, nails, dowels, or other joining methods; these may become loose, and the items can fall apart. Keeping temperature and moisture levels stable will help to prevent these structural problems.

Wood is often painted or coated with resin or varnish. These applied layers are more fragile than the wood, often decomposing, fading, and flaking. When painted wood is in this condition, avoid moving it. It should be handled very carefully, kept in a stable environment, and exposed to as little light as possible.

Avoid the use of commercial wood waxes and polishes because these can damage the wood finish and leave layers of residue that are difficult to remove. Many commercial waxes today use silicone, and this is nearly impossible to remove.

Special Pest Concerns

Many insects, such as powder post beetles, silverfish, and cockroaches, feed on items made of wood and birch bark. Some traditional paints are made of natural products and may make these items even more attractive to insects. The key to controlling pests is to control the environment. Keep the relative humidity under 60 percent, and you will prevent mold from growing and discourage most insects.

Routine Handling

Wear clean gloves made of cotton, nitrile, or latex when handling items made of wood and birch bark. Because they are highly porous, wood and birch bark easily absorb hand oils when they are touched. The resulting stains can be difficult if not impossible to remove. Additionally, layers of paint may be friable (powdery) and should be handled as little as possible to reduce the chance that they will be damaged.

Display Issues

Wood and birch bark are easily degraded by overexposure to light and may darken or turn yellow. The paint on wood or birch-bark items is easily faded by exposure to light. For this reason, light levels should be minimized, and display times kept as short as possible. Follow the temperature and humidity recommendations specified in the Basic Care and Storage section.

Mounts and Supports

Mounts should not prevent wooden items from expanding and contracting with changes in relative humidity, since the resulting stress can cause cracks to form in the wood. Birch bark must be adequately supported while used for display and in storage. If not, it can warp and even crack over time. However, it should be allowed to move slightly to accommodate changes caused by temperature and relative humidity fluctuations. Items made from birch bark should be used for display as they were used. In other words, bark items should not be hung on a wall or propped up on edge, unless this is how they were used. Small three-dimensional items made of birch bark, like small boxes, bowls, and baskets, can be supported with a soft foam pad, or a cloth pillow filled with polyester batting or raw cotton. Pads or pillows should be covered with a soft clean cloth to prevent the polyester or cotton fibers from snagging on the item.

Store birch-bark scrolls in shallow curved-bottomed trays. These can be made out of acid-free corrugated cardboard. Curved bottoms can be formed by carefully slitting along all the corrugations on one side of the three-ply corrugated acid-free cardboard. Cut in this manner, corrugated cardboard will flex in one direction to form a curved shape. This cut cardboard can be placed inside a tray, padded with polyethylene foam, polyester batting, or raw cotton, and covered with a soft, clean cloth.

Acid-free paper, mat board, or cardboard are the most affordable and compatible materials from which to make storage boxes, and even display supports, for wood and birch bark. The stable plastics discussed in chapter 7 are also good materials for display and storage supports, although they can be expensive.

Cleaning and Minor Repairs

Wooden and birch-bark items that need to be cleaned can be dusted lightly with a soft brush to remove dirt and debris. Beware of items that have loose or peeling bark or paint that might be removed by a brush. Avoid using water to clean these items, as it may stain or cause them to swell and then crack when dried. Solvents such as alcohol or acetone will not leave a mark on wood and can work well to remove oily or greasy deposits such as those left by hands. Acetone, however, is highly flammable and can irritate the eyes and skin. To avoid problems with solvents, be sure to use the precautions recommended by the manufacturer or supplier. The use of any solvent on birch bark should be considered very carefully. Because of its layered structure, solvents can affect the moisture content and cause it to dry out, crack, or curl. As mentioned earlier, avoid wood cleaners, waxes, and polishes because they are so difficult to remove.

Warped or cracked wood cannot be brought back into its original shape without placing the item under a great deal of stress. Some furniture restorers use high pressure and steam to reshape wooden items into their original shape, but this will damage paint and other coatings and can also damage the wood by crushing it. Generally, conservators consider this type of treatment inappropriate.

A person skilled in making items out of birch bark may be the best person to repair these items when they are damaged, especially if they retain their general shape and only the structural joining elements have broken. However, one of the most common ways for birch bark to degrade is for the bark to curl, delaminate, and split. When this happens, repairs can be difficult for anyone to accomplish. Fresh birch bark can be almost "rubbery," but as it ages it can become very brittle and prone to splitting and cracking. It might seem that soaking the bark in water would help it to relax and unroll. Water, however, will not relax the bark or restore it to a pliable state, and it may even damage it further. In some cases, solvent fumes can be used to relax curled birch bark. Consult a conservator for advice before attempting that kind of treatment. Simply adhering layers of split or separated birch bark together can actually cause greater damage than leaving them alone, as new stresses may build up.

Under no circumstances should any type of sticky tape, staples, or sewing thread be used to repair a wood or birch-bark item. Over time, most tapes do more harm than good. They cause deep stains that are difficult if not impossible to remove. Once the sticky adhesive dries up, the plastic or paper support can fall off, and the item can fall apart again. Staples can cause permanent damage. Because sewing thread is very thin and strong, it can literally cut through birch bark.

Sometimes, very old items made of wood or birch bark may be found in dry caves, very wet environments, underwater, or in a charred state on the ground. These items are usually weak, darkly stained, and brittle. Waterlogged items can be dried in a number of ways but require the expertise and equipment available to a conservator. If these items are simply left to air dry, they can completely disintegrate. If, however, the items are dry and still recognizable as wood or birch bark, they can be treated in the same way as other wooden or bark items. Be sure to handle them with great care, as they will be very fragile.

21

Ceramics

Found in such items as vessels, toys, loom weights, pipe bowls, and decorations

THOMAS J. BRAUN

Mille Lacs Trading Post, ca. 1935

Indian people have used tribal methods and techniques to care for their cultural items for generations. These caregivers are highly skilled and knowledgeable individuals in possession of sound information. They have developed excellent methods that have been proven by the test of time. The purpose of this chapter is not to replace any of this knowledge or information. Instead, we are offering additional methods that American Indian people can use for the cultural items in their care.

Identification and General Information

Ceramics are usually made by heating natural clays at a high temperature. Typically, clays for ceramics are grouped into two general types: *red clay,* which contains primarily silicon dioxide and iron oxide; and *kaolin clay,* which contains mostly aluminum oxide and almost no iron oxide. Because red clay contains more iron, it often has a rusty brown shade somewhere between light tan and dark brown, while pure kaolin clay is white. American Indian items are rarely made from kaolin, although raw, unfired kaolin is used as a natural white pigment. This chapter will discuss only red clay ceramics.

Most traditional American Indian ceramics are red clay fired at a relatively low temperature. Ceramics are often grouped into several loose categories based on the temperature at which they were fired. Most American Indian ceramics made before 1950 were fired below 1,650°F and can be classified as "terra cotta." In recent years, many Indian artisans have been making ceramics using other materials and methods.

A general rule of thumb is that lower-fired ceramics will easily absorb water, while higher-fired ceramics will absorb little or no water. To test this, you can use a small paintbrush to apply a little water to an unglazed area of ceramic, and watch to see if it is drawn in. Because high-fired ceramics are less likely to absorb water, they have fewer salt problems (see below).

Ceramics may have different surface finishes, coloration, or impressed designs. A *glaze* is a thin layer of clear or colored glass on the ceramic surface. A *slip* is usually more like a thin layer of clay and has a matte appearance and is a different color than the clay body. Ceramics may be coated with other materials as well, including paints and inks.

Basic Care and Storage

Ceramics are decorated most commonly with a slip or glaze that is fired on, or melted onto the surface when it is fired. Ceramics with a fired-on overall glaze or other decorations are impervious to normal variations in temperature below several hundred degrees. These fired-on decorations also help protect ceramics from humidity. In recent decades, some ceramics have been initially fired but later decorated with paint or some other decoration that is never fired. These unfired decorations are very fragile and are easily damaged by exposure to water, heat, or light. If you want to know if decorations are fired on or not, consult a conservator.

Ceramics are brittle and break easily.

Repaired ceramics may suffer damage from temperature and humidity extremes. In particular, many adhesives used for repairs soften and give way at elevated temperatures. Ceramic pots with repairs may sag, collapse, or fall apart if they are stored in a hot area, such as an attic or a building that does not have air conditioning.

Salts can also damage or destroy ceramics. The clay may have originally contained a significant amount of salt, and other types of earth added to adjust the properties of the clay may include salt. Water or foods stored in ceramic vessels often leave salts behind. Contact with seawater or burial below ground can also introduce salts.

Fluctuating humidity levels aggravate the harmful effects of salts in ceramics. Above 60 percent relative humidity, the salts dissolve and can move around inside the ceramics. When the ceramics dry, the salts migrate to the surface and are left behind when the water evaporates. This is called *salt efflorescence.* Efflorescence generates tremendous forces, pushing off areas of glaze or decoration and even breaking up entire ceramics. To prevent this, ceramic items are best stored at a low humidity that does not fluctuate widely. Check ceramics frequently for salt efflorescence, which appears as fluffy, furry, or dusty deposits, as a dry white film, or as a hard, thick white crust.

Never stack ceramics, such as pots, one on top of another. This may break them or wear away parts of their surface. Store ceramics on open shelving if they are not sensitive to light. Ideally, store each ceramic item by itself in a padded cardboard box made from preservation-quality materials. Box storage may be impractical if you have a large collection, because the boxes may take up too much space, are expensive to purchase, are time-consuming to construct, and hide the pots from view. Boxes should still be considered for especially valuable items.

Special Pest Concerns

Generally, mold will not grow on ceramics, and insects will not attack them. In very wet conditions, however, mold or lichens may grow on ceramic surfaces, although the mold will not digest the ceramic itself. Insects will eat food residues left on ceramics and will eat materials such as paint, sinew, or feathers applied after firing. However, proper environmental conditions prevent mold, lichens, and insects.

Routine Handling

Ceramics can be slippery when handled with cotton gloves. For a better grip, handle ceramics with clean hands or with nitrile or latex gloves. Pick items up from their lowest, widest point, finding the center of gravity and using both hands. Ceramics are extremely brittle, and they will easily break. The best protection for brittle ceramics is to handle them on a firm, stable surface padded with cloth, pillows, or sheets of polyethylene foam. Take care that they do not roll off the surface. Ceramics with paint or other unfired decorative elements are particularly fragile and should be handled with special caution. Do not allow ceramics to touch other nearby objects that can chip or damage them. Protect lids that may be loose and fall off when the ceramic is moved. Be extra careful with handles, and never use the handles to lift an item. When moving heavy and bulky ceramics, find at least one other person to assist you in the move.

Display Issues

Many ceramics are strong but also brittle. This means that they will withstand stress up to a point, after which they will suddenly break. For this reason, they should always have solid and stable support while used for display.

Humidity fluctuations are also a major concern for all ceramics. As explained earlier, at a relative humidity over 60 percent, water-soluble salts dissolve and start to move within the ceramics, causing damage as they dry out. For this reason, the climate in display areas should be kept dry and steady.

Ceramic items with painted, unfired decorations are susceptible to fading and should be kept out of light whenever possible. Hot spots caused by intense display lights are also damaging. In some rare cases, the heat of lights causes cracks to grow. Do not place ceramics too close to lights, and avoid any intense lights that will heat ceramics from a distance.

Mounts and Supports

External supports help pots to remain stable. Support pots with rings made of polyethylene foam tubing or with blocks of polyethylene foam carved to support the sides. Cylindrical polyethylene foam tubing in several diameters is sold through various conservation suppliers. Ideally, you should use solid, not hollow, foam. To make a pot ring, cut a short length of tubing to the appropriate length to support the underside of the pot, and glue the ends together with hot-melt adhesive. For a better appearance, consider sewing cloth around the pot ring. A ring should fully support the pot so that it does not touch the shelf where it is stored. The ring will relieve some of the strain on the bottom of the pot. More information about mounts and supports can be found online at http://www.cr.nps.gov/museum/publications/conserveogram/04-12.pdf.

Above: A replica of a St. Croix Woodland earthenware pot found in Minnesota. The original is approximately 1,400 years old. Note the display mount with padded metal wire support. **Top right:** Substitute pot in custom-made storage box with two compartments: one constructed to hold round-bottom pot securely upright, and one constructed to hold the display mount when the pot is in storage.

Cleaning and Minor Repairs

You will need to regularly remove accumulated dust from ceramics. Dust may disfigure the appearance of ceramics, become imbedded in pores, and lead to surface scratches. If dust accumulates quickly on your ceramics, you need to identify the source of the dust and reduce it. Reducing the amount of dust will save you a significant amount of cleaning time.

If you only have a small number of items, you may want to do your dusting in a room separate from where the items are stored or used for display. This is to prevent the dust from returning to the air and settling on other items. This, of course, requires moving the items some distance. If they are fragile or if there are many of them, the handling required to move them to another room could be a problem. With large or fragile collections, it may be better to set up a cleaning station near the items. This cleaning station can be on a table or on a cart with locking wheels that could be moved from item to item. Great care will need to be taken to avoid scattering dust to other items nearby.

Make sure ceramics are stable during cleaning, are surrounded by padding, and are not at risk of tipping or breaking. Avoid the use of household cleaners or dusting tools on ceramics. Never use a feather duster, since broken feathers may scratch the surface, and the feathers will catch on and remove small protrusions. Instead, use a soft cotton cloth, like the "magnetic" dust cloths mentioned in chapter 9, or a soft, dry long-bristled brush.

If the dust is particularly heavy, a vacuum may help. The guidelines in chapter 9 will help you choose an appropriate vacuum. The vacuum nozzle can be placed near the ceramics, and a brush used to push dust toward the nozzle. A piece of cotton cheesecloth or flexible fiberglass screening can be stretched over the nozzle and secured with a rubber band, so that no loose

pieces will be sucked into the vacuum. More information can be found online at http://www.cr.nps.gov/museum/publications/conserveogram/08-01.pdf.

After dusting, ceramics may still appear dirty or dusty. Do not wash ceramics in water unless you have a good reason to do so. If ceramics are not completely fired, they may redissolve into soft clay when they touch water. Washing can remove fragile slip layers, flaky surfaces, unfired paints or coatings, and other elements. Washing frequently creates a water-soluble salt problem, which can badly damage or destroy the drying ceramics. Additionally, washing ceramics may also damage or remove important evidence and information, such as food residues. For these reasons, contact a conservator before washing ceramics.

Conservators can repair broken ceramics with specialized acrylic adhesives not commonly available to the public. Common emulsion adhesives, such as Elmer's white glue, should be avoided. These adhesives can be difficult to remove if the ceramics ever need to be disassembled. Do not use self-adhesive tapes on ceramics, because they can remove the glaze, slip, or other areas of decoration. Many hardware stores carry the cellulose nitrate or cellulose acetate adhesives historically used to repair ceramics. A cellulose-based adhesive, like Uhu brand glue, behaves like the acrylic adhesives conservators use and can be safely used to repair broken ceramics. The advantage of both acrylic and cellulose-based adhesives is that you can easily remove any excess adhesive with the proper solvent. With these adhesives, if reconstructed ceramics break again or any missing pieces are found, they can be easily disassembled, cleaned, and reassembled again. Consult a conservator to select and match the best adhesive to the type of ceramic and its type of damage.

Stone

Found in such items as jewelry, pipes, arrowheads, grinders, mauls, rock art, sculpture, mineral specimens, and fossils

THOMAS J. BRAUN

Indian people have used tribal methods and techniques to care for their cultural items for generations. These caregivers are highly skilled and knowledgeable individuals in possession of sound information. They have developed excellent methods that have been proven by the test of time. The purpose of this chapter is not to replace any of this knowledge or information. Instead, we are offering additional methods that American Indian people can use for the cultural items in their care.

Indian Inscription Rock at Mulberry Creek, Kansas, 1868

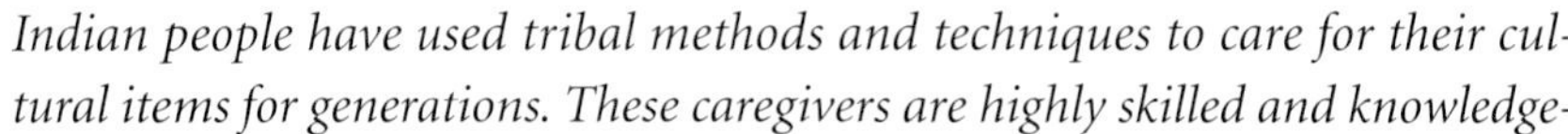

Identification and General Information

Stone items come in a wide variety of forms, including mineral specimens, sculpture, jewelry, flaked lithic tools, fossils, cave paintings, and even outdoor rock art such as petroglyphs. Some stone items are sturdy, intended for use outdoors or on the ground, while others are more polished and fragile. In general, stone is one of the most stable materials found in American Indian items as long as it is protected from physical and chemical damage.

In spite of this stability, stone can still be damaged. While it is often thought to be among the hardest materials known, it is actually softer and weaker than some metals. Most stone is brittle, and certain types are fragile and especially prone to damage. Like ceramics, if stone items are handled improperly, they will break. Some stone is so soft that it can be scratched with a fingernail. Certain types of stone, such as blue celestite, turquoise, and brown topaz, can be faded by light. Poor-quality semiprecious stones may have been dyed to accentuate their colors, and these dyes can also fade when exposed to light. Almost all stone can be deteriorated by weather and pollution.

Stone items, like metal ones, sometimes acquire a patina after many years of use. While metal patinas often originate from corrosion, patinas on stone are composed of accumulated layers of handling residues, such as oils and dirt. On outdoor stone items, patinas form also from prolonged weathering.

Geologists divide stone, or rock, into several broad categories: *sedimentary, igneous,* and *metamorphic.* Each category contains several different types of stone. The stone in each category is formed in a certain way, which influences how it performs and the use to which it can be put. In other words, each category has unique characteristics, such as hardness and the way that it fractures or breaks when struck, that determine what kinds of items are made from it. For example, manos and metates are sometimes made of basalt because it is extremely hard and has some porosity so it is abrasive. Pipe bowls are often made of catlinite or steatite, stones that are resistant to cracking when heated.

Above: Man holding a pipe, 1868
Below: Ojibwe carved stone pipe bowl

Basic Care and Storage

For the most part, stone items stored indoors have fewer problems than items made from other materials. Nevertheless there are concerns. Large stones are heavy, and heavy items are difficult to move and can break without proper support. Flaked stone can have thin, sharp, brittle edges that are easily broken. Sculpture is usually made of softer stone, which is more porous and stains easily. Gemstones and mineral specimens can be altered or damaged by light and pollutants.

Most stone can be safely stored at any temperature below 100°F and at a relative humidity below 60 percent. At higher humidity, molds and lichens can grow on stone, and soluble salts within the stone can be mobilized. Also, metallic mineral seams can corrode and stain stone, and iron pyrite can react and be converted to iron sulfate, which can turn to powder and cause the stone to fall apart.

Salt efflorescence is caused by the movement of soluble salts in stone. It looks like a powdery white film or a hard white crust and can cause spalling, flaking, and the loss of pieces of the stone. Efflorescence occurs when the stone dries out and the salts rise to the surface, being left behind as the water evaporates. The salts then crystallize and generate tremendous force, which can cause pieces of the stone to fall off. Stone items found buried or lying on the surface of the ground may contain these soluble salts. Salts are usually introduced to stone from rising dampness in the ground. This will not happen indoors but can occur when a stone item is found or used for display outside. When stone is stored or used for display on cement, even indoors, water can travel through the cement and into the stone. In these cases, rising dampness can be blocked by placing a water-impermeable material under the stone, or by placing the item on a raised shelf. Low humidity, below 35 percent, can also cause some types of stone to crack as they lose water. More information on

these problems can be found online at http://www.cr.nps.gov/museum/publications/conserveogram/11-02.pdf.

Special Pest Concerns

Insects will not attack stone items but may be attracted to residues on the stone, such as paper labels. As mentioned earlier, lichens often grow on stone that is outdoors. Lichens are extremely aggressive weathering agents for stone and generally should be removed if the item needs to be preserved (see Cleaning and Minor Repairs, below). Lichens growing on stone usually look like round patches with a soft or powdery appearance. The use of chemical poisons to control the growth of lichens should be avoided. These chemicals are damaging and will not prevent lichens from reforming. A better solution is to make sure that water, which supports the growth of lichens, is kept away from the item. This water can come from many sources, such as rain and lawn sprinklers.

Routine Handling

Smooth stone items are best handled with bare clean hands or nitrile or latex gloves, as they can be too slippery for cotton gloves. Rough-textured stones can be handled with clean dry hands, although some porous stones easily absorb oils from hands and should be handled with cotton, nitrile, or latex gloves.

Display Issues

Stone items can be used for display with fewer concerns than most other materials can. Many gemstones, however, can be faded by light. Any stone that has been painted, dyed, or otherwise decorated may also be sensitive to light. If you keep these concerns in mind, items made of stone can be used for display in higher light levels than those made of other materials.

Mounts and Supports

Even though stone is a strong material, items may still need additional support. Because of stone's heavy weight, mounts and storage supports may require additional reinforcement. Vibrations from foot or automobile traffic can shift items and put them in peril. Some stone items that are heavily weathered or thinly carved can be very weak and require significant support.

Cleaning and Minor Repairs

Stone items require only occasional dusting. Avoid using household sprays or cleaners on stone since they leave harmful residues. Cleaning stones in jewelry with commercial jewelry cleaners or common detergents can be harmful to both the stone and any metal. Stone items can usually be cleaned safely by dusting them with a soft-bristled brush or soft cotton cloth or by vacuuming using a micro-attachment as appropriate. More information can be found at http://www.cr.nps.gov/museum/publications/conserveogram/15-02.pdf.

Before cleaning a stone item aggressively, carefully consider whether the item really needs it. Some stains, such as iron stains on limestone, are practically impossible to remove without damaging the item. If cleaning with a brush, cloth, or vacuum is not sufficient, some stone may be cleaned of soil by simply washing with water. Pressurized water, such as from a pressure washer, is often used to clean outdoor stone items, but this can cause significant damage, both by breaking off pieces of loose stone and by etching lines in the stone that are cleaner than other areas. Using an everyday low-pressure garden hose is much safer. Blast-cleaning outdoor sculpture, using pressurized particles such as sand, glass beads, or powdered walnut shells, is another common cleaning technique. This is too aggressive and will rapidly cause damage. Blast-cleaning has the further disadvantage of removing protective patinas and opening up the pores on the surface of the stone to the weather, which greatly accelerates deterioration.

The presence of lichens on outdoor stone can be very damaging. Usually lichens can be removed with a stiff-bristled plastic brush and some water. The use of bleach should be avoided. Bleach will kill the lichens, but it will often weaken or damage the stone and leave a corrosive chlorine residue behind.

Some stone items can be cleaned with an eraser. Use a white vinyl block eraser such as the Staedtler Mars Plastic or the Sanford Magic Rub. Additionally, dry cleaning sponges made of vulcanized rubber, also called soot removal sponges, work well for removing fine particulate dirt from relatively smooth surfaces. Various solvents can be used to clean stone items that have been defaced by graffiti. Generally this should be done very carefully as the solvent may remove dirt around the graffiti, causing lighter areas to form. Contact a conservator for guidance.

Stone items can be difficult to repair because few adhesives are strong enough to support the weight of the stone. Avoid using the common adhesives such as epoxy resins, superglue (cyanoacrylate), ultraviolet-curing adhesives, and polyester resins, because these adhesives are difficult if not impossible to safely remove should that become necessary. Emulsion adhesives such as Elmer's glue should be avoided because they discolor and are very difficult to remove. Special adhesives used by conservators are available from conservation suppliers, but these need to be carefully prepared before use. Many hardware stores carry other adhesives that contain cellulose nitrate and cellulose acetate. These adhesives, such as Uhu brand glue, behave similarly to the adhesives used by conservators. Unlike most types of adhesives, these can be easily removed by a conservator, unless the stone is very porous. Contact a conservator to help you select the proper adhesive for the job. For very heavy fragments, dowels or pins are necessary to give the join better strength, but the pieces may be difficult to align properly. The treatment involves drilling into the item; this task should also be left to a conservator.

23

Plastics and Modern Materials

Found in such items as beads, buttons, and decorations

PAUL S. STORCH

Indian people have used tribal methods and techniques to care for their cultural items for generations. These caregivers are highly skilled and knowledgeable individuals in possession of sound information. They have developed excellent methods that have been proven by the test of time. The purpose of this chapter is not to replace any of this knowledge or information. Instead, we are offering additional methods that American Indian people can use for the cultural items in their care.

Identification and General Information

Many modern American Indian items contain plastics and other synthetic materials. In this chapter, the term *modern materials* will include synthetic materials from the 1860s to the present. European industrialists and scientists developed these materials to replace natural substances such as shell, bone, and ivory. Various American Indian cultures used items made of these materials, such as buttons and imitation pipe beads, for ornamentation. A wide variety of modern materials are found on late-twentieth-century powwow dance apparel.

Plastics are the most widely used modern material. A complete description of the many plastics available is well beyond the scope of this chapter. Identification of a particular plastic is generally not possible without conducting tests that involve cutting, burning, or dissolving part of the item, so they will not be discussed here. Contact a conservator for further information and advice on the identification of plastics.

Plastics deteriorate for a variety of reasons including heat, moisture, light, and physical stresses. Some plastics will slowly self-destruct, especially cellulose nitrate and other early synthetics. These suffer from inherent vice: they are materials that have an innate tendency to deteriorate. Cellulose nitrate turns yellow and becomes brittle over time. Although proper storage conditions will slow the process, nothing will stop the ultimate loss of the item. Deteriorating plastics release acids and other chemicals. These breakdown products can affect other, more stable plastics and nonplastic materials that are in proximity in storage or display. Problem plastics should therefore be separated from other materials if possible.

Deterioration from ultraviolet light, heat, physical stress, high relative humidity, and contact with low-quality storage and display construction materials can cause the following chemical effects:

- color changes,
- chalkiness or surface bloom,
- crazing or cracking,
- embrittlement,
- release of breakdown products, and
- softening and stickiness.

Signs of deterioration include

- distortion or dimensional change,
- crazing or cracking,
- surface deposits that are often sticky,
- less flexibility,
- odor, and
- a change in texture or color.

Above and left: Plastic hair pipes with three plastic beads at the bottom, and plastic beads hanging from the headpiece, both on modern Ojibwe powwow dance outfits

Basic Care and Storage

Since many plastic items were considered disposable, they were not manufactured to endure. You need to provide the best possible storage conditions to counteract this characteristic. Optimum basic preservation in collections involves consistent temperature and humidity. Follow the recommendations in chapter 6. Stable, cool, and dry conditions are best.

Many plastics, especially urethane foams, are particularly prone to degradation by ultraviolet and infrared light. Plastic items should be stored in the dark. Avoid storing items near radiators, heat pipes, outside windows, or incandescent lights. These poor conditions can cause excessive drying.

Never apply pressure-sensitive tape or self-adhesive labels to the surface of plastic items. The adhesives can eat into the surface of plastics and are difficult to remove without causing further damage to the item. Do not stack plastic items within one another; this will cause physical distortion over time.

Special Pest Concerns

Plastic materials can develop mold growth under extreme conditions, for example, if the relative humidity in the storage or display area is allowed to exceed 60 percent for relatively long periods. Mold infestations can be recognized by a fuzzy white or greenish growth on the surface of objects. Good ventilation

and air circulation in storage and display areas will help to prevent mold infestations. If mold growth does occur, take measures to reduce the relative humidity to which the items are exposed, and contact a conservator on how to clean the surfaces safely. Many types of mold can cause serious and permanent health problems. Personal safety is the primary concern when dealing with mold infestations.

Insects will not usually attack plastic items. In fact, the absence of insect damage can be a way to tell imitations from natural products. Natural shell and bone products are attacked by dermestid beetles and will have small round holes in them if infested. Imitation plastic products will not have any holes.

Routine Handling

The general methods and techniques for the proper handling of all items apply as well to plastic items. Always wear gloves when handling plastic items since the acids and salts in sweat and on fingerprints can permanently mark the surface. In addition, body oils can stain the porous plastic surfaces, especially those that are light colored.

When lifting and moving an item composed of or including plastic, make certain that it is supported well and that no stress is being put on weak areas or attachment points. Use a tray or other support if necessary. This can be made from a piece of acid-free corrugated board that is cut to the standard sizes of drawers or other storage units.

Display Issues

The temperature and relative humidity ranges mentioned above in Basic Care and Storage also apply to display conditions. It is important that plastic items used for display be protected from high light levels, ultraviolet radiation, and heat from incandescent lights and sunlight, because these items are especially prone to damage from light and heat. Incandescent floodlights inside cases and dioramas generate a lot of heat and can cause extreme drying. Lights should usually be outside of cases. See chapter 11 for other general display concerns.

Mounts and Supports

Avoid using adhesive mounts. These can cause irreversible damage to the surface of the items, resulting in staining and loss of surface texture. The solvents in the mounting adhesive can dissolve the surface of the plastic item, causing permanent damage. If the adhesive bond fails, the item can fall from its mount. It is better to grip items to mounts with padded wires or flat acrylic plastic clips rather than to pierce the surfaces with fasteners. Avoid using unpadded wires or attaching items through existing holes with fasteners such as screws.

External supports can be fabricated from acrylic plastic sheeting, such as Plexiglas, and shaped with heat to conform to an item's surface shape. This requires only minimal tools and training. Books on working with foam and plastic sheeting are available for those who want to fabricate their own mounts (see Barclay, Bergeron, and Dignard 2002). Standard-size mounts are available from some suppliers, though they can be expensive and hard to use with unique items.

Cleaning and Minor Repairs

Plastic materials are prone to getting dirty during storage, handling, and use because many have an electrostatic charge and attract dust. Others slowly bleed plasticizers to the surface and become tacky. Plastic items rarely develop an attractive appearance from the combined effects of aging, wear, and polishing as ivory and stone do. The few plastics that do so are those for which color is only a small part of their attraction, for example, vulcanite and molded Bakelite. In such cases, cleaning with a dry soft brush or cloth is probably all that is necessary.

The best method for the long-term preservation of plastics is periodic inspection and maintenance. Check for loose attachments before cleaning an item. Remove surface dust with a variable speed vacuum, brushes, and micro-attachments, as described in chapter 9.

In addition, plastics, with certain exceptions, can be cleaned periodically to remove surface contamination that may have built up over time. How frequently plastics should be cleaned will depend on how dirty they get. With cellulose-based materials, such as celluloid and cellulose acetate, and casein, plastics made with a milk protein, it is recommended that cleaning be done at least once every five years.

Plastic objects that are stable and have no metal, fiber, or fabric attachments should be washed with tepid water containing a small quantity of mild liquid detergent, such as unscented dishwashing soap. You may need to use a small brush for textured surfaces. Afterwards, rinse the materials with clean water, and immediately dry using an absorbent cloth. Do not soak for long periods. It is much better to rewash if soiling remains. Degrading cellulose nitrate and cellulose acetate (identified by visible crazing or porous areas) should not be washed. Be careful with objects containing metals that might corrode, or with hollow objects that may be difficult to dry on the inside. We suggest disassembling these composite objects before cleaning, if this can be done safely and without risk to the item. If items are tacky, isolate them, because a degrading plastic can affect anything else it touches.

Using commercial adhesives to repair cracks and breaks is discouraged, as these repair methods are difficult and may result in staining and further breakage as the adhesives age. In addition, breaks and cracks may provide useful information and evidence of use. Unnecessary repair of such damage can obscure historical evidence.

24

Paper

Found in such items as books, drawings, photographs, newspapers, documents, letters, maps, and prints

SHERELYN OGDEN

Indian people have used tribal methods and techniques to care for their cultural items for generations. These caregivers are highly skilled and knowledgeable individuals in possession of sound information. They have developed excellent methods that have been proven by the test of time. The purpose of this chapter is not to replace any of this knowledge or information. Instead, we are offering additional methods that American Indian people can use for the cultural items in their care.

Identification and General Information

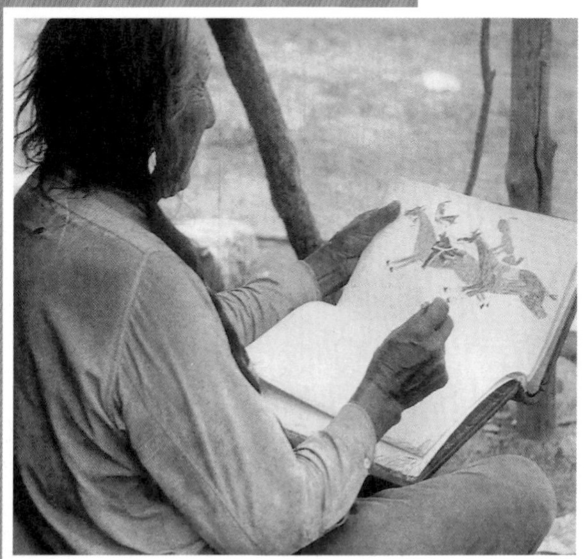

Richard Wooden Leg (Sioux) drawing in a ledger book, ca. 1928

This chapter is limited to the type of paper most commonly found in the items listed above. Other paperlike materials, such as tapa, amatl, and papyrus, sometimes referred to as semi-papers because they are not made from a slurry (see below), are not discussed here.

Paper was invented in China approximately two thousand years ago. It is generally believed that it was introduced to the Arab world by the Chinese in the eighth century, carried to Europe by the twelfth century, and spread to other parts of the world, such as North America, a few hundred years after that. Paper was originally made by hand using various similar methods. When it became accepted in Europe and demand increased, especially as a result of the industrial revolution, the papermaking process became mechanized, around 1800. Today most paper is machine-made, although very fine papers are still made by hand by highly skilled craftspeople and artists for special purposes.

Paper has been made from many different fibers over the centuries, depending on what was grown locally, readily available, and easy to use. In Europe and North America, most paper was made initially from cotton and linen cloth rags. The rags were cut up, beaten into a pulp, mixed with water to make a slurry, and then formed into sheets of paper. When the papermaking process became mechanized, there were not enough rags to meet the demand, and alternative fibers were investigated. After some experimentation, wood was found to be a suitable alternative in the early 1840s. Today most of the paper produced in Europe and North America is made from wood.

Wood, however, contains many impurities that accelerate the deterioration of paper by causing harmful acids to form. Modern newsprint, for example, deteriorates very quickly. This deterioration can be seen by its rapid discoloration. The impurities that cause the deterioration can be removed from the wood pulp by chemical means before the paper is made. Wood pulp paper is classified into two types. *Chemical* wood pulp paper has been treated chemically to remove harmful impurities. Some of the most permanent paper that we have today is this type. *Mechanical* or *ground* wood pulp paper has not been treated to remove the impurities and is very impermanent. Other factors that contribute to the deterioration of paper regardless of the fibers from which it is made are the overbleaching of the fibers to make paper whiter and the use of chemically unstable sizes, such as alum rosin, commonly added to paper so that inks will not feather.

Rag, chemical wood pulp, and mechanical or ground wood pulp papers are all found in American Indian items. Exact identification of the type of paper used in an item requires chemical or microscopic tests. Often a conservator can look at a sample and make an educated guess as to the type of paper based on its age, condition, and appearance. This level of identification is usually adequate for most purposes.

Basic Care and Storage

In general, the recommendations for care and storage provided in chapters 6 and 7 can be followed. Paper is especially vulnerable, however, to poor storage methods. Haphazard, overcrowded conditions soon result in avoidable damage, such as dirt marks, tears, and creases, while poor-quality storage containers accelerate the deterioration of the items they are intended to protect by transferring acids to them. Because most of the American Indian items made of paper fall into a limited number of specific types, the care and storage of paper are discussed here by type of item. For more detailed information on the storage of items such as these, consult the sources listed in the bibliography (Canadian Conservation Institute, *CCI Notes;* National Park Service, *Conserve-O-Gram Series;* Ogden, *Preservation of Library and Archival Materials;* Ritzenthaler, *Preserving Archives and Manuscripts*) and online at http://www.nedcc.org/plam3/tleaf41.htm and http://www.mnhs.org/preserve/conservation/reports/occasional_papers.pdf.

BOOKS

Ledgers and sketchbooks that contain drawings produced by American Indians to document their life and experiences, often made while they were in captivity, are unique cultural items. The paper used in these books is usually of relatively good quality. The images are most often in graphite, colored pencil, crayon, ink, or watercolor, and although they are sometimes smeared, they are most often in sound condition. The bindings on these books, however, are frequently fragile.

Boxing is crucial to the preservation of certain books, and these ledgers and sketchbooks are a prominent example. Storing a book in a box keeps the binding and pages clean, protects them from light and physical damage, and provides structural support for fragile or damaged bindings. Boxes should be constructed of preservation-quality materials, and they should be custom made to fit the book's dimensions exactly so that the book does not slide in the box and become abraded.

Both drop-spine and phase boxes are acceptable and are available commercially. Drop-spine boxes are preferable because they provide better support and keep books cleaner. Envelopes are sometimes used for the storage of books. These generally do not provide the support books need and should be replaced with boxes. If boxes are too expensive or take up too much space on shelves, books can be wrapped in paper. Never hold damaged books together with rubber bands or string, which can damage bindings. Box them, wrap them in paper, or tie them with a flat undyed cotton, linen, or polyester tape.

Left: Damaged book tied with flat cotton undyed tape. **Below:** Examples of custom-made drop-spine boxes *(top)* and phase boxes *(bottom)*

You may have a variety of books in your care, not just ledgers and sketchbooks. Most books have similar storage requirements. In general, maintain good air circulation. Never store books directly against walls but, instead, at least three inches away to facilitate movement of air around the books and to avoid the occurrence of pockets of damp air. This is especially important when bookshelves are positioned against the outside walls of a building.

Keep books upright on shelves rather than allow them to lean to one side or the other, because leaning causes strain on the binding. Bookends help hold books upright. Bookends with smooth surfaces and broad edges are preferred to prevent bindings from being abraded and pages from being torn or creased.

As a rule, do not stack books in piles on shelves. Small, structurally sound books can be shelved upright. Oversize, heavy, structurally weak, or damaged books can be stored flat rather than upright to give them the overall support they require. If books are stored flat, additional shelves may need to be inserted at narrow intervals to avoid having to stack these books. If it is absolutely necessary to stack books, the stacks should contain only two or three books. When possible, individually box the books that are stacked. Shelves for oversize books need to be wide enough to support the books completely so that they do not protrude into the aisles.

Ideally do not store paper and cloth bindings in direct contact with leather bindings. Acidity and oils in the leather migrate into paper and cloth and hasten their deterioration. Furthermore, degraded powdery leather soils paper and cloth. Again, when possible, box books to avoid these problems. When this is not possible, shelve paper and cloth bindings together, separate from leather bindings. Another alternative to consider is the use of polyester film book jackets or simply the placement of a piece of polyester film between the books.

Remove all acidic inserts, such as bookmarks, scraps of paper, and pressed flowers, from books. If these inserts are important to keep, they can be placed in a small plastic or paper folder or sleeve and returned to the book or stored separately. Removing these inserts will prevent acidity in them from migrating into book pages. Remove paper clips in books as well.

UNBOUND FLAT PAPER

Unbound paper items are more vulnerable to damage than books because they do not have the protection of a binding. Many of the ledgers and sketchbooks that contain drawings by American Indians have been disbound, leaving the drawings loose. Other drawings by American Indians were never part of a book but were produced on single sheets of paper. These valuable drawings and other works on paper need to be stored in some sort of container to protect them. Traditionally museums place items such as these in a mat and then store them in frames or boxes. Unless you have immediate plans to display your drawings, frames are not necessary. Matting them and then storing the matted drawings in a box is a good option. Make all the mats the same size,

that of the box, not the drawings, to prevent movement of the matted drawings in the box. If you have drawings that vary greatly in size, you may need to choose more than one standard size for the mats and boxes. A lower-cost alternative is to place each drawing in a folder instead of a mat, and then place all the folders in a box. As with mats, the folders should be the size of the box. Using folders will take up less space than mats, so if space is a concern, you may want to select this alternative. Place only one drawing in a folder. If the image on the drawing appears to be smeared, contact a conservator for suggestions on how to store the drawing to prevent further smearing. All mats, folders, and boxes should be made of preservation-quality materials. The boxes should be stored flat.

Counting Coup. Ledger drawing in graphite and colored pencil, ca. 1880, attributed to Big Cloud (Cheyenne)

For other loose paper items, such as documents and letters, keep in mind that only ones of the same general size and type should be stored together. Generally speaking, heavy objects need to be stored separately from lighter ones, as do bulky objects, which cause uneven pressure inside boxes. Because acid migrates from paper of inferior quality to any other paper with which it comes into direct contact, it is important to separate poor-quality paper from that of better quality. Remove news clippings and other obviously inferior-quality papers from direct contact with documents and letters that are on better-quality paper.

Documents and letters should be unfolded for storage if this can be done without splitting, breaking, or otherwise damaging them. If left folded, these items will eventually tear along fold lines when they are repeatedly unfolded for reading. If unfolding for storage may result in damage, consult a conservator before proceeding. Carefully remove all damaging fasteners such as staples, paper clips, and pins. Guidelines on how to do this removal are available online at http://www.cr.nps.gov/museum/publications/conserveogram/19-05.pdf. Damaging fasteners can be replaced, but *only if absolutely necessary,* with non-rusting staples or paper clips. House documents in file folders. Ideally, place no more than ten to fifteen sheets in each folder; the more valuable or fragile the item, the fewer the sheets that should be stored in one folder.

Folders can be kept in document storage boxes. Be sure all folders inside a box are the same size and conform to the size of the box. The boxes can be stored flat or upright. If boxes are stored flat, they should be stacked only two high to facilitate handling. Flat storage will give the documents overall support and will prevent crumbling edges, slumping, and other mechanical damage to which upright storage might subject them. Flat storage, however, causes documents on the bottom of the box to suffer from the weight of those above. Upright storage is preferable when documents and folders are well supported to prevent slumping and edge damage. Spacer boards made out of stable materials can be used to fill out boxes that are not quite full. Care needs to be taken to not overfill boxes because this can cause damage when items are removed, replaced, or reviewed. An alternative to boxing is storage in a file cabinet equipped with hanging racks and hanging folders. If hanging folders made of preservation-quality materials cannot be found, general office hanging folders can be used, as long as the folders within them are made of acceptable materials.

PHOTOGRAPHS

It is best for each photograph to have its own enclosure. This reduces damage to the photograph by giving it protection and physical support. Folders, sleeves, and envelopes are common choices. These can be made of either paper or plastic (see below). Because paper enclosures are opaque, the photograph must be removed when it is viewed; clear plastic enclosures have the advantage of allowing researchers to view the image without handling it, thus reducing the possibility of scratching or abrasion. Paper enclosures should be acid- and lignin-free. Plastics suitable for photographic storage are polyester, polypropylene, and polyethylene. Avoid polyvinyl chloride (PVC) at all times. Both paper and plastic enclosures should pass the Photographic Activity Test (PAT) as specified in ISO 14523:1999 (formerly ANSI IT 9.16-1993) and also meet the standard ISO 18902:2001 (formerly ANSI IT 9.2-1998). These are standards that specify criteria for storage enclosures for photographic materials.

Once photographs have been properly housed in enclosures, they can be stored flat in drop-front boxes. Glass plate negatives are an exception and need to be stored vertically to prevent breakage of plates stored on the bottom of a pile. Horizontal storage of photographs is usually preferable to vertical storage, since it provides overall support and avoids mechanical damage such as bending. Vertical storage, however, may make access to the collection easier and decrease handling. For vertical storage, place photographs in file folders or envelopes that are themselves housed in hanging file folders or document storage boxes. Avoid overcrowding. The use of hanging file folders will prevent

photographs from sliding down under each other and will facilitate their handling. Also follow these guidelines if storing photographs in albums. Make sure all materials used in an album pass the standards cited above. Avoid the use of so-called magnetic albums, which employ plastics and adhesives of questionable quality.

House boxes on metal shelves or in metal cabinets. Where possible, store items of similar size together; the mixing of different sizes can cause abrasion and breakage and can increase the risk of misplacing smaller items. Regardless of the size of the photograph, be sure all enclosures within a box are the same size, that of the box. Do not overfill boxes.

Special care needs to be given to the storage of oversize photographic prints mounted on cardboard. This board is often acidic and extremely brittle. Embrittlement of the support can endanger the image itself because the cardboard may break in storage or during handling, damaging the photograph. Such prints must be carefully stored, sometimes in specially made enclosures. Handle them with great care.

OVERSIZE ITEMS

Oversize materials, such as maps and large prints, are best stored flat in the drawers of map cases or in large covered boxes. Place the items in folders, and cut all the folders to fit the size of the drawer or box. Allow adequate room where oversize materials are stored to remove them safely from drawers or shelves, and make sure there is a place to put them down once they are removed.

If oversize items are not brittle or fragile, they can be rolled when flat storage is not possible. It is important to make sure the items are not too brittle or fragile to sustain rolling and unrolling. Depending on their condition, some items need to be rolled individually; others can be rolled in groups of similar-size items, the exact number depending on the size and weight of the paper. A tube several inches longer than the largest item being rolled and at least four inches in diameter (larger diameters are preferable) works well. If the tube is not made of preservation-quality materials, wrap it in neutral or buffered paper or polyester film. Alternatively, the items can be placed in a folder of five-mil polyester film cut several inches larger in both dimensions than the largest item being rolled. The item or items can then be rolled face out onto the tube. If a polyester film folder is used, roll it so that the fold is parallel with the length of the tube. Then wrap the assembly with neutral or buffered paper or polyester film to protect it from abrasions. Tie the wrapped roll loosely with flat linen, cotton, or polyester tape. This assembly can be stored inside a larger tube for added protection if desired. Store tubes horizontally.

NEWSPRINT

Much of the newsprint produced after the mid-nineteenth century is made of mechanical wood pulp, and its long-term preservation is difficult at best.

While it is possible to alkalize (deacidify) newsprint to retard its deterioration, this is often not practical because the paper will still continue to deteriorate at a relatively rapid rate. Also, alkalization after newsprint has become yellow and brittle will not make it white and flexible again. Most news clippings are important because of the information they contain and not because of the value of the clippings themselves. For this reason, photocopying and microfilming are the most practical preservation options for collections of news clippings. Be sure to do all photocopying on preservation-quality paper using an electrostatic copier with heat-fused images. Physically separate news clippings that must be retained from better-quality papers in an enclosure made of polyester film or paper.

Special Pest Concerns

Paper is highly susceptible to mold growth. High levels of relative humidity in combination with still air can lead to mold growth. If, however, you keep the relative humidity below 60 percent and maintain good air circulation, you will probably avoid this problem in most situations.

Insects are another concern, and their presence should be avoided at all costs. Several species will attack paper and in extreme instances can destroy items. Maintaining acceptable levels of relative humidity along with implementing a program of integrated pest management will discourage insects.

Routine Handling

Following a few basic handling guidelines will extend the useful life of items significantly. Always handle paper with care. It tears and creases easily. Also, it is very susceptible to dirt and marks easily. Be sure to wash your hands before handling paper items so that you do not leave dirty or oily fingerprints behind. These are particularly disfiguring on photographs and drawings and are often difficult, if not impossible, to remove. Use your judgment about wearing gloves. If the gloves do not fit snugly, they may get caught on the edge of paper items and tear them. Also, if you choose to wear gloves, be sure to change them as soon as they become soiled.

Do not pull books off the shelves by the headcap (the top of the binding at the spine), a practice that causes the headcap to fail, tearing the spine of the binding. Instead, books on either side can be pushed in, and the desired book pulled out gently by grasping it on both sides with the thumb and fingers. To minimize chances of dropping books, do not stack them too high when they are moved or carried. Do not stack books of special value at all. If book trucks or carts are used, they should be easy to maneuver. Avoid stacking books high on the truck and having them protrude beyond the edges.

Books are often unnecessarily damaged during photocopying. Photocopy machines with flat copy platens necessitate jamming the binding flat in order to get a good image. Better machines are those with edge platens or other fea-

tures that allow a book page to be copied with the book open to only 90 degrees instead of 180 degrees. Never press the spine of a book down with your hand or the cover of the copier to ensure a good-quality image.

In general, avoid touching a single sheet of paper, especially a drawing, any more than necessary. Handle it by using its storage enclosure. If it must be turned over, for example, accomplish this by handling only its mat or folder. If an item does not have its own storage enclosure, an acid-free paper folder can be provided. If the item itself must be handled, hold it at the edges, touching no more of it than necessary and avoiding the image if possible. Use two hands. If an item is heavy, oversize, or otherwise difficult to maneuver, two people should handle it.

When an item must be moved from one location to another, support it well. Always use a rigid support larger than the item, made of acid-free corrugated board or similar material, under it. These supports or carrying cards can be cut to the standard sizes of the storage drawers, mats, and other enclosures used in the museum. Remember that certain media on drawings can smear. Avoid touching or rubbing the image.

Display Issues

In general the suggestions provided in chapter 11 can be followed when paper items are used for display. Also, the National Information Standards Organization (NISO) has issued guidelines for displaying library and archival materials. These guidelines are ANSI/NISO Standard Z 39.79-2001. This important standard provides all the basic information you will need to safely display your paper items. The standard can be purchased for $49 from Global Engineering Documents, 15 Inverness Way East, Englewood, CO 80112, 1-800-854-7179, or online at www.ANSI.org.

Because paper is very susceptible to damage from light, exposure to light is probably the most pressing display concern. Minimize light levels and display times as much as practical, and use substitutes instead of the originals whenever possible. Newsprint, for example, degrades quickly upon exposure to light and will darken. Color photographs, with a few recent exceptions, also are extremely sensitive to light and will fade quickly. Black-and-white photographs are less sensitive, but they also will fade in time. Display a substitute instead of the original if at all possible. Some photographs also are particularly susceptible to pollution. If your display space is in a polluted area, you have another reason to display a substitute rather than the original.

Another concern when using paper items for display is adequate support of items so they do not slip, distort, or suffer structural damage. If loose sheets of paper are displayed vertically on a wall, they need to be well supported in a mat and a glazed frame or in a mat with a glass or acrylic cover. Secure them into the mat in a non-damaging way by such means as hinges, tabs, or straps. For information on this type of display, see the sources in the bibliography (e.g., Ogden, *Preservation of Library and Archival Materials*) and online at http://www.cr.nps.gov/museum/publications/conserveogram/13-04. Alternatively they can be displayed flat in a case.

This crayon enlargement of Snana Good Thunder (Dakota) was reproduced photographically and placed in storage, and the new photograph was substituted for the original on the wall. This will protect the original from light damage.

Books are best displayed flat, not leaning against a wall vertically. Unless done with great care and expense, vertical display does not provide the physical support needed by a book to prevent the binding from becoming damaged over time. If a book must be displayed at an angle so that it can be seen, use as low an angle as possible, not exceeding 30° to 45°. Ideally display a book closed, with photocopies of the significant pages displayed beside the book. If the book must be shown open, avoid opening it any farther than necessary to view it, and never open it any farther than the binding allows without force. If the book opens flat without causing stress to the binding or pages and is small and lightweight, it can probably be safely displayed without the aid of a book cradle or other type of book support. Most books, however, need to be displayed on a book cradle that fully supports them when open or with the aid of another type of support, such as blocks or wedges. These bear the weight of the book covers and text block and reduce strain on the hinges and spine of the binding. Do not leave the book open to one place for an extended period of time, because it may become altered structurally and not close properly again. Open it to one place for a limited time only, such as one to three months. If the book must be displayed open for a longer period, turn the pages regularly and as often as possible.

Various types of supports are available from conservation suppliers. Use ones made out of chemically stable, non-damaging materials that are strong enough to support the weight of the book. Directions for constructing an easy-to-make book cradle from polyester film are available in the sources in the bibliography (National Park Service, *Conserve-O-Gram Series*) and online at http://www.cr.nps.gov/museum/publications/conserveogram/18-01.pdf. This type of cradle is best suited for lightweight books but has been used successfully for other sizes of books. If, however, the cradle is positioned at an angle rather than flat, so that the book can be seen better, the cradle needs to be made out of a heavier, more rigid material, such as acrylic, and be fitted with a bottom ledge to support the book. If the book is large and heavy, the cradle also needs a text block support. Although cradles custom-made from acrylic to fit the book when open to a specific location are preferred, these are expensive. Use of polyester film cradles, adjustable cradles, and other types of book supports are an acceptable, if less than ideal, alternative.

If necessary, the leaves of an open book can be held in position by narrow (½-inch) restraining straps made of a non-damaging transparent material, such as polyester film. Wrap the straps gently around the text and binding and secure them in a non-damaging way with minimal tension. Be sure any adhesives and tapes used to secure the straps never come in contact with the book.

Mounts and Supports

Aside from the book cradles and other types of supports needed for display, paper items do not generally require special mounts and supports. Their greatest need is for storage containers, discussed on pages 179–185 under Basic Care and Storage, for example, phase boxes, drop-spine boxes, mats, frames, document storage boxes, sleeves, and folders.

Cleaning and Minor Repairs

Although removing all dirt from paper is neither necessary nor desirable, some cleaning will often improve the appearance of an item and can remove substances that may eventually harm it. The term *cleaning* refers to a variety of procedures. The simplest of these is surface or dry cleaning, which is done with a soft brush or an erasing compound. The surface cleaning technique described below can be used safely on most book pages, documents, letters, and maps. Use it very cautiously on brittle newsprint, which may tear from even gentle pressure applied during cleaning. Do not use it for photographs. Consult a conservator for advice on how to clean these. Also avoid using it on ledger drawings by American Indians. These often have graphite or colored pencil, which can smear when cleaned. In general, avoid cleaning pastels, charcoal, watercolors, or other hand-applied coloring that may not be firmly bound to the paper and may be smeared, lifted, or erased during the cleaning process. More detailed information on the cleaning process can be found online at http://www.nedcc.org/plam3/tleaf62.htm and at http://www.nedcc.org/plam3/tleaf43.htm.

To start, clear a work area that has a large, clean, smooth surface, and place the item to be cleaned on it. Begin cleaning by gently brushing the surface of the item with a soft brush to remove loose dirt and dust. Use up-and-down strokes, and work across the paper. When cleaning books, be sure to brush the dirt out of the gutter or inner margin.

If the dirt is firmly bound to the paper, you may need to use an erasing compound. These come in the form of granules and block erasers. It is probably best to consult a conservator for advice about current brands that are recommended because the compositions of these change periodically. Noncolored vinyl block erasers, such as the Staedtler Mars Plastic eraser and the Sanford Magic Rub eraser, appear at this time to have the least potential for damaging paper. These block erasers can be ground into granules, and they are commercially available in both forms. Test first in an inconspicuous spot to make sure that no damage will occur. Steady the paper with one hand, and test by gently rubbing the cleaning compound over one small area. Once you are certain the image will not be smeared or erased, begin cleaning.

Most conservators clean with granules. To clean with these, sprinkle them over the item to be cleaned. Using your fingers, gently rub the granules over the surface in small circles. Start in the middle and work toward the edges.

When cleaning near the edges, do not use a circular motion, but rub from the middle toward the edges using a straight movement. This will help prevent tearing the edges, which are fragile. Brush away granules and loosened dirt frequently. It is essential that all granules be removed from the item following cleaning because they are potentially damaging if left on the paper long-term.

While granules will remove most dirt, erasers in block form may remove even more. Block erasers can abrade soft papers, however, and need to be used with care and only when necessary. Rub gently in a single direction or in small circles.

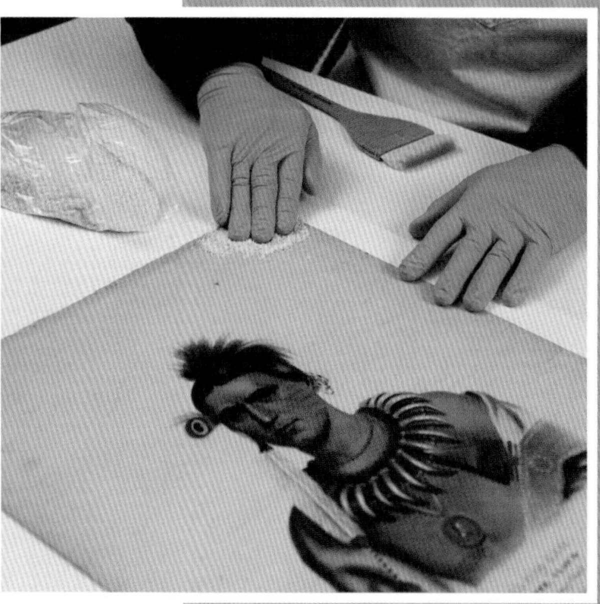

Surface cleaning a lithograph on paper of Ma-Has-Kah, or White Cloud, an Ioway chief

Dry cleaning sponges made of vulcanized rubber, which were intended originally for soot removal following a fire, are now being used increasingly for surface cleaning dirt on paper. These sponges are reported to leave no damaging residues on paper, and they appear to be nonabrasive. They are easier to use than granules and block erasers and avoid some of the hazards of these cleaning compounds. You may want to try cleaning with sponges first, especially if you have heavily soiled items. Do not use these on ledger drawings or other items with an image that may smear or lift. Because the sponges tend to degrade upon exposure to light and with age, they need to be stored in an airtight container in the dark. As the surface of the sponge becomes dirty with use, cut off and discard the dirty part.

To clean the outside of books, hold them tightly closed and wipe them with a magnetic wiping cloth like those described in chapter 9. Dry cleaning sponges also work, but they are more awkward to maneuver into the tight spots of a binding unless you cut them to the shape you need. If the books are covered with a heavy layer of dust, vacuuming may be advisable. A soft brush attachment is recommended. The suction of the vacuum may need to be decreased to avoid pulling off loose fragments of deteriorated bindings. Do not use the vacuum directly on books of special or great value. Instead, use a soft-bristled brush to sweep dust from the book into the vacuum nozzle, or use a micro-suction attachment on the vacuum. When cleaning books, it is important to hold them tightly closed so that dirt does not slip between the pages. Clean the top of the book, which is usually the dirtiest area, first followed by the rest of the book. Wipe or brush the book away from the spine to avoid pushing dirt into the endcap or down into the spine of the binding. Clean dust cloths frequently, and never use the cloths for cleaning shelves to clean books.

Several cleaning products are available for cleaning bindings; some are specified for particular types of bindings such as leather, cloth, or paper. There are advantages and disadvantages to the use of these products. Since magnetic wiping cloths and sponges are sufficient for most cleaning tasks, rely on these instead. If you have a particular stain or mark you are trying to remove, contact a conservator for advice.

Tears in paper are a common occurrence, especially if the paper is brittle or the items are used frequently. Never repair tears with self-adhering sticky

tape even though the temptation to do so is great. This is because at this time there are no tapes of this type on the market that are of preservation quality. Even though some of the tapes are reputed to be safe and are labeled as archival or of preservation quality, experience shows that these discolor and cause other problems over time, and they should not be used on any item that is intended to last long-term. The same is true of lamination that uses heat or adhesive fusion processes. Safe methods of repairing tears are available. Consult http://www.nedcc.org/plam3/tleaf63.htm. These methods, however, require hand skills that take time to master, as well as the investment in at least a small amount of supplies to get started. In most situations it is not practical to repair tears in-house. An alternative for unbound torn items is to place them in plastic or paper folders or sleeves until the tears can be repaired by a person with these skills. Plastic or paper folders for this kind of storage are available commercially in a variety of sizes. Plastic folders and sleeves have the advantage of allowing an item to be viewed without removing it, which reduces the chance of tearing it further.

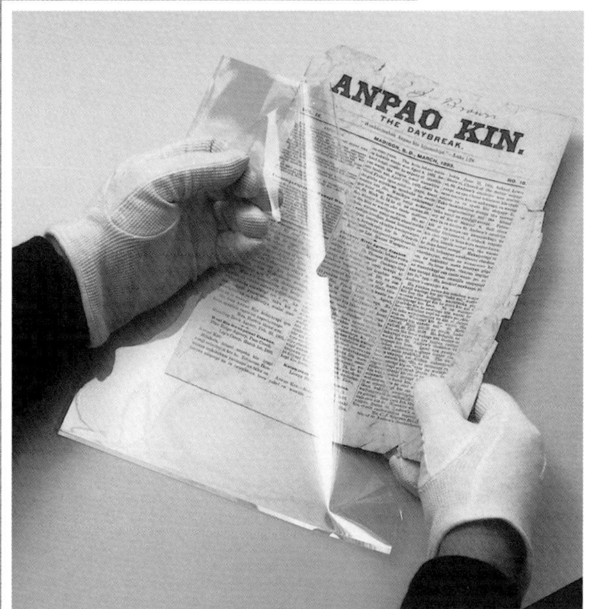

Most other repairs to paper items are best left to conservators. Do not hesitate to contact them for guidance.

25

Plant Materials

Found in such items as baskets, hats, mats, containers, and footwear

ANN FRISINA

Indian people have used tribal methods and techniques to care for their cultural items for generations. These caregivers are highly skilled and knowledgeable individuals in possession of sound information. They have developed excellent methods that have been proven by the test of time. The purpose of this chapter is not to replace any of this knowledge or information. Instead, we are offering additional methods that American Indian people can use for the cultural items in their care.

Identification and General Information

Plant materials include a wide and varied group of plant parts from many species. General categories of plant materials include grasses, rushes, barks, woods, gourds, stems, roots, seeds, and leaves. These materials can be used to construct baskets, netting, cordage, and even fabrics. Common production methods include felting, knitting, knotting, coiling, plaiting, and weaving, to name a few. Identification of plant materials is often done microscopically. Some individuals, such as those with tribal heritage, may have developed a more intimate knowledge of surrounding terrains, plants, and techniques, which allows them to identify plant species through visual examination. These versatile materials, as well as their processing and construction techniques, vary greatly from region to region.

Woman weaving a bulrush mat, ca. 1910

Basic Care and Storage

Pay extra care and attention to items made from plant materials because of their inherent fragility. The decomposition of items made from plant materials is often initiated by the fragility of the materials themselves, the construction

techniques, normal use, inadequate storage, and mishandling. Deterioration, whether it is physical, chemical, mechanical, or biological, will likely result in very fragile items that are prone to embrittlement, distortion, and areas of loss. Items constructed of plant materials, including three-dimensional items, such as baskets and hats, and two-dimensional or flat items, such as mats, should not be flexed, scraped, or abraded.

Plant materials are susceptible to damage from both humid and dry environments. A basket constructed of woven reeds, leaves, grasses, or bundles of pine needles that becomes saturated with moisture from high humidity may become too heavy to support itself. Swelling due to humidity can cause stress on many traditional construction techniques. Items made of birch bark can swell or warp. This swelling leads to breaks within woven or tied fiber bundles, allowing the bundles to splay out of position. Warping or fractures can also occur on a microscopic level within the plant materials. The risk is also greater for older, more fragile items stored within humid environments.

Color changes and stains are another concern in highly humid environments. Tide lines can occur. These form when the combination of soils and acidic by-products within fibers migrates through the plant materials, depositing in a dark wavy line, or tide line, on the surface. High humidity can cause water-based dyes or surface paints to run or bleed into surrounding areas.

While not as common, low humidity and high temperatures can also be detrimental to plant materials. Loss of moisture can further embrittle them, again resulting in distortion, delamination, and fractures.

Above: Chippewa family at their home near Grand Marais, Minnesota. Note the mat hanging on the wood pole.
Right: Birch-bark and lake-grass wigwam at Leech Lake Agency, 1896

Plant materials are especially vulnerable to light damage. Light affects components inside the fibers and accelerates embrittlement, weakening of fibers, and fading. It is important to monitor light exposure in both storage and display areas. As with textiles, a good rule of thumb is to exhibit plant material items for no more than four months in even the most controlled lighting. Displays of plant materials should never use direct or bright light.

Physical Deterioration: Swelling and shrinkage due to an excessively humid or dry environment, and fragility due to excessive light exposure; also includes tears, breaks, misshapen structures, abrasion, and soiling.

Chemical Deterioration: Reaction between the item and other materials causing a chemical *change* that leads to such problems as embrittlement.

Biological Deterioration: Mold, bacteria, fungi, soiling, or infestation of insects or rodents.

Special Pest Concerns

Fungi, which include mold and mildew, will grow on plant materials in excessively humid environments and cause discoloration, embrittlement, and structural damage. Baskets with food deposits, such as cornmeal, are particularly susceptible to fungi, insects, and rodents. If your plant material items suffer from water or humidity damage, or if mold is visible on the surface of items, isolate them and contact a conservator for advice.

Insect infestations are a special concern for plant materials. The items themselves, as well as the remains of foodstuffs and previous contents stored within them, can attract pests. Insects will feed on plant materials or use them as areas in which to lay egg cases. Rodents will use plant materials as areas for nesting. Routine inspection, regular cleaning, and an active program of integrated pest management are the best means of prevention. If any infestation is noted, isolate the item and contact a conservator immediately. Avoid the use of over-the-counter pesticides as they can stain the item and may be toxic to the user.

Routine Handling

Wash your hands prior to handling, and if acceptable given cultural concerns, wear gloves when handling items made of plant materials.

When transporting items made of plant materials, use a board or box for support to limit the stresses of handling. Three-dimensional items, such as baskets, can be especially fragile and will need extra support inside and out to prevent breakage. When moving baskets that are conical in shape, support the outer walls with supportive coils or rings made of extruded polyethylene tubing or backer rod, or of cloth tubing. Supports can be coiled around the exterior or interior of a basket, conforming to its shape, supporting either a fragile and heavy top edge or delicate footing. For information on how to manufacture these supports, see the sections on exterior and interior supports, pp. 194–195.

Display Issues

Assess the structural condition of your item before using it for display. Ask yourself if it will withstand the stress of being used for display without an exterior or interior support. For example, is a basket strong enough to be used for display without collapsing? If not, you may want to choose another item.

The form of the piece will determine the way it is used for display. For three-dimensional items, a flat board or platform, preferably within a display case, works well. A hanging piece that is both flat and flexible can be displayed by draping it over a fabric-covered rod for short periods, such as three to four months. A fabric-covered slanted mount board is best for fragile flat items that cannot be draped over a rod or cannot sustain their own weight, like a bag with a handle. A cost-effective option is to fabricate storage mounts that can double as display mounts.

A curator holds an acrylic display mount custom designed to support this basket while it hangs inside a teepee for display.

In general,

- support items, preventing undo stress to fragile fibers;
- protect items from excessive humidity or dryness; and
- protect items from excessive light exposure.

Mounts and Supports

FLAT STORAGE

Secure flat plant material items on support boards with twill tape ties, or line a board with a piece of washed cotton muslin, securing this in place with small tabs of 3M #415 double-sided tape. The texture of the fabric will prevent slippage of the item when opening and closing drawers or moving items from one location to another.

Baskets stored on shelves in a cabinet. The Hidatsa basket on the upper shelf is supported with polyethylene foam, while the Apache basket on the lower shelf is supported on a rigid mount.

If you are going to store items in drawers or boxes, line the surface on which they will sit with a sling of muslin, nonwoven polyester, or Tyvek fabric larger than the item. By gently grasping the fabric excess on the side, you can lift an item out of a box or drawer with minimal handling. This sling method will allow you to safely remove two- and three-dimensional items from deep drawers or boxes. Do not use a sling for exceedingly fragile items. Instead, choose a flat board, and create two handles with twill tape secured through slots in the board. You should be able to lift the board by the twill tape handles without touching the item. As always, protect an item stored on an open shelf from dust and dirt by covering it with unbuffered tissue or cotton muslin.

EXTERIOR FLEXIBLE SUPPORTS

Rings and coils are often wrapped around the exterior of baskets to support the walls from the outside. The rings can be constructed of polyethylene tubing available from conservation catalogs, which comes in $\frac{3}{4}$-inch or $1\frac{1}{4}$-inch diameter rolls. Once cut to the appropriate size, these tubes can be hot-glued together, creating stable doughnut supports.

If you do not have access to polyethylene tubing, you can create support rings out of rolled lengths of thermal-bonded polyester batting wrapped in washed cotton knit fabric or Tyvek fabric. Once the fabric length is positioned, pin and then secure it with hand stitching. Take care not to make your stitches so large that they may snag on the item.

INTERIOR FLEXIBLE SUPPORTS

When a basket is collapsing, internal polyethylene rings may be too stiff and unwieldy to insert. In this instance, it may help to insert softer, more supple tubing made of thermal-bonded polyester batting covered in washed cotton knit fabric. Another option is to fill the space with soft crumpled, unbuffered, acid-free tissue.

This Ojibwe woven cedar-bark bag is filled with polyester batting covered with muslin. The interior support is formed to the shape of the interior of the basket.

When storing a flat woven item in a box, such as a large mat that requires folding, pad out the folds with rolls of crumpled acid-free tissue to prevent knife-edge creases from developing. Protect against abrasion between layers by lining with flat sheets of acid-free tissue. If you are storing items on open shelves, cover them with a piece of acid-free tissue or washed de-sized muslin fabric to prevent dust and dirt from settling on the items.

Hats and headdresses may need a support to rest upon. You can often build structural shapes with corrugated acid-free board, and then pad them with thermal-bonded polyester felt or batting, and cover them with muslin or cotton knit fabric. These forms should easily fit the item and not cause undue stress to it. Make a base for these forms with a board so that they are stable and will not tilt over.

Cleaning and Minor Repairs

Storing items in protective boxes or a cabinet and displaying them in cases are a good defense against dust and dirt accumulation. The less dust accumulation you have, the less handling and abrasion your items will receive during cleaning.

Since plant materials are so susceptible to damage from water, only dry surface cleaning is recommended. Vacuuming with the aid of a soft brush can help remove loose dust and dirt with minimal risk to plant materials. However, thoroughly examine your item for broken and unstable areas prior to any surface cleaning. Brushing the surface gently with a soft bristled brush will help loosen dirt, which can then be picked up with a vacuum micro-attachment. Take care to have the vacuum on a low suction setting. Remember to vacuum the surface in a methodical row-by-row manner. This will facilitate the overall cleaning of the item so that no one area is brighter than another.

Do not remove unknown substances found in storage containers without thoroughly examining them. Foodstuffs, herbs, or other materials found on items may provide significant clues about an item's previous use. If the surface of an item will not be abraded, distorted, or affected by soil and loose particu-

lates found within it, you may want to leave the item as is for later testing and documentation. A tribal member may be able to help you decide whether to maintain or discard such information. However, if you must clean a basket to prevent further damage, you may want to keep a sample of the material and take photographs and notes to document the area.

Items made from plant materials often have areas of loss due to use, fragility of materials, or handling and storage procedures. No one method of repair answers the needs of all plant materials. Adhesives, patches, and solvents can cause irreversible changes to the item and may be inappropriate for museum objects. For this reason, it is recommended that you choose repair methods that will not alter the item permanently. Exceptions to this rule are past or current repairs by tribal members.

When making the decision to mend an item, ask yourself the following questions:

- Will the mend help the item hold together structurally?
- Will the mend fill in an area of loss to create a whole looking item?
- Will the mend be stronger than the surrounding area and cause more breaks or damage in the future?
- Will the mend be visible to the viewer?

Remember that the overall goal of mending is to prevent further deterioration and to stabilize the item. Small areas of loss that do not affect the structural integrity of the item may be better left alone. Certain types of mending, for example, the joining or binding of plant materials, can be a reversible treatment. However, such detailed mending must be executed with extreme care. In general, mends are designed to help hold an item together. Unfortunately, mending practices can split and tear plant fiber. Filling in areas of loss with new or secondary materials can be a complex and difficult procedure. In many cases, it is recommended that a conservator or tribal member be consulted.

A simple mending technique, however, can stabilize rims and footings within woven, plaited, or bundled plant materials and prevent further deterioration. A mend should not be stronger than the surrounding area. Too much strength often causes fragile plant materials to form new breaks at the joins, promoting damage rather than preventing it.

Wrapping and tying original materials with single strands of cotton embroidery floss and splints of thin Japanese paper or Tyvek can mend or bind broken areas together. Be sure to wash the floss first because of potential dye bleeding. This type of repair is commonly used on baskets that are woven or sewn together with bundles of plant materials, like pine needles or grasses. Use cotton embroidery floss that is an appropriate color. The thread can be wrapped around broken reeds or bundles, attaching them to one another, and preventing further breakage. If the bundles are exceedingly fragile, try wrapping a splint of thin Japanese paper or Tyvek around the area first before securing it with the cotton embroidery floss. You can tone the paper to match the surrounding area with a thin wash of acrylic or artist color paint.

When choosing a needle, test it in an inconspicuous area to make sure it will not make a hole in the plant materials. A size 24 tapestry needle with a duller point and large eye for thread is a common choice. Insert the needle between fibers and stalks rather than through them. Take care not to pull the thread too tight; this will cause a break in the plant materials and lead to more damage. It is important to document all repairs made. Diagrams, photos, notes, and a small sample of materials used should be kept in a file about the item.

Do not remove deteriorated or broken repairs made by tribal members without first seeking tribal advice. Contacting a member of the tribal community with experience in construction and repair of items made of plant materials may yield access to traditional repair techniques that may be preferable.

Audiotapes and Videotapes

Such items as audiocassette tapes, videocassette tapes, and reel-to-reel tapes

THOMAS J. BRAUN

Identification and General Information

Audiotapes and videotapes are included in this book because you may have in your care tapes of songs, interviews, and other events that record the experiences of Native people. These tapes are one way that oral traditions can be carried forward. Sound and video recordings range from the earliest wax cylinders to today's most advanced digital formats. The most common types in your collection, however, are probably audiotapes and videotapes. These are two types of what are referred to as magnetic media or magnetic tapes.

Magnetic tapes first appeared in North America just after World War II. Most types of magnetic media are made of a plastic film coated with a magnetic material that has an iron-containing compound. The tapes used in audiotapes and videotapes are made of identical materials but are different widths. Usually, magnetic tapes are easily identified by their appearance. They are brown or almost black in color, sometimes with a slight metallic sheen. They are stored on reels, which are usually in a cassette or occasionally loose and exposed.

Frequently, information identifying the origin of the recording on a magnetic tape may be sparse, if present at all. For this reason, it is especially important to retain and preserve any original written information about the tapes in your care. Any additional information about these tapes that you gather over the years should also be carefully documented. If you need to make marks for identification, ownership, classification, or tracking purposes, you should make these on the recording's housing, not on the tape itself, as this can interfere with playback.

Additional sources of related general information are listed online at http://palimpsest.stanford.edu/bytopic/motion-pictures.

Basic Care and Storage

Audiotapes and videotapes are not as permanent as many of the other materials discussed in this book. Most types of magnetic media cannot be expected to last more than approximately thirty years, even when stored under the best of conditions. Today the standard preservation recommendation for magnetic tapes is to make at least two copies of the original tape, a master copy and a use copy. The master copy should be played only to make an additional use copy or when it needs to be exercised (see below). The master copy should be made to the highest standards possible. The use copy should be used for listening or viewing instead of the original or the master. It is wise to store the master copy in a different location from the original and the use copy so that if a fire or other disaster occurs, it is less likely that all copies will be destroyed.

Some people believe that transferring the information stored on magnetic media to a digital format (such as an optical disk or digital tape) is the best way to preserve this information. Most preservation professionals, however, disagree. Although digital recordings provide access to the material, concerns about lack of standards, data compression, and software obsolescence make these recordings unsuitable for preservation.

When making copies of magnetic media, use the highest-quality magnetic tape you can find, as usually this is the thickest, making it less prone to breakage. Use the fastest recording speed available on your equipment, as this will result in the best-quality recording. Of course, recording information in this manner adds to the cost. After making a copy, be sure all of the tabs from the cassette are broken off to prevent accidentally recording over the tapes in the future. Carefully keep track of all copies of magnetic media; take careful notes as to which "generation" any particular copy is from the original.

Some experts recommend a practice referred to as exercising: rewinding the tape reels periodically to release tension on the tape and to prevent the transfer of magnetic information from adjacent areas of tape. When magnetic tape is tightly rolled, areas of magnetic material lay next to each other in many successive layers. With time, these magnetic materials sometimes start to affect each other, and the magnetic information passes from one area of tape to another, resulting in faint sounds in the background when the tape is played. Exercising magnetic tapes will help prevent this. Exercising a tape is simply done by slowly rewinding or playing the reel. Recommendations vary on how often tapes should be exercised, ranging from once every three years to once every ten. The master tape should only be played when it is being exercised or copied. When copying a master, it is a good idea to listen to the audiotape, and watch and listen to the videotape. At that time, you can assess the quality of the tape's preservation.

Eventually magnetic recordings may no longer be produced commercially. Even if magnetic tape is available, the device needed to playback the information may no longer be manufactured or available. Eight-track tapes are an example. Decades ago these were common recording media. Today, eight-track

You may find in your collections old movie film or photographic negatives, or even plastic objects that are made with cellulose nitrate. Cellulose nitrate is one of the oldest and most unstable forms of plastic. It releases noxious nitric acid vapors as it degrades, which can be harmful to people and collections. Additionally, the plastic is a fire hazard and may spontaneously combust when exposed to a heat source. A later type of plastic, cellulose acetate, is not as unstable as cellulose nitrate, but can release acetic acid vapors and smell like vinegar if stored improperly. If you suspect that you have items made out of these types of plastics, you should contact a conservator.

tapes are difficult to find, and their players are even more difficult to obtain. If a collection contains many types of magnetic media, the equipment necessary to play all of them must be regularly maintained to ensure that playing these tapes will be possible. This equipment should be regularly cleaned according to the manufacturer's recommendations. Dustcovers are advisable for all such equipment. When you decide to copy the information on a tape to a more current format, this equipment will be needed to play the tape. Thus, the information will be preserved, although the recording media itself may not be.

Reels of tape should be stored upright and on their narrow edges, rather than flat, to prevent the tape from slipping from the reels around which it is wrapped. Dirt, dust, and particulates can cause abrasion to the magnetic media and subsequent loss of recorded information, so store tapes in as clean and dust-free an area as possible. Avoid dropping magnetic media as the shock can disorient the magnetic particles on the tape and cause a loss of recorded information. Excessive heat can cause the film to fuse together and make it impossible to unwind the tape from the reel. For this reason, magnetic tape should never be left inside a hot car. Additionally, the information on magnetic tape can be altered by radiation from the sun, so it should not be exposed to direct sunlight. Excessive humidity encourages tapes wound on reels to stick together and can cause the tape to undergo decay at a faster rate.

Temperature and relative humidity in a storage vault for magnetic media are carefully monitored at the Minnesota Historical Society using two different types of data loggers.

Magnetic media are best stored in cool, dry conditions. The American National Standards Institute has established a standard for the storage of polyester-based magnetic tape (ANSI/NAPM IT9.23 – 1996). Store tapes that are in continual use at 65 to 70°F and at a relative humidity of 40 to 50 percent. Tapes in long-term storage, such as master tapes, should be at as low a temperature as possible but not under 50°F and 30 percent relative humidity. If tapes are stored at low temperatures, however, they must be allowed to acclimate for several hours at room temperature before they are used.

Access to master copies of magnetic media should be restricted. The master copy should be in the most restricted storage area to decrease the chance that it will be used for anything other than making a copy or being exercised. Use copies can be more accessible, depending on how often they are requested.

It is also important to store magnetic media away from strong magnets and magnetic fields such as television sets, computers, high-tension power lines, and anything with electric motors. Magnets and magnetic fields can permanently alter the magnetic recording on a tape and effectively erase the information recorded on it. If magnetic media are stored on metal shelving, it should be grounded. Magnetic media are believed to be safe to pass through airport walk-through metal detectors and x-ray machines, but this should still be avoided if possible.

Special Pest Concerns

Insects and rodents are not a problem for magnetic media. Mold, however, can grow on magnetic tape in humid conditions. If you find magnetic media in your collections that are moldy, immediately contact a conservator or a magnetic media recovery service for advice.

Routine Handling

The magnetic tape that is most subject to damage from handling is reel-to-reel tape. Since the roll of tape is not protected by a cassette, it is relatively easy for dirt, dust, and fingerprints to damage the tape. Magnetic tape should never be handled with bare hands. Always wear clean, lint-free white cotton gloves. Ideally, these reels should be stored inside a paper or plastic box that protects the roll from dirt. Many varieties of these containers can be purchased through conservation suppliers. Some cassette tapes do not need an additional container because the cassettes protect the magnetic tapes stored inside of them, preventing them from being touched and from getting dirty and dusty. Videocassette tapes usually have an added layer of protection in that the tape itself is protected behind a plastic shield, which is only lifted away by the videocassette player during playback of the tape. Many cassette tapes come with a paper or plastic case designed to further protect the tape from dust and dirt. Generally, the tapes should be stored in these cases. Paper or plastic cases for cassette tapes are also available from conservation suppliers.

Avoid pausing tapes during play, as this places stress on the tape. When finished playing the tape, rewind it to the beginning tape leader and only then eject it, as this protects the tape from potential damage.

Display Issues

Magnetic tapes are rarely used for display since their value is the information they contain rather than their appearance. If it is necessary to display a cassette or magnetic tape, a prop tape can be used instead of the actual tape. If, however, a sound or video recording is going to be played as part of an exhibit, great care should be taken to make several high-quality copies from the master tape for use in the display, recording the tape to a digital format if possible.

Cleaning and Minor Repairs

Cleaning and repair of magnetic tapes is an area of conservation that is still emerging. Typically, the best people to help you with problems are electronics experts who specialize in recovering lost information from magnetic media. Consult a conservator for the names of commercial companies that specialize in this work.

27

Framed Items

Such as prints, drawings on paper, paintings, photographs, and textiles

THOMAS J. BRAUN

Identification and General Information

This chapter discusses framed items that are flat and in a frame of some sort. They can be drawings, photographs, maps, textiles, ornaments, or anything that can be fitted into a frame. Items that are framed can have a variety of conservation problems. The more common problems include "mat burn" caused by poor-quality acidic mat materials, damage from light, tears and perforations, and damage or losses to the frame itself.

Basic Care and Storage

Since framed items are usually designed for vertical display, they are best stored in this manner. Generally, when not hung on a wall, they are best stored upright rather than flat and not on their sides. The exception to storing framed items upright is when they are torn, flaking, or otherwise unstable. In these cases, it is often best to store items flat and facing upwards on large shelves. When stored flat, they need to have adequate shelf space because they should never be stacked on top of each other or left hanging over the edges of shelves. They should be covered to protect them from the accumulation of dust.

Flat storage for framed items that are unstable

Frames that are stable can be stored in narrow vertical bins. They should be placed upright in the bins, standing on edge. They should be positioned face-to-face and back-to-back, and separated by pieces of sturdy acid-free corrugated board or foam core that are larger than the items they separate. Acid-free cardboard sleeves should be made for items in ornate frames, such as plaster and gold-leaf ones, to prevent pieces from breaking off. Ideally, each bin should not house more than three or four framed items. The bins should be large enough to accommodate items easily; using bins that are too small may lead to damage to the frames. The bins should also be deep enough so that items do not extend out into walkways. Small items, however, should not be stored in deep bins, as they can be difficult to retrieve and can be damaged by larger items adjacent to them. Having bins of different heights and depths avoids these problems. The bottoms of bins should be covered with a soft carpet, if possible one of preservation quality, to protect the edge of the frames on which they are standing. More information can be found online at http://www.cr.nps.gov/museum/publications/conserveogram/01-11.pdf. Clearly marked labels affixed to the exposed sides of the frames will provide ready identification and eliminate the need for haphazard rummaging to find a specific item. Additionally, the bottoms of bins should be several inches above the floor for cleanliness as well as for protection in case of a flood.

Framed items on movable wire screens

Another alternative for the storage of framed items is to hang them on wire screens or racks, stationary or movable. Screens allow many items to be hung in a relatively small space, but depending on the type, they can be expensive to install. Screens work particularly well for the storage of three-dimensional and oversized items and are suitable for ornate plaster and gold-leaf frames as well. They also work well for odd-sized items, which can be hung wherever they fit in order to use all available space; such items tend to take up greater space in a bin. Fragile works, such as pastel, charcoal, and chalk drawings, should not be stored on sliding screens because the vibrations may loosen particles. More information on storage screens for paintings can be found online at http://www.cr.nps.gov/museum/publications/conserveogram/12-01.pdf.

Ideally, framed items should be stored in a windowless room that is used for no other purpose. When the framed items are not being accessed, the lights should be turned off to prevent unnecessary light damage. Framed items should be kept in as stable an environment as possible, especially paintings that are stretched on cloth supports such as linen or cotton. These paintings can be under extreme tension, and major changes in the humidity or temperature can cause these items to sag and warp, or become so tight that they suddenly tear.

Framed items in vertical bins

Special Pest Concerns

Frames that are made of wood are susceptible to insect attack. Insects are not usually a problem, however, if proper integrated pest management procedures are followed.

One of the most common concerns with framed items is damage from mold. Mold can easily grow on the back of the frame, the side that faces the wall, where air circulation is poor. Mold growth is a problem in humid areas and where walls are made of masonry, brick, stone, or concrete. Masonry and concrete walls can "wick up" water from the ground, which will then vaporize behind the framed item, creating a space that is high in humidity and favorable for mold to grow. This problem can be avoided by hanging only on interior walls and on walls that are not made of masonry.

Routine Handling

Damage to framed items is usually due to improper handling, poor environment, or a disaster. Damage includes scrapes, scratches, broken glass, tears, punctures, food spills, water damage, burns, and exposure to smoke from a fire. Possibly the most common handling damage to framing occurs when the screw eyes on the back of a frame scratch the front of another frame or item. Avoid this damage when handling items by placing them back-to-back and front-to-front.

Frames should always be handled with extreme care, because they can be damaged if dropped. Frames are often heavy, and the image areas are usually thin, under significant tension, and easily warped, perforated, or torn. Often it is advisable when removing framed items from a wall to have a team of at least two people: one to hold the frame, and one to look behind the item and make sure the hanging hooks and wires are free. Often the wires distort after they are released from the hook, and you should be sure to secure them so that they do no damage. Handle and move framed items only when necessary. Check to make sure the item is stable before moving it. As always when handling items, you should make sure there is a padded, secure place to set the item down before you begin to move it. Make sure your hands are clean and dry before holding the framed item, or wear gloves. Generally, it is best to hold framed items by the sides of the frames, not by the top and bottom moldings.

Display Issues

Framed items are different from many of the other materials discussed in this book because, in essence, they are already in a protective housing that helps preserve them. The frame usually protects the item inside it from physical damage, and the glazing, mat board, and other mounting materials usually protect it from dust, light, and mechanical damage. If the mat boards are made of acid-free materials, they will help to preserve the item. The glazing protects the face of the item from physical damage and can filter out some types of damaging light, such as ultraviolet. If the entire framing package is well designed and made of good-quality materials, it will in effect create a microclimate that helps preserve the item long-term.

It is important to display framed items only in areas with a moderate and stable climate. Avoid areas over radiators, near air vents, over fireplaces, and on exterior masonry walls. Hang framed items away from direct sunlight or high levels of light, as these are very damaging. Kitchens and bathrooms are inappropriate places to hang framed items because of the moisture fluctuations, problems with water condensation, and the food residues present in these places.

Mounts and Supports

Many framed items have raw wood, cardboard, or mat board on the back, as part of the original package. Usually these materials are included to support the item and keep it flat. Ideally, only preservation-quality matting and framing materials should be used for this purpose because poor-quality materials can deteriorate, become brittle and acidic, and damage the item inside the frame. Poor-quality mat board often causes a mat burn around the edges of prints, and raw wood backing boards frequently transfer an image of the wood grain to the item, which is damaging as well as disfiguring. Unless the original acidic support materials are crucial to the interpretation of a framed item, they should be replaced with preservation-quality materials. Make sure the matting materials are acid-free and lignin-free. They should be 100 percent cotton or linen rag board or an otherwise lignin-free, chemically purified conservation mounting board. Framed items should have a rigid backboard behind them to protect them from damage. For this purpose use acid-free corrugated cardboard, acid-free foam core, or Coroplast, a plastic corrugated board made of polypropylene and polyethylene. Avoid acidic brown cardboard and standard-quality foam core. Lastly, the back of the frame should be sealed from dust with a dust sheet made of good quality paper and sealed to the back of the frame with an adhesive or tape of preservation quality.

Careful consideration should go into the method of attaching the item to the mat, support, or mount that will hold it in the frame. Many different methods are appropriate, depending on the type of item that is being framed. For example, the methods suitable for a drawing on paper are different from those for a textile. In addition, several methods are available for specific types of items. Works on paper can be attached to a mat by paper hinges and a starch paste adhesive, or they can be attached to a mat without applying adhesive directly to the paper, using corners made of polyester film. Selecting the appropriate method of attachment is important because the wrong method can prove damaging and lead to serious problems in the future. Contact a conservator for advice on the best method to use for the specific item you want to frame, and pass this information on to your framer, or suggest that the framer contact the conservator directly.

Most framed items are hung with metal hardware and braided metal wire. Brass or stainless steel mounting hardware is best, though many commonly available types of other metal mounting hardware will work well. Frequently the manufacturer will rate these pieces of hardware for a certain weight. Make sure the hardware you choose is capable of holding significantly more than the weight of your framed item.

Either glass or acrylic glazing is appropriate for framing, though items with loosely bound particles on the surface, most notably pastels, charcoal, or chalk drawings, should be covered with glass rather than acrylic. The static charge in the acrylic sheet can pull particles off the surface. Make sure that the item is not in direct contact with the glass or acrylic glazing in the frame because humidity can cause the item to stick to the glass. Finally, if available and you can afford it, you should consider using glass or acrylic sheeting that will filter out damaging ultraviolet light.

There are many commercial framing companies that use high-quality materials to mount and frame items. Usually their services are quite expensive. In fact, if framers offer their services at an inexpensive price, it is almost certain that preservation procedures will not be followed because preservation-quality materials alone are expensive, and the labor of the framer adds to the cost. Before hiring any commercial framer, get a recommendation from someone who is familiar with museum-quality framing. At the very least, make sure the framer you hire is a Certified Picture Framer and is a member of the Professional Picture Framers Association and uses materials of the highest quality. Check http//www.ppfa.com for members, certification programs, and framers. If possible, observe the framer as he or she works and question the materials used. Additional guidelines for framing that you can take to your framer can be found in the sources listed in the bibliography (Canadian Conservation Institute, *CCI Notes*) and online at http://www.nedcc.org/plam3/tleaf410.htm, http://www.AIC.Stanford.edu.htm, http://www.cr.nps.gov/museum/publications/conserveogram/13-01.pdf, and http://www.cr.nps.gov/museum/publications/conserveogram/14-01.pdf.

Cleaning and Minor Repairs

Frames should be cleaned as needed but no more than necessary. In parts of the country that are dry, windy, and dusty, frames may need cleaning as often as every few months. As a rule, no cleaning solutions of any type should be used on frames. If frames are simply metal or wood, they can be cleaned with a magnetic wiping cloth, which uses static electricity to draw dust away and hold it on the cloth. Both the front of the frame and the back of the framed item can be cleaned in this way. If, however, the frames are highly carved or gilt ones, they will require more care in cleaning. They can be lightly dusted with a dry, soft-bristled brush. The use of a cloth or a feather duster should be avoided, as they can scratch the frame or catch on loose parts and either leave a part of the cloth or duster on the frame or, even worse, remove part of the frame. A vacuum cleaner can be used to catch the dust as it is brushed, which has the advantage of removing the dust from the area so that it cannot settle on other items nearby. Hold the nozzle of the vacuum close but not touching the frame. A piece of cotton cheesecloth can be stretched over the nozzle and secured with a rubber band so that if any pieces fall off, they will not be sucked into the vacuum. The vacuum should be on as low a suction level as possible. As the frame is brushed, you will see the dust drawn into the vacuum. Once the front of the frame is cleaned, clean the back of the framed item also using a vacuum or a magnetic wiping cloth.

Many framed items will be glazed, or covered with a sheet of glass or acrylic plastic. Determining whether the glazing is made of one or the other of these materials can be difficult, but the more familiar you become with these two materials, the easier it is. There are a few ways to differentiate the two materials. Generally, a glass sheet is much heavier than an acrylic sheet. It also more commonly has minor imperfections in it, such as small bubbles, lines, or wavy areas, especially if the glass is more than fifty years old. It is rare for glass to be scratched, although it is possible. Also, glass usually feels slightly cold to the touch at room temperature. In comparison to glass, an acrylic plastic sheet is remarkably lightweight, and it rarely has any imperfections in it, unless it has been scratched, which is easily done. Typically, acrylic will not feel cold at room temperature.

As with cleaning frames, cleaning the glazing should only be done when necessary. If the glazing is glass and there is a heavy accumulation of dust or gritty dirt on it, this should be removed with a magnetic wiping cloth. Be sure to clean the area where the glazing meets the edge of the frame, as dust and dirt will often settle there. A vacuum with a micro-suction attachment may be helpful with this. If the glass needs further cleaning, rub a slightly damp cloth over the surface, using the least amount of pressure possible. Avoid touching the edges of the frame next to the glass, as this can damage the frame after repeated cleanings, and immediately dry the glass with another cloth to avoid streaking. If the dirt on the glass is not removed with a cloth dampened with water, add a few drops of ammonia to a quart of water and dampen a cloth with this solution. Another alternative is to use one part isopropyl (rubbing) alcohol to three parts water. Dry immediately, and make sure that the cleaning solution, no matter which one you use, does not touch the frame, as it may quickly damage the finish on the frame.

If the frame has acrylic glazing, special care must be taken because acrylic is easily scratched. If there is a heavy accumulation of gritty dirt, it may be best to vacuum the surface of the acrylic, as a magnetic wiping cloth will probably scratch it. Then use the mixture of isopropyl alcohol and water mentioned above. Avoid the use of the ammonia mixture on acrylic. Another possibility is the use of a commercial Plexiglas cleaner. Several products are available that are intended for use on acrylic glazing, and the manufacturer's instructions should be followed. When cleaning acrylic, be sure to use the softest, lint-free cloth or paper you can obtain because acrylic scratches easily. When cleaning

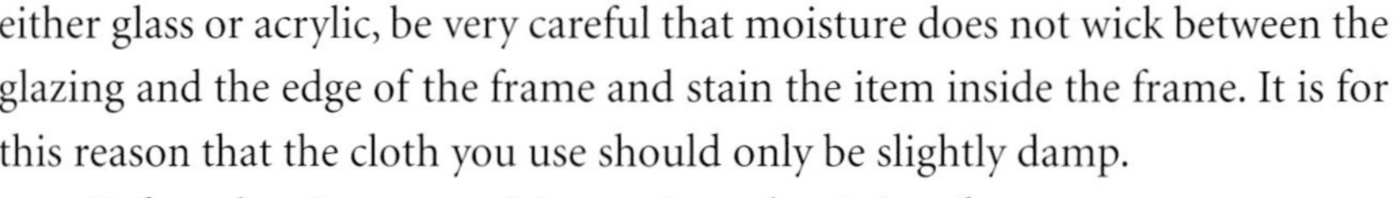

either glass or acrylic, be very careful that moisture does not wick between the glazing and the edge of the frame and stain the item inside the frame. It is for this reason that the cloth you use should only be slightly damp.

Before cleaning or repairing an item that is in a frame, contact a conservator for advice. During the process of cleaning, some items in a frame can be irreparably damaged. Cleaning an oil painting, for example, is a procedure that seems straightforward but is not. Household remedies that suggest a freshly cut potato or onion to clean paintings do not work and will cause damage. Oil paintings are usually made up of many different pigments, resins, and other materials, and knowing what these materials are and how they will react with cleaning agents is crucial when cleaning them. Severe and irreversible damage can easily occur if the wrong cleaning agents are used.

The same is true for repairing frames. Frames frequently are damaged during exhibit and display, and commercial frame shops often can repair them. Be sure, however, that the frame shop will do exactly as you desire before you approve the work. Frequently, the appearance of a frame may be changed radically after a frame shop repairs it, and it may look "new." This can be disappointing if the item in it has a distinguished-looking "old" or antique appearance. Additionally, frame shops will frequently use materials to repair a frame that are difficult if not impossible to remove, so the appearance of a frame before treatment may be completely lost. Take careful and exacting photographs of a frame before it is brought to a commercial framer for work. Generally, it is inappropriate and risky to have conservation work completed on the item within a frame by a frame shop, unless the shop contracts out that work to a recognized conservator.

Epilogue

The Value of Preserving the Past: A Personal Journey

NOKOMIS PAIZ ***(ANISHINABE/OJIBWE)***

My name is Nokomis Paiz. I am from the Red Lake Indian Reservation in northern Minnesota. Like most other Native people, I live in two worlds, the world of my people and the world of general society. I was raised knowing who I am, where I come from, and where I am going. My family has always fought to protect the rights of Native people throughout the country. My Great-Uncle Roger Jourdain, who was chairman of the Red Lake Band of Chippewa Indians, dedicated his life to the betterment of Native people not only here in Red Lake but throughout the country. My mother was involved in the 1969 occupation of Alcatraz, where she fought to assert treaty rights and to establish a Native Cultural Center. In 1970 both my parents were actively involved in taking over land in California on which DQ University is now. Together they traveled to Wounded Knee in 1973 to support the people of Pine Ridge. I grew up hearing these stories and knowing that being Native comes with responsibility. There is the responsibility to protect myself, my family, my tribe, and what my ancestors have passed down to me. These are the values that are instilled in me and that I try to live my life by.

My mother, Kathryn "Jody" Beaulieu, is the director of the Red Lake Nation Archives and Library, the NAGPRA representative for the Red Lake Indian Reservation, and a longtime member of the Minnesota Historical Society (MHS) Indian Advisory Committee (IAC). This all-Native committee is made up of representatives from each of the eleven reservations in Minnesota plus six at-large members. The IAC was established in 1989 to assist in the planning, development, and evaluation of MHS activities and initiatives that deal with Indian history and culture. My mother's involvement with this group sparked my interest in the museum field and how museums and NAGPRA are affecting the lives of Native people in the twenty-first century. My involvement with museum work and NAGPRA began during an internship at the MHS that focused on acquisitions from the Red Lake Indian Reservation.

For most Native people in the twenty-first century, museum collections and research come as a double-edged sword. My mother and I talk about the oftentimes difficult relationship between Native people and museums. For Native people, there is no easy answer when it comes to the museum field and the issues that arise in dealing with preservation, acquisitions, study, and so on. Many Native people and tribes are struggling to survive and do not have the resources to even start to deal with these issues. Living on the reservation, I see how complicated our lives can get just dealing with survival. A high level of unemployment makes attaining the simple things in life a struggle sometimes. Tribal politics touches all aspects of our lives on the reservation; you cannot be a Native person living on the reservation and not be affected by politics. Family is a strong bond, and if your family is hurting, you are hurting too. These are things that are ever present in our lives that make it difficult to delve into the museum field, which can often be a very unwelcoming place to Native people.

While at the MHS, I learned about the Beatrice Blackwood collection, which contains information from Red Lake. Blackwood was an ethnographer who was especially interested in Native people. She did fieldwork in Red Lake and Nett Lake from 1924 to 1927 and again in 1939. In the course of this work she collected drawings, hair samples, and photographs from and of Ojibwe people. In 1935 she joined the staff of the Pitt Rivers Museum in Oxford, England, where her research materials are now housed. This museum is an important part of the University of Oxford and is devoted to the study of human cultures. In March 2000, I had the opportunity to travel to England to do research on the Beatrice Blackwood collection. The research that I conducted while in England was not only important to me but was about me and my people. I was excited about traveling abroad, but I knew that the collections contained sensitive materials, and therefore my journey would be difficult.

Prior to the visit, I had long conversations with my mother in regard to the collection and all of the possible ramifications that this visit could have. We talked about how it is difficult to see a part of our culture in the midst of something so new, so strange, so foreign. Minnesota Indian people are at the heart of activism in this country and have done a lot to bring up issues of importance to Indian people. The American Indian Movement (AIM), the Minnesota Indian Affairs Act (MIAA), the National Indian Education Association (NIEA), the Private Cemeteries Act, Indian gaming, license plates for Indians on reservations, and the Indian State Scholarship Fund all came about as a result of the efforts of Minnesota Indians. NAGPRA issues extend beyond U.S. boundaries even though the law does not. My initial concern and motives for making the trip were to represent my tribe and to try and understand why Blackwood studied my ancestors. I also wanted to get a clearer understanding of who this woman was who traveled so far so long ago.

This was my first trip overseas. I was the first in my family (besides those who joined the military) to travel off of our home continent, so this was an important event and an amazing experience from the start. Initially I was going to travel alone, but through some intervention, arrangements were made for me to travel with staff from the MHS. Having visited the Pitt Rivers Museum previously, they were going to be my guides.

When I reached England, I experienced culture shock. Everything was so different and new to me, and it was all coming at me very fast. There is so much history everywhere, and people take it for granted. I saw buildings, books, barns, and wall paintings that were several hundred years old and had survived for generations. I was overwhelmed. And still the culture shock came.

We traveled by train from London to Oxford, and there I was confronted by the Pitt Rivers Museum, where the colonial exploits of Europeans were proudly paraded in overcrowded museum cases. I walked into the galleries and felt suffocated/smothered by all of the objects and their stories that were emanating from every case. It still saddens my heart as I am writing this to think of all of the emotions and power that are tied to those objects, and yet there they are, thousands of miles away from the people who created them, their people who may not know that they are there or even exist.

I needed air. After I got my wits about me, I decided to walk through the museum a little on my own. I was cautious about venturing too far because I did not know what I would encounter. I came across a lot of objects from North American Indians, some of which, to my knowledge, should not have been displayed in the manner in which they were.

That first evening we visited a barn that was at least seven hundred years old. How nice it must be to have your history clearly visible everywhere you look, to not have to search and seek it out. If the English want to know what life was like for their ancestors, they merely have to walk through their front door, attend church, visit one of hundreds of museums, or eat pizza at a restaurant where the exposed walls have murals dating back to medieval times.

Native North American people do not have it so easy. We are a tribal people with widely varied languages, beliefs, and cultures who passed our way of life on through stories, lessons, and shared experiences. We used biodegradable materials that were returned to the earth. We survived governmental attempts at everything from assimilation to genocide. Given what little material culture we do have left, how odd it is that these items that are so precious are kept in a place that is completely alien to the cultures that created them and still survive.

The second day we had our first opportunity to see the Red Lake items that Blackwood collected in Minnesota. Since the items were not on display, we traveled to the conservation lab to view them. We saw collections of drawings by Indian children and hair samples of children. We viewed physical objects such as wooden ladles, basswood dolls, beadwork belts, breechcloths, birch-bark samples and containers, and birch-bark scrolls, all of which had a Minnesota association.

Viewing these items raised a lot of questions for me because I am still learning about my cultural traditions and practices. I am a young person still trying to learn what is culturally appropriate and how to address issues and find answers. I did not know if reviewing this material for my community was something that I could do or should do. I was put in a position where I did not have enough experience to be considered the expert. But I thought that if I were not to deal with this, then who would? How often do Native people visit here? This was my thinking. I trusted my upbringing and tried to let my knowledge, intuition, and commitment to my people guide me to do and say the right thing.

We looked at each of the objects separately, and I asked that any objects with spiritual significance not be stored in plastic. I believe the museum staff present listened to my concerns and were respectful. I was feeling the enormous responsibility put on me, and a voice kept saying, "Why am I here? Why am I doing this? Why was I chosen? Why have I come here to do this? After all of this time, all of this way, why am I the person who is supposed to be here?" I do not regard myself as an expert on anything, yet here I was.

So I decided to listen to that higher power that got me here and to let it guide me. I have learned a lot from my mother. She has taught me well about the ways of our people. Her influence has affected a lot of the choices that I have made. Although this journey had been anything but emotionally comfortable, I felt honored to be there, yet at the same time uneasy about how what I said would be interpreted. I felt that while I was there to study the museum's collections, the museum's staff was studying me.

The third day we returned to the Pitt Rivers Museum, where we studied the drawings that Blackwood collected, which were made by children at the Red Lake and Ponemah boarding schools. The information recorded on the drawings was extensive and included who the students were, where they were from, their age, their grade, and frequently a comment on their blood quantum. Viewing the drawings gave me a new direction for the use of the collection in the community. I thought of how the elders of our community would react to seeing the drawings and in that way seeing back into their boarding school days. I was permitted to make photocopies of the original drawings to take home with me.

I was aware that seeing the photocopies would not be easy or comfortable for everyone back at Red Lake, and that all of the memories would not be good ones, but I realized the importance of having a tangible personal connection to the community's past. It was an amazing experience to look through these drawings and get a glimpse through the eyes of a young Native child away at boarding school. Some of the artists are still alive, and all have family in the community. I imagined all the stories and memories the drawings might conjure up.

The visit to England answered many of my questions and led to many more. The hair samples Blackwood collected were taken from children at boarding schools. An initial motivation for me to visit the museum was concern for the elders from whom the hair was collected. Some of these people are still alive and are now elders in the community. My first objective was to try to deal with the sensitive issue of the hair samples and the importance of returning them to the community from which they came. On the other hand, I knew that this was a preliminary visit, and I was merely viewing them and seeing where they were, how they were stored and cared for, if they were used at all, and if so, for what purposes. At this point in Great Britain, repatriation was not an option that museums were willing to consider.

What the visit ultimately provided was a line of communication between the museum and Red Lake. Shortly after my return, a professor from the University of Oxford visited Red Lake. The summer following my visit, the curator from the Pitt Rivers Museum visited Red Lake and had the privilege of meeting with my mother, my grandmother, and an elder from the community who had a personal involvement with the collection. She was a young girl at the time Blackwood traveled to the boarding school she attended. She had no memory of that visit, but seeing her drawing brought up a lot of memories. Also, she was very concerned to learn of the hair sample taken from her so long ago. She was very gracious and articulated some of her memories of her boarding school days.

I feel that this was as overwhelming an experience for her as visiting the museum was for me, and she was not adequately prepared for what was to come. She had long conversations with my mother after that visit. I cannot imagine how it must have been to be such a young child living away from home in a foreign environment. Revisiting that time, I am sure, brought up a flood of emotions for her.

Ultimately we would like to have these collections back. For younger Natives, such as myself, collections can be used to learn about how times were for our elders. We are recapturing things from our past, and we should use museum collections as a small piece of the puzzle we are trying to put back together. Museums should let their collections be known and used by Indian communities to give back some of what was taken. Also, so many times non-Indian people have done the research and the writing about collections, and it is long overdue to involve Native people. Indian communities in Minnesota have been very fortunate to have such an open and inviting resource as the MHS. The MHS should be used as a role model for other museums to make Native communities aware of and involve them in their collections. To have more Native people involved in the collections would be mutually beneficial.

Now, three years after my trip, I am living and working as a teacher on my reservation. I am here with my mother, writing these concluding words to the story of my journey and once again revisiting that difficult trip, and again getting frustrated by the issues that preservation brings up for our people. We are all treading on new ground. I am happy that my voice can be included in this book on preservation. My mother and I think of how much our cultural items mean to our people and how important it is to preserve our way of life. We look to the time when our efforts are no longer confined to just the day-to-day business of survival, when once again we can create and utilize our "objects" of beauty, purpose, and spirit. It is imperative that Native people be an equal partner with museum staff, sharing the research, the writing, the decision making, and the responsibility for the care of our items, or, better still, that we preserve our heritage ourselves in our own museums and cultural centers.

CONCLUSION

This book is the beginning. It is basic and introductory. More in-depth information on the care of objects is available for those who want it. This information is from standard museum preservation practice. Preservation professionals know little about tribal methods of care. We hope that non-Indian preservation professionals can learn more about these methods. Balancing standard museum practice with tribal practice will benefit everyone. Sharing knowledge of both approaches will enrich standard museum practice, enhance care of American Indian cultural items, and further the preservation of the American Indian cultures. We hope this book is the beginning of a mutually beneficial collaboration.

Appendix 1

Recommendations for Applying Accession Numbers to Museum Items

GINA NICOLE DELFINO

Labeling museum items with accession numbers is an important responsibility. An accession number identifies the item as part of your collection, links the item with its documentation, and allows you to keep track of your inventory. Without this number, an item may become virtually inaccessible.

The following are suggestions for labeling items in a sound manner for preservation. Remember, however, that there are variations within most collections, so in placing labels you must often employ your common sense.

An item's label must not only be durable enough to remain legible over time but must also be removable, should the need arise to make a change. The process of labeling should never cause harm to the item. The label should be easy to find yet be in an unobtrusive place so as to not be distracting while the item is used for display. The writing should be as small as possible while still legible. Write numerals as clearly as possible, for example:

0 1 2 3 4 5 6 7 8 9

There are several methods for labeling items. The type of label used depends on the type of item to be marked.

Textiles, Clothing, Basketry, and Beadwork

MATERIALS TO USE

- Black Sakura Micron Pigma pen (waterproof, fade proof, does not "bleed")
- White, plain-weave, 100 percent cotton tape, 3/8-inch wide, without sizing or other additives (and *non*-adhesive)
- White or black fine 100 percent cotton sewing thread
- Fine ball-pointed needles
- Scissors

WHERE TO LABEL

Clothing with a neckline: inside center back of neck (do not obscure existing label)

Clothing with a waistline: inside center back of waistband (do not obscure existing label)

Hats: inside center back, where crown and brim meet

Flat, long, or large textiles: two labels: back, lower right and upper left corners

Basketry: bottom or back, depending on structure

Fragile or fragmented textiles that cannot withstand stitching: on storage support

METHOD OF LABELING

Marks should not be made directly on textiles. The number is written onto a piece of cotton cloth tape that is then carefully sewn onto the item.

First, be sure the textile is out of potential harm's way (i.e., away from pens, scissors, etc.).

Keeping the pen away from the textile, use the Micron Pigma pen to write the accession number clearly onto a piece of cotton cloth tape before attaching the tape onto the textile. Leave about ¼ inch on each end to fold underneath; this saves the edges from fraying.

Choose white thread for light-colored pieces, and black thread for darker ones. If black or white is still too obvious, colored thread may be used as long as it is 100 percent cotton and colorfast. Make three backstitches (see figure 1) on the cotton cloth tape tag (not the textile) to anchor the thread without using a knot. Make small whipstitches all the way around the label, using as *few* as necessary to securely attach the label (see figure 2).

The aim is to make certain the label cannot later be snagged, causing damage to the item. When making stitches, use a single strand of thread, and be sure not to pierce fibers. Instead, sew between fibers, through gaps in the weave (see figure 3). Use a magnifying glass if necessary. Finish with three more backstitches, on the tag only, and without using knots.

Figure 1

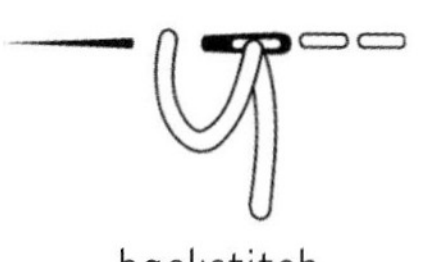

backstitch

Figure 2

whipstitch around tag

Figure 3

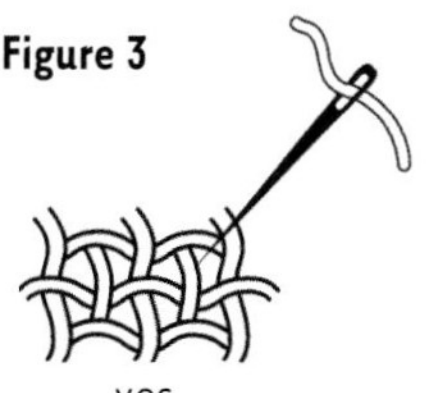

yes

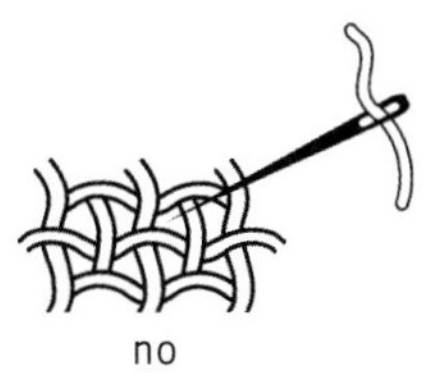

no

When it is inappropriate to attach labels directly, for example, with fine basketry, the labels can be sewn in a loop around large, stable fibers. First, apply the number to the cotton tape, wrap the cotton tape around a stable point, and then sew the ends of the tape together, forming a slightly loose loop.

Note: Never sew onto a textile that is in poor condition. If sewing a label onto an item could cause it harm, it may be necessary to label only its storage support (see Fragmentary and Fragile Items, p. 219).

Deciding how to label beadwork can be difficult. If the beadwork is sewn onto a textile (appliquéd or "lazy stitched"), proceed as you would for other textiles, taking extra care not to harm the beads or the threads that hold them to the textile. If the beadwork is woven or loom-work, you may be able to sew a label onto the underside. Stitch between the threads that hold the beads *only* if those threads are strong and in good condition. If the beadwork is sewn onto leather, sew on a label only if you can do so using pre-existing holes. Otherwise, use a cotton tape loop if possible (see above), or simply label its storage support. Do not try to apply a label directly onto fragile beadwork; proceed as for other fragile pieces (see Fragmentary and Fragile Items, p. 219).

To remove a sewn-on label, carefully snip the threads against the tag, being especially careful not to let the scissors touch the item. Pull the snipped threads slowly, without tugging or causing any strain to the item.

Three-Dimensional Items

MATERIALS TO USE

- Acryloid B-72, 20 percent solution in a 50:50 mixture of acetone:toluene*
- Black Sakura IDenti-pen, 441 series, permanent ink, dual-point marking pen

- Titanium white Golden fluid acrylic paint, Golden Artist Colors, Inc.
- Polymer medium (gloss), Golden Artist Colors, Inc. (water-based acrylic emulsion)
- Acetone, 100 percent*

**Note:* These solvents are considered hazardous and should be handled accordingly. Read the health hazard information on pages 219–220.

WHERE TO LABEL

Three-dimensional items come in all shapes and sizes. Choose an unobtrusive area, usually on the back or bottom of the item; the back lower right-hand corner is preferable, if it is appropriate. Clear or transparent items are difficult, so try to label along an edge where it will be least noticeable. If possible, the label should not be visible while the item is used for display.

If an item is made of lacquer, plastic, or wax, or if it has a corroded or porous surface, do not apply a direct label; instead, use a paper-and-string tag (see Hard-to-Label Items and Secondary Labels, p. 218) or cotton cloth tape loop (see Textiles, Clothing, Basketry, and Beadwork, p. 214). Some lacquers, plastics, and waxes are soluble in the solvents used. A friable, crumbling surface is not stable enough to hold a label, and a porous surface could absorb the B-72. Directly applying a B-72 label to these types of surfaces could damage an item irreparably.

METHOD OF LABELING

Most three-dimensional items can receive B-72 and ink labels. This method requires some extra care and concentration, because you are making an application directly onto the item. A clear B-72 barrier is applied to the item to create a removable writing surface onto which the number is marked; this is followed by a clear gloss seal that protects the number from scratches.

First, make sure the surface you will mark is clean and free of corrosion. It is to your advantage to label a group of items at one time, since this method requires a waiting period between steps. Be aware of drips sliding down your brushes. Try to remove as much excess as possible before approaching the item. When writing with the IDenti-pen, be certain the surface you are writing on is completely dry. If it is at all tacky, you may clog the pen's nib, rendering it unusable.

1. Barrier Layer

Brush on a barrier layer of B-72. Apply a thin rectangular layer. Its size should not be excessive, yet it should be able to accommodate the number and a top coat within its boundaries. Allow the B-72 to dry for at least thirty minutes, so that it is not tacky to the touch. If the barrier layer surface is irregular or porous, a second thin layer may be applied to improve the writing surface. Allow it to dry completely again. If the B-72 remains tacky for more than an hour, remove it with acetone, discard your supply and make a fresh batch.

If your supply of B-72 becomes too thick, it may be thinned with a *very* small amount of acetone, added two to three drops at a time. Adding too much acetone at once will make your supply too thin. If your supply becomes yellow, discard it and make a fresh batch.

2. Accession Number

For light-colored items, neatly write the item's accession number directly onto the barrier layer, using the extra-fine nib of the black IDenti-pen (*Note:* Both ends of the pen have writing nibs; use the smaller one.) Do not extend your writing beyond the edges of the barrier layer. Allow the ink to dry completely (at least five minutes).

For dark-colored items, first brush a thin layer of white acrylic paint over the barrier layer, making sure to stay within its boundaries. *Do not brush the acrylic paint directly onto the item's surface.* Once the white layer dries completely (about forty-five minutes), you may proceed as for light-colored items.

Some people prefer to use ink and a steel-nibbed pen to write their numerals; however, these pens present the danger of blotting and scratching due to their hard, sharp metal nibs. Instead of taking this risk, the method described above should be adopted.

3. Seal

Brush a thin coat of acrylic gloss medium over the number to ensure it will not be abraded. The gloss will go on white but will dry to a clear finish. This top coat should be smaller than the barrier layer. By using this material instead of a second layer of B-72, you remove the risk of dissolving the barrier layer and smudging the number when applied. Again, allow it to dry completely before moving the item.

If your supply of acrylic gloss medium becomes too thick, it may be thinned with a *very* small amount of water, added two to three drops at a time. Adding too much water at once will make your supply too thin.

4. Removal

If a mistake or change is made in an attached label, it can be carefully removed with solvents. All layers can be removed with acetone applied with a small cotton swab on a stick. Be sure never to redip a dirty swab into your supply of solvent. It is important to keep your solvents clean.

Use solvents sparingly. They should not come in contact with an item's surface more than necessary.

Do not pour solvents into the sink. Dispose of solvents in accordance with local, county, state, and federal regulations.

ALTERNATIVE METHODS

The approved methods for labeling three-dimensional artifacts can vary widely, both because of the multitude of materials that make up three-dimensional items, and the number of acceptable methods available for labeling them. There are several alternatives to the method described above that may be more appropriate for your collections or staff.

Other Barrier Layers

Acryloid B-67 dissolved in mineral spirits (or other petroleum distillates such as petroleum benzine, naphtha, or Stoddard's Solvent) is slightly less aggressive on most material surfaces and slightly less hazardous to people; however, it may yellow slightly over time, and it requires a longer drying period.

Rhoplex is a water-based acrylic emulsion similar to the acrylic gloss medium used for the seal coat, and it is much less hazardous to people. Once dry, it is most readily soluble in ethanol or acetone, though it is sometimes easier to peel off mechanically. Like the acrylic gloss medium, it is not as durable as the Acryloid B-72 and therefore not the ideal barrier layer for most materials.

Other Labels

Some museums do not like to have a white field used for labeling their dark items. While there are no suitable white markers that can be used with the same ease as the IDenti-pen, there are a few fillable pen options available. The white Zig pen has been found to be acceptable, as well as the Tria pen filled with white fluid acrylic paint or ink. Special care needs to be taken any time open bottles of paint or ink are near museum items. Both of these pens require some practice and skill to use, as the paint is liable to blot or smear easily and may be more prone to clogging.

If consistently good penmanship is a problem, some have found that cut-out printed accession numbers are a useful alternative. On your computer, select a small font size, usually between size 4 and size 8. Also, use a font that is easy to read, such as Arial or Helvetica. Use a preservation-quality paper. Also, be sure to use a laser printer. If you use an inkjet or bubblejet printer, the ink may run in your adhesive. The number is cut out and placed on the barrier layer while it is still tacky. A seal coat is still advisable, once the barrier layer is dry.

Paper and Photographs

MATERIALS TO USE

- Hard pencil, 2H
- Soft pencils, 2B and 6B
- White Staedtler Mars-Plastic vinyl eraser

WHERE TO LABEL

Both paper and photographs are labeled on the backside (verso), lower right corner. Try to write behind the border of a photograph, rather than behind the printed image. If a paper article has printing on both sides, choose the side where the label would seem least obtrusive for display.

METHOD OF LABELING

Make sure the surface on which you lay the front of the paper or photograph is clean and dry. It is a good idea to put a piece of white paper on the surface first.

With a suitable pencil, as prescribed below, lightly write the accession number onto the appropriate area. The pencil should not be dull, yet not so sharp that it could cause damage. Be certain *not* to press so hard that the pencil leaves an imprint. You should *not* be able to see the writing from the front side.

Most normal papers with smooth surfaces and in stable condition can be labeled with a 2H pencil. Some papers are very fibrous and could be damaged by a hard pencil. For these, use the softer, 2B or 6B pencils. They are more likely to smudge, but they will not tear the fibers in the paper. Photographs can be labeled with a 6B pencil.

Mistakes may be erased with a gentle touch of the white vinyl eraser unless the paper is soft and fibrous.

Hard-to-Label Items and Secondary Labels

MATERIALS TO USE

- 2H pencil
- Archival paper tags with soft cotton string

WHERE TO LABEL

Items made of fur pelts or leather or that have heavily corroded or porous surfaces usually cannot hold an applied label. Instead, their primary label will be a paper-and-string tag or, if appropriate, a cotton cloth tape loop (see Textiles, Clothing, Basketry, and Beadwork, p. 214).

Textiles and three-dimensional items can receive a secondary, paper-and-string tag label for storage. Paper-and-string tags are not used alone (unless the material demands it, as above) because they can be easily lost or mutilated. For storage purposes, they provide more accessible identification, reducing the amount of handling of the items, and also allow you to include more information.

Choose a strong holding point that will not break, tear, or abrade easily if the tag is pulled or caught. If the sharp edges of the tag seem to be a potential hazard, round them off, or use soft Tyvek paper instead. If no safe area can be found, the tag may lie next to the item without being attached. If a garment is stored on a hanger, attach the tag to the hanger, and make sure it does not rest on the fabric. If a textile lies flat in storage, situate the tag to its side, again so it does not rest directly on the fabric.

METHOD OF LABELING

With a 2H pencil and all uppercase letters, neatly write the following information onto a tag:

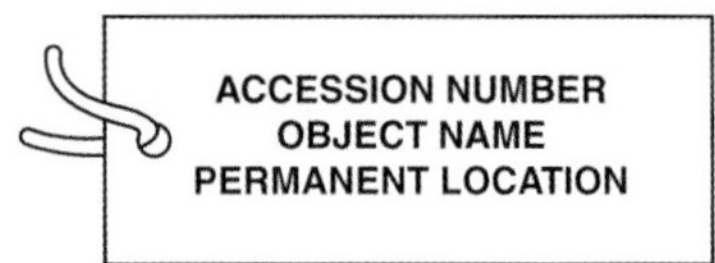

The backside may have various additional kinds of information such as date, style, source, and so on.

Attach the tag by pulling it through a loop in the string (see figure 4). If the point of attachment is too wide to pull the tag through without stressing the item, remove the pre-attached string, and add a longer one (100 percent cotton) that will comfortably accommodate the item.

Figure 4

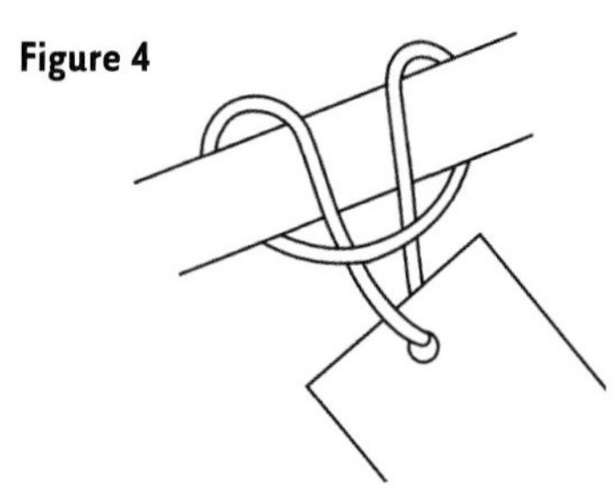

Fragmentary and Fragile Items

If you are uncertain about the safety or possibility of labeling an item, do not apply one. Even a paper-and-string tag is unusable in certain cases. Sometimes it is appropriate to label the housing or support for an item as opposed to the item itself. This not only saves the item from being harmed by the act of labeling it, it also reduces further handling of fragile pieces to locate their identity.

Sacred or Ceremonial items

A minimalist approach is applied to items that are considered sacred or ceremonial. While it is often highly important that these types of items are clearly identified, it is best to label them as you would fragmentary or fragile items, described above. Always work with great respect and handle items as little as possible. Marking the outside of a room or cabinet in which these types of items are housed is advisable, including a list of the accession numbers contained within, so that they do not need to be disturbed more than necessary. Do not remove the contents of an item, such as a medicine bag, to number them separately, unless you have been advised to do so by a member of the appropriate American Indian community.

Dangerous Materials Warning

Removable self-stick notes, as well as any other adhesive tapes or labels, leave a residue (sometimes unseen) that will attract dirt or cause yellow stains over time. *Do not use these for temporary labels or for any purpose.* While convenient, they ultimately cause harm, and they are not appropriate for use with museum items. Nail polish and correction pens or fluids are also potentially unstable and should not be substituted for the proper materials listed here. Not even all materials labeled as "archival" or sold by "archival" suppliers are *necessarily* appropriate for these specific purposes.

Health Hazard Information

Acetone and toluene are considered moderate-to-serious hazardous materials and can cause health complications if not handled properly. If you will be using these solvents, either alone or in solution with Acryloid B-72, read the Material Safety Data Sheet (MSDS) for each solvent. MSDSs can be obtained upon request from the solvent supplier. When handling these solvents, take the following precautionary steps.

1. Work in a space with good ventilation. Avoid breathing vapors, and use a respirator if necessary. A half-mask respirator fit-tested by a qualified person for individual use with Organic Vapor filters is recommended.
2. If your hands will be in direct contact with solvents, wear solvent-resistant gloves.
3. If the potential for splashing exists, wear chemical safety goggles.
4. Alert yourself to the nearest accessible location of a water supply in anticipation of an accidental spill or splash.
5. Keep containers tightly closed and upright when not in use.
6. Never place solvents near a heated area or source of ignition. They are highly flammable.
7. Make sure your workspace is neat and solvents are not in danger of tipping over.
8. Store solvents securely in a metal container or cabinet.

Warning signs of overexposure are as follows:

- irritation of the skin, eyes, nose, throat, or mucous membranes;
- drowsiness, headache, dizziness, nausea, loss of coordination, or fatigue;
- redness, burning, drying, and cracking of the skin; and
- burning, tearing, and redness of the eyes.

If you are experiencing any symptoms of overexposure, discontinue your work in the exposure area and get some fresh air. Wash directly exposed skin with soap and large amounts of water for fifteen to twenty minutes. In the event of a spill or splash, flush hands, eyes, or any other affected body part with water immediately. Flood directly exposed eyes with large amounts of water for fifteen to twenty minutes. Alert your supervisor to your symptoms, and seek medical help if problems persist.

Do not dispose of any solvents in the sink or garbage. Dispose of solvents in accordance with local, county, state, and federal regulations.

References

Alten, Helen. "Materials for Labeling Collections," *Collections Care Network* 1, 6 (Winter 1996). Minneapolis: Upper Midwest Conservation Association.

Denton, P. Lynn, and Sara J. Wolf. "Labeling Museum Specimens," *Conservation Notes*, no. 11 (January 1985). Austin: Texas Memorial Museum.

QUICK REFERENCE

Material/Item Type	Primary Label Type	Label Location
Glazed ceramics, glass, metals, wood, stone, ivory, bone, some kinds of basketry	B-72 and ink	Unobtrusive area (usually bottom or back)
Leather or skin (fur), moccasins, heavily corroded metals, unglazed ceramics, plastic, wax, lacquered surfaces, other porous surfaces	Paper-and-string tag or cotton cloth tape loop	Unobtrusive spot that will not be harmed by the string; tie loosely
Clothes with neckline	Cotton cloth tape	Inside center back of neck
Clothes with waistline	Cotton cloth tape	Inside center back of waistband
Hats	Cotton cloth tape	Inside center back, where crown and brim meet
Shoes without leather soles	B-72 and ink	Bottom of sole, close to heel
Socks, gloves	Cotton cloth tape	Inside opening
Flat, long, or large textiles	Cotton cloth tape	Back, lower right corner
Fine basketry	Cotton cloth tape loop	Unobtrusive area (usually bottom or back)
Paper, photographs	Pencil	Back, lower right corner
Fragile or fragmented items	Pencil	Storage support
Sacred or ceremonial items	Pencil	Storage support

Appendix 2

Storage Furniture (Wardrobes, Cabinets, Shelves, Drawers)

SHERELYN OGDEN

The selection of storage furniture requires careful investigation. Many of the currently available furniture choices contain materials that produce by-products that contribute to the deterioration of the collections they house. In addition, some construction features are damaging and also contribute to deterioration of collections. The information that follows is intended to serve as an introduction to the subject and as a guide to what to look for in selecting storage furniture.

Baked Enamel

Until recently only baked enamel furniture was recommended. Constructed of steel with a baked enamel coating, this furniture was thought to be made of chemically stable materials. Because it is readily available, competitively priced, strong, and durable, it has been a particularly attractive choice. Questions, however, have been raised about the possibility that the baked enamel coating may give off formaldehyde and other volatiles harmful to collections if it has not been properly baked (not long enough at high enough temperatures). This concern is especially serious when collections are stored in furniture that is closed or has poor air circulation around it.

Because of this concern about off-gassing, baked enamel furniture is no longer widely recommended unless it has been properly baked. To be certain that it has, the furniture must be tested. Testing should comply with ASTM (American Society of Testing Materials) E-595.[1] This testing requires the use of sophisticated analytical equipment. Furniture can be less conclusively tested in-house with the organic solvent methyl ethyl ketone (MEK).[2] If this crude test, known as the MEK rub test, indicates that the coating may not be properly baked, the furniture should perhaps be tested by a professional testing service to determine for certain if it is off-gassing.

Powder Coatings

Steel storage furniture with various powder coatings appears to avoid the off-gassing problems associated with baked enamel. Powder coatings of finely divided, synthetic polymer materials are fused onto the steel. Testing done thus far indicates that the coatings are chemically stable, present minimal threat of off-gassing, and so are safe for the storage of valuable items. Nevertheless, conducting the MEK rub test in an inconspicuous area where the steel is the heaviest gauge will confirm that the coating is properly cured and that off-gassing is not a concern.[3]

Anodized Aluminum

Anodized aluminum storage furniture is another option. This uncoated metal is extremely strong yet light in weight. The metal itself is reported to be nonreactive, and since it has no coating, off-gassing problems are eliminated. Many people consider anodized aluminum to be the best choice, especially for highly sensitive materials, but it tends to be the most expensive.

Chrome-Plated Steel Shelving

Open chrome-plated steel shelving, made of heavy-gauge, chrome-plated steel wire, is a storage choice suitable for boxed items. The shelving is durable, and the open-wire framework is light in weight and provides good air circulation. The wires, however, can leave permanent marks on items that are not protected, so materials should be boxed, or the shelves should be lined.

Wood

Storage furniture, especially shelving, made of wood has traditionally been popular for reasons of aesthetics, economy, and ease of construction. Harmful acids and other substances, however, are emitted by wood, wood composites, and some sealants and adhesives. Although the levels of emissions are highest initially, in most cases volatiles are present for the life of the furniture. To avoid potential damage to collections, storage furniture made of wood or wood products should be avoided. If this is not possible and wood must be used, precautions are necessary. Certain woods and wood composites are more potentially damaging than others. For example, oak, which has been used extensively for the storage of library and archival materials, is considered the wood with the most volatile acidity and should not be used. Also, many wood composites that are advertised as formaldehyde-free may contain potentially damaging acids or other aldehydes. Current information should be obtained prior to selecting new furniture made of wood or a wood product so that the least damaging wood can be chosen. All wood and wood composites should be tested to determine their safety for use.[4]

Sealants for Wood

For wooden storage furniture that is already in use, safeguards should be taken. You should consider coating all wood. It should be noted, though, that no sealant will completely block the emission of acids and harmful volatiles for prolonged periods of time, but it can be useful for short-term exposure. Also, some sealants are better than others at blocking damaging substances. Great care must be taken in selecting a sealant to make sure that the one chosen forms the most effective barrier and does not itself emit harmful substances.

The most readily available sealant recommended at this time is a waterborne polyurethane. Many kinds of polyurethane are available. Oil-modified polyurethanes are the most common. However, oil-modified polyurethanes, oil-based paints, and other products that contain oil or alkyd resins should be avoided. Only waterborne polyurethanes are recommended. Unfortunately, not all waterborne polyurethanes on the market are safe for use. Also, formulations often change without notice. For these reasons, the polyurethane selected should be tested prior to use to guarantee its acceptability.[5] Contact a preservation professional for brand names of waterborne polyurethanes that are currently being recommended, and begin testing with these. Because these urethanes do not completely prevent the escape of volatiles, choosing low-emission wood products is critically important.

Paints can also be used to coat wood if the natural appearance of the wood does not have to be retained. Oil-based paints and stains should not be used because of the potentially damaging effects of the acids in the drying oils. Two-part epoxy paints form an excellent barrier, but they are difficult to use. Latex and acrylic paints form a less effective barrier but are easier to use.[6] All sealants should be tested prior to use. Contact a preservation professional for current information before making a decision. After furniture is coated, it should be allowed to air before items are placed on it. No one seems to know how long the airing period should be. A frequent recommendation is three to four weeks. Because of the toxicity of various components of most sealants, the sealants should be used with caution and appropriate safety measures observed.

Additional Barriers

In addition to coating wood, surfaces with which items come in direct contact should be lined with an effective barrier material. Barriers that are recommended at present include a laminate of aluminized polyethylene and polypropylene sold under the trade name of Marvelseal, PCTFE (polychlorotrifluoroethylene) high-barrier films (e.g., Alclar), sheet aluminum, glass, polymethyl methacrylate sheeting (e.g., Plexiglas), or a combination of these.[7] Polymethyl methacrylate sheeting can absorb pollutants and reemit them, so this material should not be reused once it has served as a barrier. Note that printing inks found on some of these barrier materials may be corrosive.[8] Contact the manufacturer to request information on the printing inks, or request products without printing. If these barriers do not provide an appropriate surface for the storage of items, 100 percent rag board can be used in addition. Rag board, however, should not be used by itself, because it does not provide a sufficient barrier. Another alternative is polyester film, but this does not provide a complete barrier either.

Construction Features

Regardless of the construction material chosen, storage furniture should have a smooth, nonabrasive finish. If steel furniture is painted or coated, the finish should be resistant to chipping since chips will leave steel exposed and susceptible to rust. The furniture should be free of sharp edges and protrusions. Exposed nuts and bolts are particularly hazardous. The furniture should be strong enough that it will not bend or warp when filled. Shelving should be bolted together as well as to the floor and perhaps the ceiling so it will not wobble when collections are housed on it. Shelves should be adjustable to accommodate items of various sizes, particularly oversized ones. The lowest storage area in the furniture should be at least four to six inches off the floor to protect collections from water damage in the event of a flood.

Cabinets with doors are often preferred when security and protection from dust are special concerns. The use of piano hinges for the attachment of the doors is advisable, as opening the doors flat will facilitate safe removal of items from the cabinet. Condensation can be a problem in closed steel cabinets when the relative humidity where the cabinets are stored fluctuates.[9] Condensation can result in rusting or mold growth in cabinets. If possible, the use of closed steel cabinets should be avoided unless the cabinets are well ventilated or the relative humidity is closely controlled and monitored.[10]

Drawers in flat files should have stops to prevent them from coming out of cabinets. Also, they should have ball bearings rather than slide-in grooves because they will open and close more smoothly, causing less vibration to items, and the risk that they will fall out of the grooves and become stuck is eliminated. Drawers can be lined with polyethylene foam for cushioning as added protection from jarring and vibration.

High-Density Storage Systems

High-density storage systems, often referred to as compact or movable shelving, are used by many museums with space limitations. These systems minimize the amount of space needed by compacting rows or ranges of shelves or cabinets of drawers tightly together. The ranges slide along tracks so they can be moved apart for retrieval of items on a particular range and then moved back together again. Moving systems such as these can be damaging because of the vibrations to which they subject items. Also, items can be jostled off shelves, causing further damage. If a high-density storage system must be used, a design should be chosen that minimizes these hazards. It is crucial with high-density storage systems that items do not extend beyond the edge of the shelves to avoid having the items on opposite shelves collide when the ranges are closed. When installing high-density systems, enough overall space should be allowed to ensure that sufficiently wide aisles are formed between the ranges for the safe removal of items, particularly oversized ones, from shelves and drawers.

Floor overloading is a serious concern and should be taken into account if many heavy items are stored in a confined space. Weight estimates need to include floor treatment, furniture tracks and fittings, and shelf and drawer loads as well as the furniture. A structural engineer should be consulted.

Fire detection and suppression are additional concerns. A space of a few inches always should be left between the ranges so that a fire between them can be detected and suppressed. Leaving a small space will also enhance air circulation, avoiding the buildup of pockets of damp or stagnant air. Another concern is the behavior of compact shelving during floods, fires, or earthquakes, and how to gain access to materials if the shelving fails to open because of increased weight, distortion of the tracks, or failure of electricity. Consult the manufacturer about this subject.

Things to Remember

The selection of suitable storage furniture and the specification or modification of wooden storage furniture are complicated tasks. Poor-quality storage greatly accelerates the deterioration of collections. Opinion on what constitutes acceptable storage furniture is changing rapidly. A preservation professional should be consulted for the most up-to-date information before decisions with far-reaching impact are made. Making the right choice will add immeasurably to the useful life of collections.

Notes

1. Pamela Hatchfield, Conservator, Objects Conservation and Scientific Research, Museum of Fine Arts, Boston, Massachusetts, personal communication.

2. *Note:* The solvent used in this procedure is considered hazardous and should be handled accordingly. Read the health hazard information below. Saturate a small-tip cotton swab on a stick with methyl ethyl ketone (MEK), available in hardware stores, and rub it vigorously over a small inconspicuous area of the furniture to be tested. Rub the swab over the furniture backward and forward thirty times in each direction. The finish on the furniture may soften, take on a moist look, or discolor slightly. This is not a concern. Look at the swab to see how much, if any, paint has been removed. Minimal or slight discoloration on a swab is a reasonable assurance that the coating is properly cured. Medium to heavy discoloration indicates that the coating may not be properly cured and may need to be tested further. *Please note that MEK is toxic and flammable. It must be used in a well-ventilated area, and appropriate protective measures must be taken. Remaining solvents and used swabs must be disposed of in accordance with local, county, state, and federal regulations.* B. W. Golden, Vice President, Engineering, Interior Steel Equipment Co., Cleveland, Ohio; and Bruce Danielson, President, Delta Designs, Topeka, Kansas, personal communication.

3. Golden, personal communication.

4. This procedure is used for testing wood products, sealants, and a variety of other materials. If you are testing a wood or other material, place a sample of the material in a glass jar. If you are testing a sealant, coat a clean glass slide with the sealant you want to test, and place the coated slide in a glass jar. Also place in the jar a piece each of cleaned and degreased lead, silver, and iron; rub the metal pieces with 600-grit sandpaper or steel wool, and then wipe them with denatured alcohol available from hardware stores *(see the toxicity warning in Note 2)*. Next dampen a piece of cotton with deionized water and place it in the jar with the metal pieces and wood sample or glass slide. Place the dampened cotton in a small glass beaker or glass vial in the jar so that it is not in direct contact with the metal pieces and glass slide and to slow the evaporation rate. Cover the jar with two thicknesses of aluminum foil, and secure the foil tightly with brass or other wire. Prepare a second jar exactly the same way as the first but without the sample or coated glass slide. This jar will serve as a control. Place both jars in an oven at 170°F for three weeks or on a windowsill for as long as possible. Watch for changes in the appearance of the metals. Looking under magnification will be helpful. Changes will probably occur in both the test samples and the control samples. If the changes in the test samples differ from those in the control samples, unacceptable substances are probably present. In the testing of wood composites, it is impossible to determine if the reaction is caused by the wood or by the adhesives in the composite. If a positive reaction is observed, the material is probably unsuitable for use. Hatchfield, personal communication.

5. Hatchfield, personal communication.

6. Hatchfield, personal communication.

7. Pamela B. Hatchfield, "Choosing Materials for Mu-

seum Storage," in *Storage of Natural History Collections: Basic Concepts,* edited by Carolyn L. Rose and Catharine A. Hawks (Pittsburgh, Pa.: Society for the Preservation of Natural History Collections, 1994), 7.

8. Hatchfield, "Choosing Materials for Museum Storage," 5–6.

9. Margaret Holben Ellis, *The Care of Prints and Drawings* (Walnut Creek, Calif.: AltaMira Press, 1995), 148.

10. Ellis, *The Care of Prints and Drawings,* 148–49.

Suggested Further Readings

Hatchfield, Pamela B. "Choosing Materials for Museum Storage." In *Storage of Natural History Collections: Basic Concepts,* edited by Carolyn L. Rose and Catharine A. Hawks. Pittsburgh, Pa.: Society for the Preservation of Natural History Collections, 1994.

———. *Pollutants in the Museum Environment: Practical Strategies for Problem Solving in Design, Exhibition and Storage.* London: Archetype Publications Ltd., 2002.

Hatchfield, Pamela B., and Jane Carpenter. *Formaldehyde: How Great Is the Danger to Museum Collections?* Cambridge, Mass.: Harvard University, 1987.

Miles, Catherine E. "Wood Coatings for Display and Storage Cases." *Studies in Conservation* 31, 3 (August 1986): 114–24.

National Park Service. *Exhibit Conservation Guidelines.* Washington, D.C.: CD-ROM publication by SANAD Support Technologies, Inc., 1999.

Tétreault, Jean. *Coatings for Display and Storage in Museums.* Technical Bulletin No. 21. Ottawa, Ont.: Canadian Conservation Institute, 1999.

Sources of Supplies

This list was provided by Pamela Hatchfield, Conservator, Objects Conservation and Scientific Research, Museum of Fine Arts, Boston, Massachusetts. The list is not exhaustive, nor does it constitute an endorsement of the suppliers listed. Obtain information from a number of vendors so that you can make comparisons of cost and assess the full range of available products.

Alfa Products
30 Bond Street
Ward Hill, MA 01835
Telephone: 978-521-6300
Fax: 978-521-6350

Metal foils for materials testing

Camger Company
364 Main Street
Norfolk, MA 02056
Telephone: 508-528-5787
http://www.camger.com

Camger Polyglaze 1-146 (waterborne polyurethane)

Conservation Resources
8000-H Forbes Place
Springfield, VA 22151
Telephone: 703-321-7730
Fax: 703-321-0629
http://www.conservationresources.com

Carbon-based paint in acrylic binder
(Microchamber Emulsion MCE-750)

Dexter Brothers
59 Amory Road
Roxbury, MA 02119
Telephone: 617-445-7755

Sancure 878 waterborne polyurethane

Fisher Scientific
3970 Johns Creek Street
Suwanee, GA 30024
Toll Free: 800-766-7000
Fax: 800-926-1166
http://www.fishersci.com

Glass beakers and vials and other testing supplies

Honeywell International
98 Westwood Road
Pottsville, PA 17901
Telephone: 800-934-5679
Fax: 800-445-0040
http://www.honeywell-films.com

Alclar transparent vapor barrier

International Paint Co.
2270 Morris Avenue
Union, NJ 07083
Toll Free: 800-INTRLUX

Interprotect 1000 2-part epoxy paint (clear)

Ludlow Packing Corp.
Laminating & Coating Division
4058 Highway 79
Homer, LA 71040
Telephone: 318-927-9641

Nylon or polyethylene aluminum laminates
(e.g., Marvelseal) for lining shelves and drawers

Noveon, Inc.
9911 Brecksville Road
Cleveland, OH 44141-3247
Telephone: 216-447-5000
http://www.noveoninc.com

Sancure 878 waterborne polyurethane

NuSil Technology
1050 Cindy Lane
Carpinteria, CA 93013
Telephone: 805-684-8780
Fax: 805-684-2365
http://www.nusil.com

Low out-gassing materials testing service; testing in compliance with ASTM E-595

Sure Pure Chemetals
5 Nottingham Drive
Florham Park, NJ 07932
Telephone: 973-377-4081
Fax: 973-377-4081
http://www.surepure.com

Metal foils for materials testing

Sources of Storage Furniture

This list is not exhaustive. Nor does it constitute an endorsement of the suppliers listed. We suggest that you obtain information from a number of vendors so that you can make comparisons of cost and assess the full range of available products.

Crystallization Systems, Inc.
640C Broadway Avenue
Holbrook, NY 11741
Telephone: 631-567-0888
Fax: 631-567-4007
Contact: Pat Ellenwood
E-mail: csistorage@aol.com
http://www.csistorage.com

Powder coated

Delta Designs Ltd.
PO Box 1733
Topeka, KS 66601
Telephone: 785-234-2244
Toll Free: 800-656-7426
Fax: 785-233-1021
E-mail: bdanielson@deltadesignsltd.com
http://www.deltadesignsltd.com

Powder coated

Charles J. Dickgiesser & Co.
257 Roosevelt Drive
Derby, CT 06418
Telephone: 203-734-2553
Fax: 203-734-9221

Powder coated and anodized aluminum
Custom builder

Equipto
4550 Beltway Drive
Addison, TX 75001
Telephone: 214-443-9800
Toll Free: 800-323-0801
Fax: 888-859-2121
E-mail: CustomerService@Equipto.com
http://www.equipto.com

Powder coated

Lane Science Equipment
225 West 34th Street
New York, NY 10122-1496
Telephone: 212-563-0663
Fax: 212-465-9440
E-mail: info@lanescience.com
http://www.lanescience.com

Powder coated

Light Impressions
205 South Puente Street
Brea, CA 92821
Toll Free: 800-828-6216
Fax: 800-828-5539
http://www.lightimpressionsdirect.com

Powder coated

Lyon Metal Products Inc.
PO Box 671
Aurora, IL 60507
Toll Free: 800-323-0082
Fax: 603-892-8966
E-mail: lyon@lyon-metal.com
http://www.lyon-metal.com

Powder coated

Montel, Inc.
Office in Canada
225, 4th Avenue, C.P. 130
Montmagny, Quebec
G5V 3S5 Canada
Toll Free: 877-935-0236
Fax: 418-248-7266

Office in USA
1170 Highway A1A
Satellite Beach, FL 32937
Toll Free: 800-772-7562
Fax: 321-777-3539
E-mail: system@montel.com
http://www.montel.com

Powder coated

Russ Bassett
8189 Byron Road
Whittier, CA 90606
Telephone: 562-945-2445
Toll Free: 800-350-2445
Fax: 562-698-8972
E-mail: marketing@russbassett.com
http://www.russbassett.com

Powder coated

Spacesaver Corp.
1450 Janesville Avenue
Fort Atkinson, WI 53538
Telephone: 920-563-6362
Toll Free: 800-492-3434
Fax: 920-563-2702
E-mail: ssc@spacesaver.com
http://www.spacesaver.com

Powder coated

Steel Fixture Manufacturing Corp.
PO Box 917
Topeka, KS 66601-0917
Telephone: 785-233-8911
Toll Free: 800-342-9180
Fax: 785-233-8477
E-mail: stan@steelfixture.com
http://www.steelfixture.com

Powder coated

Viking Metal Cabinet Co.
5321 West 65th Street
Chicago, IL 60638
Telephone: 708-594-1111
Toll Free: 800-776-7767
Fax: 708-594-1028
E-mail: Linda@vikingmetal.com
http://www.vikingmetal.com

Powder coated and anodized aluminum

Acknowledgments

The author gratefully acknowledges the assistance of Pamela Hatchfield in the preparation of this appendix and the Northeast Document Conservation Center for permission to reprint it here.

Appendix 3

General Procedures for Freezing Museum Collections to Eliminate Insect Pests

NANCY ODEGAARD

Freezing is a nonchemical technique that kills insects in the egg, larval, pupal, and adult stages. As there is no residual effect, however, this technique does not prevent insects from attacking the same item in the future. Great care should be taken in selecting items for this procedure. Some materials are sensitive to the severely cold temperatures required (i.e., resinous coatings, oil paintings, glass, and photographs) and need special consideration. Most materials prone to insect attack, including wool, fur, feather, and basketry items, may be safely treated using the following procedures.

1. Place the item that is infested or suspected of insect infestation in a clear polyethylene bag (3 or 4 mil in thickness). Items should be bagged individually and immediately at the place where the infestation is discovered. In the freezer room, items such as textiles and costumes should be loosely arranged in their bags with minimal folding or compression. Remove as much air as possible from the bag, and securely close the opening by twisting it and securing it with rubber bands.
2. The freezer temperature should be viewed using a remote-reading thermometer and then recorded on a form. An indoor/outdoor thermometer with a probe that has been mounted on the exterior of the freezer is usually adequate. Also record the date and time on the form.
3. When the freezer is opened, view an interior thermometer (a high-rated freezer shelf thermometer), and record the temperature on the form.
4. Place the bagged items in the freezer with as much room around them as possible to allow good air circulation. When possible, the freezer's baskets can also be used (for smaller items). Too many items tend to keep the interior temperature from reaching the critical low that is necessary to kill insects rapidly enough. Be sure to record the catalog number and item name on the record sheet.
5. Items should be left in the freezer at –2°F to –4°F for at least 48 hours. Many museums utilize a freezer system that goes below this. Most domestic chest freezers, however, will not get below this range.
6. The temperature surrounding the insects should reach 32°F within four hours. This tem-

perature is recorded by careful placement of the indoor/outdoor thermometer probe inside one of the bagged items.

7. Prior to removal of the items from the freezer, record the interior temperature of the freezer again. Also record the date and time that the item is removed.

8. Bagged items may be removed from the freezer and placed on a table or flat surface. The polyethylene bags should not be opened until the item has come to room temperature as condensation will form. It is preferable to have the condensation form on the exterior of the plastic bag rather than the item.

9. To ensure a total kill, repeat the freeze-thaw process.

10. Finally, once the item has been removed from the plastic bag, examine it thoroughly on a table in the freezer room. Record the types of insect evidence found with the item and the degree and location of the activity.

11. The item may then be vacuumed. Brushes and tweezers may be of assistance when removing the insect frass, eggs, larvae, webbings, and adults. Record the date of this examination and vacuuming.

12. If possible the item should be returned to storage in a polyethylene bag or placed in secure cabinetry, as freezing will kill insects but will not repel or prevent a reinfestation.

Appendix 4

Vendors of Preservation Supplies

The following is a partial list of vendors of preservation supplies. The list is not exhaustive. Also, local vendors may be available to you. Museums and conservators in your area may know of these. This list does not constitute an endorsement of the suppliers listed. We suggest that you obtain information from a number of vendors so that you can make comparisons of cost and assess the full range of available products.

The numbers listed at the end of each address indicate the type of supplies predominantly carried by the vendor. The supplies are categorized as follows:

1. **storage/display supplies**
2. **equipment/tools**
3. **treatment supplies**

Archival Products
PO Box 1413
Des Moines, IA 50305-1413
800-262-4091
http://www.archival.com
1

Archivart
PO Box 428
Moonachie, NJ 07074
800-804-8428
http://www.archivart.com
1, 2, 3

Bookmakers
6701B Lafayette Avenue
Riverdale Park, MD 20737
301-927-7787
bookmakers@earthlink.net
2, 3

Conservation Resources International
8000-H Forbes Place
Springfield, VA 22151
800-634-6932
http://www.conservationresources.com
1, 2, 3

Conservator's Emporium
100 Standing Rock Circle
Reno, NV 89511
775-852-0404
http://www.consemp.com
2, 3

Franklin Distributors Corporation
Box 320
Denville, NJ 07834
973-267-2710
http://www.franklindistribcorp.com
1

Gaylord Brothers
PO Box 4901
Syracuse, NY 13221-4901
800-448-6160
http://www.gaylord.com/archival
1, 2, 3

The Hollinger Corporation
PO Box 8360
Fredricksburg, VA 22404-8360
800-634-0491
http://qshost.com/hollingercorp

1

Light Impressions
PO Box 22708
Rochester, NY 14692-2708
800-828-6216
http://www.lightimpressionsdirect.com

1, 2, 3

Metal Edge West, Inc.
6340 Bandini Boulevard
Commerce, CA 90040
800-862-2268
http://www.metaledgeinc.com

1, 2

William Minter Bookbinding and Conservation, Inc.
4364 Woodbury Pike
Woodbury, PA 16695
814-793-4020

3 (vinyl cleaning granules)

The Paige Company
400 Kelby Street
Fort Lee, NJ 07024
800-957-2443
http://www.armannj.org/paige/Paige.html

1

Print File
PO Box 4100
Schenectady, NY 12304
518-374-2334
http://www.pfile.com

1

Russell Norton
PO Box 1070
New Haven, CT 06504
203-281-0066
http://www.stereoview.com

1

Talas
568 Broadway
New York, NY 10012
212-736-7744
http://www.talasonline.com

2, 3

Testfabrics
PO Box 26
West Pittston, PA 18643
570-603-0432
http://www.testfabrics.com

1, 3

University Products, Inc.
PO Box 101
Holyoke, MA 01041-0101
800-628-1912
http://www.universityproducts.com

1, 2, 3

This list does not constitute a recommendation by the Minnesota Historical Society (MHS) of any vendor or products, nor will the MHS assume liability for the products supplied by a vendor.

Appendix 5

Sources of Help

The sources listed are organized by the following categories:

- Organizations and professional associations
- Regional conservation centers and outreach offices
- Funding agencies for preservation and conservation activities
- Preservation and conservation training
- Information resources for preservation and conservation and related concerns

This list is not exhaustive. It is intended only to get you started on your search for help. Contact cultural institutions and organizations in your area for the names of local sources. Also see additional sources of help listed in the various chapters in this book.

ORGANIZATIONS AND PROFESSIONAL ASSOCIATIONS

American Association of Museums (AAM)
1575 Eye Street NW, Suite 400
Washington, DC 20005
Telephone: 202-289-1818
Fax: 202-289-6578
http://www.aam-us.org

American Association for State and Local History (AASLH)
1717 Church Street
Nashville, TN 37203-2991
Telephone: 615-320-3203
Fax: 615-327-9013
E-mail: history@aaslh.org
http://www.aaslh.org

American Indian Library Association
50 East Huron Street
Chicago, IL 60611
Toll Free: 800-545-2433
Fax: 312-440-9374
http://www.nativeculture.com/lisamitten/aila.html

American Indian Ritual Object Repatriation Foundation
463 East 57th Street
New York, NY 10022
Telephone: 212-980-9441
Fax: 212-421-2746
E-mail: circle@repatriationfoundation.org
http://www.repatriationfoundation.org

American Institute for Conservation of Historic and Artistic Works (AIC)
1717 K Street NW, Suite 200
Washington, DC 20006
Telephone: 202-452-9545
Fax: 202-452-9328
E-mail: info@aic-faic.org
http://aic.stanford.edu

American Library Association (ALA)
50 East Huron Street
Chicago, IL 60611
Toll Free: 800-545-2433
Fax: 312-440-9374
E-mail: membership@ala.org
http://www.ala.org

Association on American Indian Affairs
Box 268
Sisseton, SD 57262
Telephone: 605-698-3998
Fax: 605-698-3316
E-mail: aaia@sbtc.net
http://www.indian-affairs.org

Association of Moving Image Archivists
1313 North Vine Street
Hollywood, CA 90028
Telephone: 323-463-1500
Fax: 323-463-1506
E-mail: amia@amianet.org
http://www.amianet.org

Association of Records Managers and Administrators (ARMA)
13725 West 109th Street, Suite 101
Lenexa, KS 66215
Telephone: 913-341-3808
US and Canada 800-422-2762
Fax: 913-341-3742
E-mail: hq@arma.org
http://www.arma.org

Canadian Association for Conservation of Cultural Property (CAC) (formerly International Institute for Conservation – Canadian Group)
280 Metcalfe, Suite 400
Ottawa, Ontario K2P 1R7
Canada
Telephone: 613-567-0099
Fax: 613-233-5438
E-mail: info@museums.ca
http://www.cac-accr.ca

Canadian Association of Professional Conservators (CAPC)
280 Metcalfe, Suite 400
Ottawa, Ontario K2P 1R7
Canada
Telephone: 613-567-0099
Fax: 613-233-5438

Heritage Preservation
1625 K Street NW, Suite 700
Washington, DC 20006
Telephone: 202-634-1422
Fax: 202-634-1435
E-mail: info@heritagepreservation.org
http://www.heritagepreservation.org

International Council of Museums (ICOM) Committee for Conservation Canadian Conservation Institute
1030 Innes Road
Ottawa, Ontario K1A 0M5
Canada
Telephone: 613-988-3721
Fax: 613-998-4721
E-mail: cci-icc_services@pch.gc.ca
http://www.cci-icc.gc.ca

International Institute for Conservation of Historic & Artistic Works (IIC)
6 Buckingham Street
London WC2N 6BA, UK
Telephone: +44 20-7839-5975
Fax: +44 20-7976-1564
E-mail: iicon@compuserve.com
http://www.iiconservation.org/index.html

National Trust for Historic Preservation
1785 Massachusetts Avenue NW
Washington, DC 20036
Toll Free: 800-944-6847
Telephone: 202-588-6000
Fax: 202-588-6038
http://www.nationaltrust.org

Native American Studies Association University of Wyoming, Casper
125 College Drive
Casper, WY 82601
Telephone: 307-268-2713
Fax: 307-268-2416
E-mail: mmurdock@uwyo.edu
http://www.apsanet.org/ps/organizations/related/nasa.cfm

Society for American Archaeology (SAA)
900 Second Street NE #12
Washington, DC 20002-3557
Telephone: 202-789-8200
Fax: 202-789-0284
E-mail: headquarters@saa.org
http://www.saa.org

Society of American Archivists (SAA)
527 South Wells, 5th Floor
Chicago, IL 60607-3922
Telephone: 312-922-0140
Fax: 312-347-1452
E-mail: info@archivists.org
http://www.archivists.org

Society for the Preservation of Natural History Collections (SPNHC)
PO Box 797
Washington, DC 20044-0797
http://www.spnhc.org

NONPROFIT REGIONAL CONSERVATION CENTERS AND OUTREACH OFFICES

Services provided include one or more of the following: educational workshops, disaster assistance, response to consultation inquiries, loaning of equipment and books, treatment, microfilming, scanning.

AMIGOS Library Services
14400 Midway Road
Dallas, TX 75244-3509
Telephone: 972-851-8000
Toll Free: 800-843-8482
Fax: 972-991-6061
E-mail: amigos@amigos.org
http://www.amigos.org

Balboa Art Conservation Center (BACC)
PO Box 3755
San Diego, CA 92163-1755
Telephone: 619-236-9702
Fax: 619-236-0141
E-mail: janetbacc@cs.com
http://www.rap-arcc.org/welcome/balboa.htm

Canadian Conservation Institute (CCI)
1030 Innes Road
Ottawa, Ontario K1A 0M5
Canada
Telephone: 613-998-3721
Fax: 613-998-4721
E-mail: cci-icc_services@pch.gc.ca
http://www.cci-icc.gc.ca

Colorado Preservation Alliance
c/o The Colorado State Archives
1313 Sherman
Denver, CO 80203
Telephone: 303-275-2214
E-mail: kjones@jefferson.lib.co.us
http://www.archives.state.co.us/cpa

Conservation Center for Art and Historic Artifacts (CCAHA)
264 South 23rd Street
Philadelphia, PA 19103
Telephone: 215-545-0613
Fax: 215-735-9313
E-mail: ccaha@ccaha.org
http://www.ccaha.org

Gerald R. Ford Conservation Center
1326 South 32nd Street
Omaha, NE 68105
Telephone: 402-595-1180
Fax: 402-595-1178
E-mail: grfcc@radiks.net
http://www.nebraskahistory.org/sites/ford/index.htm

Intermuseum Conservation Association
Allen Art Building
83 North Main Street
Oberlin, OH 44074-1192
Telephone: 440-775-7331
Fax: 440-774-3431
E-mail: albert.albano@oberlin.edu
http://www.oberlin.edu/~ica/

The Michigan Alliance for the Conservation of Cultural Heritage
The Detroit Institute of Arts
5200 Woodward Avenue
Detroit, MI 48202
Telephone: 313-833-7900
http://www.dia.org/information/host.html

Minnesota Historical Society Conservation Department
345 Kellogg Boulevard West
St. Paul, MN 55102
Telephone: 651-259-3388
Fax: 651-296-9961
E-mail: conservationhelp@mnhs.org
http://www.mnhs.org

Northeast Document Conservation Center (NEDCC)
100 Brickstone Square
Andover, MA 01810-1494
Telephone: 978-470-1010
Fax: 978-475-6021
E-mail: nedcc@nedcc.org
http://www.nedcc.org

Regional Alliance for Preservation
http://www.rap-arcc.org/index.htm

Solinet Preservation Program
1438 West Peachtree Street NW
Suite 200
Atlanta, GA 30309-2955
Telephone: 800-999-8558
Fax: 404-892-7879
http://www.solinet.net

Straus Center for Conservation
Harvard University Art Museum
32 Quincy Street
Cambridge, MA 02138-3383
Telephone: 617-495-2392
Fax: 617-495-0322
http://www.artmuseums.harvard.edu/straus/

Textile Conservation Center
American Textile History Museum
491 Dutton Street
Lowell, MA 01854-4221
Telephone: 978-441-0400
Fax: 978-441-1412
http://www.athm.org

Upper Midwest Conservation Association (UMCA)
Minneapolis Institute of Arts
2400 Third Avenue South
Minneapolis, MN 55404
Telephone: 612-870-3120
Fax: 612-870-3118
E-mail: umca@aol.com
http://www.preserveart.org

Vermont Collections Care Program
Vermont Museum and Gallery Alliance
c/o Fairbanks Museum
1302 Main Street
St. Johnsbury, VT 05819-2224
Telephone: 800-639-2330
Fax: 802-748-1893
E-mail: vmga@valley.net
http://www.vmga.org/aboutvmga/memberpage/collectioncare.html

Williamstown Art Conservation Center
225 South Street
Williamstown, MA 01267
Telephone: 413-458-5741
Fax: 413-458-2314
E-mail: wacc@williamstownart.org
http://www.williamstownart.org

NATIONAL FUNDING AGENCIES FOR PRESERVATION AND CONSERVATION

Check locally for state and other funding opportunities in your area.

American Institute for Conservation of Historic and Artistic Works (AIC)
1717 K Street NW, Suite 200
Washington, DC 20006
Telephone: 202-452-9545
Fax: 202-452-9328
E-mail: info@aic-faic.org
http://aic.stanford.edu

Andrew W. Mellon Foundation
Arts and Cultural Programs
140 East 62nd Street
New York, NY 10021
Telephone: 212-838-8400
Fax: 212-888-4172
http://www.mellon.org

The Getty Grant Program
1200 Getty Center Drive
Suite 800
Los Angeles, CA 90049-1685
Telephone: 310-440-7320
Fax: 310-440-7300
E-mail: info@getty.edu
http://www.getty.edu/grants/index.html

Institute of Museum & Library Services
1100 Pennsylvania Avenue NW, Room 510
Washington, DC 20506
Telephone: 202-606-8536
Fax: 202-606-8591
E-mail: imlsinfo@imls.gov
http://www.imls.gov

National Center for Preservation Technology and Training (NCPTT)
645 College Avenue
Natchitoches, LA 71457
Telephone: 318-356-7444
Fax: 318-356-9119
E-mail: ncptt@ncptt.nps.gov
http://www.ncptt.nps.gov

National Endowment for the Arts, Museum Program Creation & Preservation
1100 Pennsylvania Avenue NW
Washington, DC 20506
Telephone: 202-682-5400
E-mail: webmgr@arts.endow.gov
http://arts.endow.gov

National Endowment for the Humanities Division of Preservation and Access
1100 Pennsylvania Avenue NW
Washington, DC 20506
Telephone: 202-606-8570 or 800-NEH-1121
Fax: 202-606-8639
E-mail: info@neh.gov
http://www.neh.fed.us

National Historic Publications and Records Commission (NHPRC)
National Archives & Records Administration
NHPRC Room 111
700 Pennsylvania Avenue NW
Washington, DC 20408-0001
Telephone: 202-501-5610
Fax: 202-501-5601
E-mail: nhprc@nara.gov
http://www.archives.gov/nhprc_and_other_grants/about_nhrprc/about_nhprc.html

National Park Service
1849 C Street NW
Washington, DC 20240
Telephone: 202-208-6843
http://www.nps.gov

Pew Charitable Trusts
2005 Market Street, Suite 1700
Philadelphia, PA 19103-7077
Telephone: 215-575-9050
Fax: 215-575-4939
E-mail: info@pewtrusts.com
http://www.pewtrusts.com

PRESERVATION AND CONSERVATION TRAINING

Also check the section on Regional Conservation Centers and Outreach Offices for additional training opportunities.

American Association for State and Local History Workshop Series
1717 Church Street
Nashville, TN 37203-2991
Telephone: 615-320-3203
Fax: 615-327-9013
E-mail: history@aaslh.org
http://www.aaslh.org

Campbell Center for Historic Preservation Studies
203 East Seminary
Mount Carroll, IL 61053
Telephone: 815-244-1173
Fax: 815-244-1619
E-mail: campbellcenter@internetni.com
http://www.campbellcenter.org

The Center of Southwest Studies
Academic minor in heritage preservation studies; graduate courses being planned
Fort Lewis College
1000 Rim Drive
Durango, CO 81301
Telephone: 970-247-7456
Fax: 970-247-7422
E-mail: Gulliford_a@fortlewis.edu
http://swcenter.fortlewis.edu

Note: Fort Lewis College has free tuition for all federally enrolled American Indians.

The Conservation Center of the Institute of Fine Arts New York University
14 East 78th Street
New York, NY 10021
Telephone: 212-992-5848
Fax: 212-992-5851
E-mail: conservation.program@nyu.edu
http://www.nyu.edu/gsas/dept/fineart/index.htm?http&&&www.nyu.edu/gsas/dept/fineart/html/cons.htm

Fleming College
Collections Conservation and Management (CCM)
Sutherland Campus
Brealey Building
Brealey Drive
Peterborough, Ontario K9J 7B1
Canada
Telephone: 705-749-5530
Fax: 705-749-5540
http://www.flemingc.on.ca/programs

George Eastman House, Inc.
Advanced Residency Program in Photographic Conservation
900 East Avenue
Rochester, NY 14607
Telephone: 585-271-3361
Fax: 585-271-3970
E-mail: romer@gch.org
http://www.eastman.org

International Centre for the Study of the Preservation and the Restoration of Cultural Property (ICCROM)
Via di San Michele 13
1-00153 Rome, Italy
Telephone: +39-06 585-531
Fax: +39-06 585-3349
E-mail: iccrom@iccrom.org
http://www.iccrom.org

National Center for Preservation Technology and Training (NCPTT)
645 College Avenue
Natchitoches, LA 71457
Telephone: 318-356-7444

Fax: 318-356-9119
E-mail: ncptt@ncptt.nps.gov
http://www.ncptt.nps.gov

National Preservation Institute
Seminars in historic preservation
and cultural resource management
PO Box 1702
Alexandria, VA 22313
Telephone: 703-765-0100
E-mail: info@npi.org
http://www.npi.org

Queen's University
Art Conservation Programme
Queen's University
99 University Avenue
Kingston, Ontario K7L 3N6
Canada
Telephone: 613-533-2000
Fax: 613-533-6889
E-mail: art@post.queensu.ca
http://www.queensu.ca

Rutgers University School of Communication,
Information and Library Studies,
Biennial Preservation Management Institute
4 Huntington Street
New Brunswick, NJ 08901-1071
Telephone: 732-932-7169
Fax: 732-932-9314
http://scils.rutgers.edu/programs/pds/pmi.jsp

Smithsonian Center for Materials
Research and Education
Museum Support Center
Smithsonian Institution
Washington, DC 20560
Telephone: 301-238-3700
Fax: 301-238-3709
E-mail: ABN@SCMRE.si.edu
http://www.si.edu/scmre

State University College at Buffalo
Art Conservation Department
Rockwell Hall 230
1300 Elmwood Avenue
Buffalo, NY 14222-1095
Telephone: 716-878-5025
Fax: 716-878-5039
E-mail: artcon@buffalostate.edu
http://www.buffalostate.edu/depts/artconservation/

Straus Center for Conservation
Harvard University Art Museum
32 Quincy Street
Cambridge, MA 02138
Telephone: 617-495-2392
Fax: 617-495-0322
http://www.artmuseums.harvard.edu/straus/index.html

University of British Columbia
2329 West Mall
Vancouver, BC V6T 1Z4
Canada
Telephone: 604-822-2211
http://www.ubc.ca/about/index.html

University of Texas at Austin
Preservation & Conservation Studies Program
Graduate School of Library and Information Science
SZB #564
1 University Station D7000
Austin, TX 78712-1276
Telephone: 512-471-3821
Fax: 512-471-3971
E-mail: info@gslis.utexas.edu
http://www.gslis.utexas.edu/

Winterthur/University of Delaware Program in the
Conservation of Historic and Artistic Works
303 Old College
University of Delaware
Newark, DE 19716
Telephone: 800-448-3883
Fax: 302-831-4330
E-mail: webmaster@winterthur.org
http://www.winterthur.org

INFORMATION RESOURCES FOR PRESERVATION AND CONSERVATION AND RELATED CONCERNS

Also check the section on Regional Conservation Centers and Outreach Offices for information resources.

American Institute for Conservation of
Historic and Artistic Works (AIC)
1717 K Street NW, Suite 200
Washington, DC 20006
Telephone: 202-452-9545
Fax: 202-452-9328
E-mail: info@aic-faic.org
http://aic.stanford.edu

American National Standards Institute (ANSI)
New York City Office
25 West 43rd Street, 4th Floor
New York, NY 10036
Telephone: 212-642-4900
Fax: 212-398-0023
E-mail: info@ansi.org
http://www.ansi.org/

American Society of Appraisers
555 Herndon Parkway, Suite 125
Herndon, VA 20170
Telephone: 703-478-2228
Fax: 703-742-8471
E-mail: asainfo@appraisers.org
http://www.appraisers.org/

AMIGOS Library Services
14400 Midway Road
Dallas, TX 75244-3509
Telephone: 972-851-8000
Toll Free: 800-843-8482
Fax: 972-991-6061
E-mail: amigos@amigos.org
http://www.amigos.org

Arts, Crafts and Theatre Safety
181 Thompson Street, #23
New York, NY 10012-2586
Telephone: 212-777-0062
E-mail: ACTS@CaseWeb.com
http://www.caseweb.com/acts/

Centers for Disease Control and Prevention
1600 Clifton Road
Atlanta, GA 30333
Telephone: 404-639-3311
http://www.cdc.gov

Conservation OnLine (CoOL)
http://palimpsest.stanford.edu

Federal Emergency Management Agency (FEMA)
500 C Street SW
Washington, DC 20472
Telephone: 202-566-1600
http://www.fema.gov/

Getty Conservation Institute
1200 Getty Center Drive, Suite 700
Los Angeles, CA 90049-1684
Telephone: 310-440-7325
Fax: 310-440-7702
http://www.getty.edu/conservation/

Image Permanence Institute
Rochester Institute of Technology
70 Lomb Memorial Drive
Rochester, NY 14623-5604
Telephone: 585-475-5199
Fax: 585-475-7230
E-mail: ipiwww@rit.edu
http://www.rit.edu/~661www1

Institute of Paper Science & Technology
500 10th Street NW
Atlanta, GA 30318-5794
Telephone: 404-894-5700
Toll Free: 800-558-6611
Fax: 404-894-4778
http://www.ipst.edu

Leather Conservation Centre
University College Campus
Boughton Green Road
Northampton, NN2 7AN
UK
Telephone: +44 1604 719766
Fax: +44 1604 719649
E-mail: lcc@leatheruk.com
http://www.leatheruk.com/lcc.htm

Library of Congress
Preservation Directorate
101 Independence Avenue SE
Washington, DC 20540
Telephone: 202-707-5213
Fax: 202-707-3434
http://www.loc.gov/preserv/

Material Safety Data Sheets
http://www.ilpi.com/msds

Minnesota Historical Society
Conservation Department
345 Kellogg Boulevard West
St. Paul, MN 55102
Telephone: 651-259-3388
Fax: 651-296-9961
E-mail: conservationhelp@mnhs.org
http://www.mnhs.org

Museum Security Network
Rechter Rottekade 171
3032 XD Rotterdam
The Netherlands
Telephone and Fax: +31-10-4653837
Cellular: +31-6-242-24620
E-mail: securma@xs4all.nl
http://www.museum-security.org

National Archives & Records Administration
8601 Adephi Road
College Park, MD 20740-6001
Telephone: 866-272-6272
Fax: 301-837-6272
http://www.archives.gov/index.html

National Center for Film & Video Preservation
American Film Institute
2021 North Western Avenue
Los Angeles, CA 90027
Telephone: 323-856-7708
http://www.afi.com/index.asp

National Fire Protection Association (NFPA)
1 Batterymarch Park
Quincy, MA 02269-9101
Telephone: 617-770-3000
Fax: 617-770-0700
http://www.nfpa.org/Home/index.asp

National Information Standards Organization (NISO)
4733 Bethesda Avenue, Suite 300
Bethesda, MD 20814
Telephone: 301-654-2512
Fax: 301-654-1721
E-mail: nisohq@niso.org
http://www.niso.org

National Media Laboratory
PO Box 33015
St. Paul, MN 55133-3015
Telephone: 651-733-1110
http://www.nta.org/AboutNTA/AboutNML/index.html

National Museum of the American Indian
http://www.nmai.si.edu/index.asp

Cultural Resources Center
4220 Silver Hill Road
Suitland, MD 20746
Telephone: 301-238-6624
Fax: 301-238-3200

George Gustav Heye Center
Alexander Hamilton U.S. Custom House
One Bowling Green
New York, NY 10004
Telephone: 215-514-3700

On the National Mall
scheduled to open in 2004
Washington, DC
Telephone: 202-287-2020

National NAGPRA Program
National Park Service
1849 C Street NW (2253)
Washington, DC 20240
Telephone: 202-354-2200
Fax: 202-371-5197
E-mail: NAGPRAInfo@nps.gov
http://www.cr.nps.gov/nagpra

National Park Service
Museum Resource Division
3300 Hubbard Road
Landover, MD 20785-2010
Telephone: 301-341-0706
Fax: 301-583-0953
E-mail: pam_west@nps.gov
http://www.nps.gov

National Park Service
Division of Conservation
Harpers Ferry NHP
PO Box 65
Harpers Ferry, WV 25425
Telephone: 304-535-6298
Fax: 304-535-6055
http://www.nps.gov/hafe

National Preservation Institute
Seminars in historic preservation
and cultural resource management
PO Box 1702
Alexandria, VA 22313
Telephone: 703-765-0100
E-mail: info@npi.org
http://www.npi.org

New York State Office of Parks,
Recreation and Historic Preservation
Bureau of Historic Sites
Collections Care Center
Peebles Island, PO Box 219
Waterford, NY 12188
Telephone: 518-237-8643
Fax: 518-235-4248
http://nysparks.state.ny.us

Occupational Safety & Health Administration
U.S. Department of Labor
200 Constitution Avenue NW
Washington, DC 20210
Telephone: 1-800-321-OSHA (6742);
emergency number only.

Check local telephone book for the number of the nearest office or online. http://www.osha.gov

Professional Picture Framers Association
4305 Sarellen Road
Richmond, VA 23231
Telephone: 804-226-0430
Fax: 804-222-2175
E-mail: ppfa@ppfa.com
http://www.ppfa.com

Regional Alliance for Preservation
http://www.rap-arcc.org

SOLINET Preservation Program
1438 West Peachtree Street NW, Suite 200
Atlanta, GA 30309-2955
Toll Free: 800-999-8558
Telephone: 404-892-0943
Fax: 404-892-7879
E-mail: helpdesk@solinet.net
http://www.solinet.net

Tribal Archives, Libraries, & Museums
Project Director, Alyce Sadongei
Arizona State Museum, University of Arizona
PO Box 210026
Tucson, AZ 85712-0026
Telephone: 520-621-4500 or 520-626-9448
Fax: 520-621-2976
E-mail: sadongei@email.arizona.edu
http://www.statemuseum.arizona.edu/aip/5stateproject/index.shtml

UNESCO-ICOM Information Centre
Maison de l'UNESCO, 1 rue Miollis
F-75732 Paris cedex 15, France
Telephone: +33 1 47 34 05 00
Fax: +33 1 43 06 78 62
E-mail: jani@icom.org
http://icom.museum/centre.html

Western Association for Art Conservation (WAAC)
5835 North Concord
Portland, OR 97217
Telephone: 503-288-8414
Fax: 503-286-6023
E-mail: waac@nwartsource.com
http://palimpsest.stanford.edu/waac

Much of this information was taken from the book *Preservation of Library and Archival Materials* with the kind permission of the Northeast Document Conservation Center.

Glossary

acid A class of chemicals having a pH less than 7.0. Acids contained in objects or in contact with them generally cause deterioration [depending upon the materials from which the objects are made]. (Long)

acid-free Term used for materials with pH value of 7.0 or higher. (Long)

acidic/acidity The quality of being acid. (Long)

acid migration Transfer of acidity from an acidic material to a less acidic material through physical contact or vapors. (Long)

acrylic A plastic noted for transparency, light weight, weather resistance, color fastness, [impact resistance], and rigidity. Important in preservation because of its resistance to change over time. [Often used in mounts and supports.] (Long)

activated charcoal/carbon Amorphous carbon produced from charcoal that has been subjected to high heat (800–900° C) with steam or CO_2 to produce porous, high surface area (about 3,600 square feet/gm) particles capable of efficient adsorption of gases, vapors, and colloidal solids. (Ellis)

alkaline A class of chemicals having a pH value of 7.1 or higher. Used to neutralize acids. (Long)

alkaline reserve An alkaline buffer. See **buffer**.

alloy Two or more elemental metals that have been melted together.

anodized aluminum Aluminum subjected to electrolytic action and coated with a protective film. (Long)

buffer A chemical reserve that helps maintain a pH range by counteracting acids or bases. It can be added during manufacture or deacidification. (Long) A preservation material that is buffered can be assumed to have an alkaline reserve added to it to neutralize any acids that form, while one that is unbuffered does not contain an alkaline reserve.

calcium carbonate An alkaline chemical that is used as a buffer [alkaline reserve] in paper and storage boxes to inhibit the formation and migration of acids. (Long)

cellulose Chief component of cell walls of all plants and plant products, including paper, wood, and cloth. (Long)

chemical stability The ability of certain chemical bonds to resist degradation when exposed to other chemicals. Not easily decomposed or otherwise modified chemically. A desirable characteristic for materials used in preservation. Also referred to as stable. (Long)

conservation The profession devoted to the preservation of cultural property for the future. Conservation activities include examination, documentation, treatment, and preventive care, supported by research and education. (AIC)

conservator A professional whose primary occupation is the practice of conservation, and who through specialized education, knowledge, training, and experience, formulates and implements all the activities of conservation in accordance with an ethical code such as the AIC *Code of Ethics and Guidelines for Practice.* (AIC)

cultural property Objects, collections, specimens, structures, or sites identified as having artistic, historic, scientific, religious, or social significance. (AIC)

deterioration The gradual aging and ultimate destruction of materials due to the action of chemical, biological, and physical processes. (Ellis)

documentation The recording in a permanent format of information derived from conservation activities. (AIC)

efflorescence As used in this book, a white powder, bloom, or crust composed of various salts; on a ceramic or stone object, it is usually caused by the evaporation of salt-laden water due to fluctuating high and low relative humidity or exposure to water.

element The primary form of matter; materials that cannot be further purified or reduced. Listed in the periodic table of the elements in chemistry.

examination The investigation of the structure, materials, and condition of cultural property including the identification of the extent and causes of alteration and deterioration. (AIC)

fluorescent lamp [A source of light that uses] mercury vapor. Has a higher ultraviolet (UV) output than an incandescent lamp but less than the amount of UV in natural light. (Long)

foam A material composed of small bubbles of gas in a liquid or solid, and typically characterized as bulky but lightweight and flexible. Most foams used in conservation are solid. Flexible solid foams made with polyethylene are typically useful as insulators from shock and damage for items in storage.

footcandle A measurement of visible light equal to a unit of illuminance on a surface that is everywhere one foot from a uniform point source of light of one candle and equal to one lumen per square foot. (Ellis)

formaldehyde A volatile organic compound that is released from wood and many adhesive products. Very reactive with most metals and other materials, especially under highly humid conditions. Has been used as an insecticide and for embalming.

frass The excrement, shell casings, or other detritus of insects. (Ellis)

glaze As used in this book, a thin coating of clear or colored glass fired to the surface of a ceramic; glass or acrylic in a picture frame or display case.

gut The tissue found in stomachs and intestines. It is usually processed into a type of rawhide and is used for clothing, fishing floats, and other items.

HEPA An acronym for High Efficiency Particulate Air Filter, which is a filtration system that retains a minimum of 99.97 percent of particles that are 0.3 microns and larger (Stavroudis, *WAAC Newsletter* 24 [May 2002]: 13).

hide The skin of a larger animal such as elk, moose, or bison.

hygroscopic The ability of a material to absorb or release moisture. This property makes objects vulnerable to damage from frequent or dramatic changes in relative humidity. (Long)

incandescent lamp [Light source that] produces light by heating a metal filament to luminescence. Has low UV component but gives off heat. (Long)

inherent vice The chemical or structural instability of the materials that compose an item.

integrated pest management (IPM) A strategy that relies on nonchemical means to prevent and manage pest infestations. Chemical treatments are used only as a last resort when other methods have failed or when serious damage is occurring rapidly.

lignin A component of cell walls that provides strength and rigidity in plants. It is believed to contribute to the chemical degradation of paper. It can be removed [from paper] to a large extent during manufacturing. (Long)

lumen A unit of measurement of light intensity; one footcandle equals approximately one lumen over an area of one square foot.

lux A unit of measurement of light intensity; one footcandle equals 10.78 lux. (Ellis) One lux equals 1 lumen/m^2, metric equivalent of footcandles.

magnetic wiping/dust cloth [A lint-free] cloth that captures dust particles through electrostatic or "magnetic" attraction. (Long) It attracts dust with only light contact with the item being dusted, reducing the risk of scratching the item.

mat burn Discoloration on matted items, most often paper ones, caused by acidic window mats. Acid migrates from the mat to the item and leaves a disfiguring stain that follows the outline of the window in the mat. Deterioration of the item is hastened in the area where the discoloration occurs.

metal coupons Thin strips of metal specially prepared for use in scientific testing.

microclimate/environment A self-contained and passively controlled environment, typically in a display or storage case. (Ellis)

microwatts per lumen A measure of ultraviolet illumination energy.

molecular trap A zeolite system having an open-network structure allowing it to selectively [adsorb] gases and liquids. (Ellis)

NAGPRA The Native American Graves Protection and Repatriation Act. On November 16, 1990, President George Bush signed this act into law. It addresses the rights of lineal descendants, Indian tribes, and native Hawaiian organizations to certain American human remains, funerary objects, sacred objects, and objects of cultural patrimony with which they are affiliated.

neutral Having a pH value of 7.0; neither acidic nor alkaline. (Long)

off-gassing The process of slowly releasing volatile materials that often contribute to the deterioration of objects. A property of wood and some paints that should be avoided in storage and display. (Long)

pH A measure of acidity and alkalinity on a scale [of 1 to 14] where 7.0 indicates neutrality, lower numbers indicate acidity, and higher numbers indicate alkalinity. The scale is logarithmic. (Long)

photochemical Visual or mechanical changes resulting from the action of radiant energy. (Ellis)

photographic activity test (PAT) A test to assess the possibility that an image will fade or become stained by materials with which it comes into contact. The test gauges how reactive photographic images are to contaminants contained in materials used to display or store photographs, such as mat board and album pages. The PAT is conducted in accordance with the International Standards Organization (ISO 14523.1999). (Long)

polycarbonate Thermoplastic linear polyesters of carbonic acid used to manufacture very clear and strong transparent plastic sheets used in glazing and vitrines. (Ellis)

polyester film Common name for the [family of] plastic called polyethylene terephthalate. Characteristics include chemical stability, transparency, and high tensile strength. (Long)

polyethylene A chemically stable, highly flexible, transparent or translucent plastic [composed solely of carbon and hydrogen atoms]. (Long)

polypropylene A chemically stable plastic of the same family as polyethylene that resists heat and is stiffer than polyethylene. (Long)

polystyrene A thermoplastic material produced by the polymerization of styrene. Used in solution as an adhesive or formed into foams. (Ellis)

polyurethane A polymer derived from the reaction of a polyisocyanate with a polyhydroxyl compound normally of polyester or polyether structure. Polyurethane foams and most varnishes are not stable on a long-term basis, and [most] should not be used for conservation purposes. (Ellis)

polyvinyl chloride (PVC) A chemically unstable plastic that can emit hydrochloric acid. May also be called simply vinyl. (Long)

potassium permanganate As used in this book, a chemical compound used in building and exhibit case air filtration systems as a gaseous pollutant adsorber.

powder coated A surface coating applied via dry powder fused through heat. Seals and eliminates off-gassing. (Long)

preservation The protection of cultural property through activities that minimize chemical and physical deterioration and damage and that prevent loss of informational content. The primary goal of preservation is to prolong the existence of cultural property. (AIC)

preservation professionals Conservators, scientists, teachers, administrators, and other individuals who have extensive specialized training that enables them to plan and implement preservation activities, conduct research, or perform treatment.

preventive care/conservation The mitigation of deterioration and damage to cultural property through the formulation and implementation of policies and procedures for the following: appropriate environmental conditions; handling and maintenance procedures for storage, exhibition, packing, transport, and use; integrated pest management; emergency preparedness and response; and reformatting/duplication. (AIC)

provenance The origin or source of an object. The object's history. Same as *provenience,* a term that is used primarily with archaeological collections. (Long)

rawhide Animal skin that has been soaked, dehaired, scraped, stretched, and allowed to dry. Very stiff, durable material that can be worked when moist. Will revert to an uncured condition if it gets wet.

relative humidity The percentage of moisture in the air relative to the maximum amount the air can hold at that temperature. (Long)

restoration Treatment procedures intended to return cultural property to a known or assumed state, often through the addition of nonoriginal material. (AIC)

rheostat A variable resistor used to regulate electrical equipment, such as a tacking iron [or vacuum cleaner]. (Ellis)

rule/law of reciprocity As used in this book, the rule that limited exposure to a high-intensity light will produce the same amount of damage as long exposure to a low-intensity light. For example, if the exposure time is kept the same but the light level is halved, the resulting damage will be halved.

scavengers Substances that remove undesirable environmental elements, such as sulfur, through chemical or physical means. (Long)

silica gel A commercially available granular form of silica that can be conditioned to maintain a specific level of humidity in a closed container.

sinew The connective tissue of larger mammals such as deer; it is generally used as a sewing thread.

skin Outer covering of a vertebrate animal, usually a smaller one.

slip As used in this book, a thin layer of clay that covers a ceramic. It has a matte appearance and is a different color than the ceramic it covers.

sponge (vulcanized rubber) A sponge used for dry cleaning; originally developed for soot removal following a fire and now being used increasingly for cleaning storage shelves and objects. These sponges are reported to leave no damaging residues on items, and they appear to be nonabrasive. They degrade upon exposure to light and with age, so they need to be stored in an air-tight container and in the dark. As the surface of the sponge becomes dirty with use, it can be sliced off and discarded.

stabilization Treatment procedures intended to maintain the integrity of cultural property and to minimize deterioration. (AIC)

treatment The deliberate alteration of the chemical and/or physical aspects of cultural property, aimed primarily at prolonging its existence. Treatment may consist of stabilization and/or restoration. (AIC)

ultraviolet (UV) filter A filter that can be placed over windows, skylights, and fluorescent light tubes to remove or reduce harmful ultraviolet radiation. (Long)

ultraviolet (UV) radiation Radiation of wavelengths shorter than 400 nanometers. Found in light from the sun and most artificial light sources. It is invisible, highly energetic, and has a strongly damaging effect on objects. Should be filtered from light sources. (Long)

unbuffered Containing no chemical reserve to maintain a pH range. Opposite of buffered. (Long)

visible light That portion of the electromagnetic spectrum detectable as colors by the human eye, extending from violet (400 nanometers) to red (700 nanometers). (Ellis)

zeolite An inert crystalline aluminosilicate (Na_2O Al_2O_5 $(SiO_2)_x$ H_2O) that is used as a molecular sieve/trap due to its ability to exhibit base exchange properties and [adsorb] water as well as small organic molecules. It is found naturally but is often made or refined by humans to meet specific performance characteristics. (Ellis)

Sources

American Institute for Conservation of Historic and Artistic Works. "AIC Definitions of Conservation Terminology." Pages 21–22 in *Directory.* Washington, D.C.: American Institute for Conservation of Historic and Artistic Works, 2001. (AIC)

Long, Jane S., and Richard W. Long. *Caring for Your Family Treasures.* New York: Harry N. Abrams, 2000, 147–51. (Long)

Ellis, Margaret Holben. *A Glossary of Paper Conservation Terms.* Unpublished. (Ellis)
Ellis' definitions were selected and edited from forty-six different sources identified in her glossary.

Terms without a source were defined by staff members of the Minnesota Historical Society Conservation Department.

Bibliography

This short bibliography is by no means exhaustive. The body of preservation literature is vast, and these are just a few of the works that are good introductory sources of information. The books listed here are useful tools to help you begin your work preserving the cultural items in your care. They provide the information that will enable you to implement the suggestions in this book. See also the additional sources of information suggested in the various chapters in this book.

CULTURAL CONSIDERATIONS

Clavir, Miriam. *Preserving What Is Valued: Museums, Conservation, and First Nations.* Vancouver, B.C.: University of British Columbia Press, 2002.

A good exploration of the cultural differences between First Nations peoples and others with regard to items, museums, and conservation. Very useful in helping us understand each other.

Cooper, Karen. *American Indian Protests of Museum Exhibition Policies and Practices.* Master's thesis, University of Oklahoma, 1996.

An interesting historical discussion of American Indian resistance to museum display policies and practices and the changes that occurred in museums as a result of these protests; interesting case studies.

Gulliford, Andrew. *Sacred Objects and Sacred Places/ Preserving Tribal Traditions.* Boulder, Colo.: University Press of Colorado, 2000.

Comprehensive discussion about the ways American Indians try to preserve their traditions and identity. A good historical overview that is intended to increase public support for tribal preservation.

Montegut, Denyse, ed. *Caring for American Indian Cultural Materials: Policies and Practices/A Two-Day Symposium October 19–20, 1996.* New York: Fashion Institute of Technology, Graduate Division, 1996.

Papers given at a symposium aimed at better understanding the meaning of American Indian cultural items. Case studies of particular items, displays, and events.

GENERAL COLLECTIONS CARE

Barclay, Robert, André Bergeron, and Carole Dignard. *Mount-Making for Museum Objects.* Illustrations by Carl Schlichting. 2d ed., rev. Ottawa, Ontario: Canadian Conservation Institute, 2002.

Simple easy-to-follow instructions for making a variety of mounts with helpful background information; very useful.

Canadian Conservation Institute. *CCI Notes.* Ottawa, Ontario: Canadian Conservation Institute, ongoing.

A series of leaflets that provide practical information on the care, handling, storage, and display of cultural items; very useful.

Ellis, Margaret Holben. *The Care of Prints and Drawings.* Walnut Creek, Calif.: AltaMira Press, 1995.

Excellent comprehensive discussion of all aspects of the care of works of art on paper.

Hatchfield, Pamela B. *Pollutants in the Museum Environment: Practical Strategies for Problem Solving in Design, Exhibition and Storage.* London: Archetype Publications Ltd., 2002.

Comprehensive and technical discussion of pollutants in museums and ways to protect cultural items; advanced treatment of the subject.

Hoveman, Alice R. ***Conservation Wise Guide.*** **Juneau, Alaska: Alaska State Museum, 1985.**

Excellent brief discussion of preventive conservation with specific information on conservation of particular materials.

Mending the Circle. A Native American Repatriation Guide. Understanding and Implementing NAGPRA and the Official Smithsonian and Other Repatriation Policies. **New York: American Indian Ritual Object Repatriation Foundation, 1997.**

"[I]ntended to guide all concerned with matters of repatriation through the maze of pertinent law, policies and procedures to the opportunities and solutions they offer"; introduction by Suzan Shown Harjo (Cheyenne and Hodulgee Muscogee).

National Park Service. ***Conserve-O-Gram Series.*** **Harpers Ferry, W.Va.: National Park Service, ongoing. Also available on the Web at http://www.cr.nps.gov/csd/publications/conserveogram/conserv.html.**

Practical and very useful series of leaflets on many aspects of collections care; designed to assist staff of national parks in caring for cultural items.

National Park Service. ***Exhibit Conservation Guidelines.*** **Washington, D.C.: CD-ROM publication by SANAD Support Technologies, Inc., 1999.**

Comprehensive detailed information on all aspects of display of cultural items; very useful for anyone involved in an ongoing display program.

Odegaard, Nancy. ***A Guide to Handling Anthropological Museum Collections.*** **Illustrated by Grace Kattermann. Western Association for Art Conservation (WAAC), 1991. Available from WAAC (see Appendix 5) for a nominal fee.**

Humorously illustrated pamphlet on a serious subject; excellent educational tool.

Ogden, Sherelyn, ed. ***Preservation of Library and Archival Materials: A Manual.*** **Andover, Mass.: Northeast Document Conservation Center, 1999. Also available on the Web at http://www.nedcc.org.**

Practical basic information on preservation planning, emergency management, environment, storage, handling, reformatting, and conservation; very useful for anyone overseeing library or archival collections.

Ogden, Sherelyn. ***The Storage of Art on Paper: A Basic Guide for Institutions.*** **Urbana-Champaign: University of Illinois, 2001.**

Brief, practical, and basic guide for the storage of works of art on paper; useful.

Ritzenthaler, Mary Lynn. ***Preserving Archives and Manuscripts.*** **Archival Fundamentals Series. Chicago: Society of American Archivists, 1993.**

Excellent work on various aspects of the preservation of archival materials including handling, storage, and conservation; very useful for anyone caring for archival collections.

Rose, Carolyn L., and Amparo R. de Torres, eds. ***Storage of Natural History Collections: Ideas and Practical Solutions.*** **Pittsburgh: Society for the Preservation of Natural History Collections, 1992.**

Contains 113 well-illustrated practical suggestions for the storage of items; provides easy-to-follow instructions for producing mounts, supports, and microenvironments; very useful.

Rose, Carolyn L., Catharine Hawks, and Hugh Genoways, eds. ***Storage of Natural History Collections: A Preventive Conservation Approach.*** **Society for Preservation of Natural History Collections, 1995.**

A comprehensive discussion of various aspects of preventive conservation including creating, managing, and monitoring storage facilities and environments, selecting and testing storage equipment and materials, and collections care as a catalyst for funding.

CARE OF FAMILY TREASURES

Bachmann, Konstanze. ***Conservation Concerns: A Guide for Collectors and Curators.*** **Washington, D.C.: Smithsonian Institution Press, 1992.**

General information on storage, display, and different types of items such as photographs, paintings, and furniture; useful sections describing when specific types of items need conservation.

Landrey, Gregory J., et al. ***The Winterthur Guide to Caring for Your Collection.*** **Winterthur, Del.: Henry Francis Du Pont Winterthur Museum, 2000.**

Sound and thorough discussions on caring for various items and materials with an explanation of the role science plays in conservation.

Long, Jane S., and Richard W. Long. ***Caring for Your Family Treasures.*** **New York: Harry N. Abrams, 2000.**

Excellent practical introductory work on caring for family items; easy to read and understand with useful checklists; a wide variety of materials and items are discussed; very useful.

National Committee to Save America's Cultural Collections. *Caring for Your Collections.* New York: Harry N. Abrams, 1992.

Basic information on preserving and protecting art and other personal collectibles, addressing such topics as environment, handling, display, storage, and packing and moving.

ARCHAEOLOGICAL MATERIALS

Cronyn, J. M. *The Elements of Archaeological Conservation.* London: Routledge, 1992.

In-depth coverage of the objectives and principles of archaeological conservation.

Ewen, Charles. *Artifacts.* The Archaeologist's Toolkit, vol. 4. Walnut Creek, Calif.: AltaMira Press, 2003.

A discussion of the removal and processing of objects from archaeological excavations and of a wide range of archaeological techniques.

Hester, T. R., H. J. Shafer, and K. L. Feder. *Field Methods in Archaeology.* 7th ed. Mountain View, Calif.: Mayfield Publishing, 1997.

Comprehensive up-to-date guide providing an overview of the methods used in field archaeology, including the handling and conservation of items in the field.

Sease, Catherine. *A Conservation Manual for the Field Archaeologist.* 3d ed. Los Angeles: Institute of Archaeology, University of California, 1994.

Basic field manual for conservators working in archaeological excavations; good discussion of how to set up a lab and the materials to use in the treatment of large quantities of items; very useful for organizing projects.

Sullivan, Lynne P., and S. Terry Childs. *Curating Archaeological Collections from the Field to the Repository.* The Archaeologist's Toolkit, vol. 6. Walnut Creek, Calif.: AltaMira Press, 2003.

Review of the curation crisis in American archeological collections and discussion of the methods and issues surrounding the curation of various object types.

PESTICIDE CONTAMINATION

***Contaminated Collections: Preservation, Access and Use.* Proceedings of a Symposium held at the National Conservation Training Center (NCTC), Shepherdstown, W.Va. April 6–9, 2001. Collection Forum, vol. 17.**

Papers given at a symposium that discuss various aspects of pesticide contamination of American Indian cultural items. Helpful in understanding the problem.

***The Contamination of Museum Materials and the Repatriation Process for Native California.* Proceedings of a Working Conference at the San Francisco State University, 29 September to 1 October 2000. Collection Forum, vol. 16, 1-2, Summer 2001. Washington, D.C.: Society for the Preservation of Natural History Collections.**

Similar to above but with more case studies and emphasis on NAGPRA items and scientific testing.

Odegaard, Nancy, Alyce Sadongei, and Marilen Pool, eds. *Old Poisons, New Problems.* In press.

Proceedings of a workshop titled "Contaminated Cultural Materials in Museum Collections" held at the Arizona State Museum, University of Arizona in March 2000. Additional information, tables, charts, and guidelines have been added for further reference.

Reigart, Routt, and James Roberts, eds. *Recognition and Management of Pesticide Poisonings.* 5th ed. Office of Pesticide Programs, U.S. Environmental Protection Agency, 1999. Also available on the Web at http://www.epa.gov/oppfead1/safety/healthcare/handbook.

Manual for health care professionals that provides information on the health hazards of pesticides currently in use and recommendations for managing poisonings caused by them.

Contributors

Faith G. Bad Bear (Crow/Sioux)
Assistant Curator of Ethnology
Science Museum of Minnesota
120 West Kellogg Blvd.
St. Paul, MN 55102
Telephone: 651-221-9432
Fax: 651-221-4525
E-mail: badbear@smm.org

Faith G. Bad Bear is an enrolled member of the Crow Tribe of Montana. She has been working in the museum field for the past fifteen years beginning with an internship at the Buffalo Bill Historical Center in Cody, Wyoming. Currently she is an assistant curator of ethnology for the North American Indian Collections at the Science Museum of Minnesota in St. Paul. She is also actively involved in teaching classes, workshops, and seminars and in consulting on creating and managing museums and cultural centers. Most of her efforts, however, are spent helping Indian tribes understand the NAGPRA law and its processes, and to this end she consults and serves on panels about NAGPRA and its many issues.

Thomas J. Braun
Objects Conservator
Minnesota Historical Society
345 Kellogg Boulevard West
St. Paul, MN 55102-1906
Telephone: 651-259-3382
Fax: 651-297-2967
E-mail: tom.braun@mnhs.org

Tom Braun is an objects conservator at the Minnesota Historical Society in St. Paul, Minnesota. He received a B.A. in art history from the University of Minnesota, an M.A. in art history from Tufts University, and an M.S. in art conservation from the Winterthur/University of Delaware Program in Art Conservation. During his conservation training, he completed internships at the Field Museum in Chicago, the Gordion excavation in Turkey, and the Arizona State Museum in Tucson, and he also worked at excavations in Pakistan and Arizona. He has done conservation work at the Peabody Museum of Harvard University, the Northeast Document Conservation Center, and the Frederick Law Olmsted National Historic Site, all in the Boston area.

Gina Nicole Delfino
Central Registrar
Minnesota Historical Society
345 Kellogg Boulevard West
St. Paul, MN 55102-1906
MHS telephone: 651-259-3272
MHS fax: 651-296-9961
MHS e-mail: nicole.delfino@mnhs.org
ACS telephone: 651-457-5399
ACS e-mail: nicole@sylvanstreet.net

Gina Nicole Delfino is the central registrar at the Minnesota Historical Society (MHS) and owner of Archival Collection Systems (ACS), a supplier of artifact labeling materials. She worked in the MHS museum collections department prior to her present position there. She has also been an objects conservation technician at the Science Museum of Minnesota and with Conservation Technical Associates in Connecticut, and worked as an intern in paper conservation at the Cooper-Hewitt National Museum of Design in New York City.

Ann Frisina
Textile Conservator
Minnesota Historical Society
345 Kellogg Boulevard West
St. Paul, MN 55102-1906
Telephone: 651-259-3385
Fax: 651-296-9961
E-mail: ann.frisina@mnhs.org

Ann Frisina received her M.A. in 1997 from the Fashion Institute of Technology Museum Studies Program with a concentration in textile conservation. She has extensive work experience, having held conservation positions at the Cathedral of St. John the Divine, the Society for the Preservation of New England Antiquities, and the Textile Conservation Workshop. She has also worked at the Metropolitan Museum of Art and with several conservators in private practice in New York City. She is currently the textile conservator for the Minnesota Historical Society.

Sven Haakanson Jr. (Alutiiq-Sugpiaq)
Executive Director
Alutiiq Museum and Archaeological Repository
215 Mission Road, Suite 101
Kodiak, AK 99615
Telephone: 907-486-7004
Fax: 907-486-7048
E-mail: sven@alutiiqmuseum.com

Sven Haakanson Jr. is the executive director of the Alutiiq Museum and Archaeological Repository in Kodiak, Alaska. He manages the museum, represents it at professional meetings and public functions, and is the lead spokesperson and fund-raiser. He also works with the Alutiiq Heritage Board to increase collaboration with Kodiak's Alutiiq villages. He received his Ph.D. in June 2000 in anthropology from Harvard University. His doctoral research focused on the Nenets reindeer herders in the Yamal Peninsula, Russia. He is of Alutiiq descent and was born and raised in the village of Old Harbor on Kodiak Island.

Joseph D. Horse Capture (A'aninin [Gros Ventre])
Associate Curator
The Minneapolis Institute of Arts
2400 Third Avenue South
Minneapolis, MN 55404
Telephone: 612-870-3175
Fax: 612-870-3004
E-mail: jhorsecapture@artsmia.org

Joe Horse Capture is the associate curator of the Department of Africa, Oceania, and the Americas at the Minneapolis Institute of Arts. He has contributed to many publications including *Beauty, Honor and Tradition: The Legacy of Plains Indian Shirts, Warrior Artists: Historic Cheyenne and Kiowa Indian Ledger Art,* and *Sacred Legacy: Edward S. Curtis and the North American Indian,* and he has organized many exhibitions. He has also been a consultant for many projects, including Monticello: The Home of Thomas Jefferson, and the Lewis and Clark Interpretative Center located in Great Falls, Montana. He was raised in Montana and Wyoming and currently lives in Minneapolis.

Brian M. Kraft
Registrar
The Minneapolis Institute of Arts
2400 Third Avenue South
Minneapolis, MN 55404
Telephone: 612-870-3122
Fax: 612-870-3121
E-mail: bkraft@artsmia.org

Brian Kraft grew up in Cedarburg, Wisconsin, a historic mid- to late-nineteenth-century Germanic town where preservation is cherished. His grandmother influenced him early in life by taking him to museums often. He received a B.A. in art history from the University of Minnesota. He began working at the Minneapolis Institute of Arts in 1991 as an intern in the Decorative Arts Department. Since then he has held several positions at the museum, including curator at the museum's Purcell-Cutts Residence, exhibition coordinator, and several positions of increasing responsibility in the Registrar's Office. His current position is as the museum's registrar.

Pollyanna Nordstrand (Hopi)
Exhibit Planner
National Park Service
PO Box 1376
Harpers Ferry, WV 25425
Telephone: 304-535-6725
Fax: 304-535-6251
E-mail: polly_nordstrand@nps.gov

Polly Nordstrand is an exhibit planner for the National Park Service. She has an M.A. from California State University, Fullerton, in exhibition planning and design. She is interested in furthering the involvement of tribes in museums and is the cochair of the Native American and Museum Collaboration Professional Interest Committee, American Association of Museums. She was curator of collections and exhibits for the Ah-Tah-Thi-Ki Museum of the Seminole Tribe of Florida. She has been involved in numerous exhibitions, among which are *Survival and Success: Florida's Unconquered Seminole; Seminole Patchwork: An Historic Overview;* and *War Bonnets, Tin Lizzies and Patent Leather Pumps: Kiowa Culture in Transition.*

Nancy Odegaard
Conservator, Head of Preservation, Arizona
State Museum; and Professor, Department
of Anthropology, University of Arizona
Arizona State Museum
University of Arizona
Tucson, AZ 85721
Telephone: 520-621-6314
Fax: 520-621-2976
E-mail: odegaard@u.arizona.edu

Nancy Odegaard is a practicing conservator specializing in the preservation of ethnographic items, movable objects of art, and archaeology. She is actively engaged in research, teaching, and service activities that relate to the protection, study, care, and management of material culture. Much of her recent work has focused on the development of materials characterization testing protocols and the study of contaminated objects by pesticide residues. She holds an M.A. from George Washington University with a Certificate in Conservation from the Smithsonian Institution, and a Ph.D. from the University of Canberra. She has published extensively.

Sherelyn Ogden
Head of Conservation
Minnesota Historical Society
345 Kellogg Boulevard West
St. Paul, MN 55102-1906
Telephone: 651-259-3380
Fax: 651-296-9961
E-mail: sherelyn.ogden@mnhs.org

Sherelyn Ogden received an M.A. from the Graduate Library School at the University of Chicago and was trained in book and paper conservation at the Newberry Library in Chicago. She held the positions of director of book conservation at the Northeast Document Conservation Center in Andover, Massachusetts, and director of field services at the Upper Midwest Conservation Association in Minneapolis, Minnesota. In her current position she oversees all conservation activities for the Minnesota Historical Society, including treatment, microfilming, photo duplication, and outreach. She has more than thirty years experience as a practicing book and paper conservator and has taught, consulted, and lectured widely on a range of preservation issues. She has published numerous articles, reviews, and books.

Nokomis Paiz (Anishinabe/Ojibwe)
Schoolteacher
Box 297
Red Lake, MN 56671
Telephone: 218-679-3978
npaiz@hotmail.com

Nokomis Paiz works as an elementary art teacher in Red Lake, Minnesota. She attended the University of Minnesota from 1994 to 1998, where she earned a B.A. in studio arts and American Indian studies. During this time she completed two internships at the Minnesota Historical Society, one dealing with FBI photographs of the 1973 Wounded Knee occupation and the other working with the Society's American Indian collection. After graduation she returned home and worked with families and children at Red Lake Head Start. She decided to become a teacher when this opportunity was provided through a Red Lake teacher training scholarship. She earned a B.S. from Bemidji State University. She is currently completing her third year of teaching and will soon seek a master's degree.

Alyce Sadongei (Kiowa/Tohono O'Odham)
Assistant Curator for Native American Relations
Arizona State Museum
University of Arizona
PO Box 210026
Tucson, AZ 85721-0026
Telephone: 520-621-4500
Fax: 520-621-2976
E-mail: sadongei@email.arizona.edu

Prior to her current position at the Arizona State Museum, Alyce Sadongei worked at the Smithsonian Institution in the Office of Museum Programs and at the National Museum of the American Indian. She has extensive experience in delivering training programs on museum practice and cultural programming to tribal communities across the country. She holds a B.A. from Lewis and Clark College. She was awarded the director's chair for the Western Museum Association, 2002, for her contributions to museums and has received other national awards for her creative writing.

Paul S. Storch
Senior Objects Conservator
Daniels Objects Conservation Laboratory (DOCL)
B-109.1, Minnesota History Center
345 Kellogg Boulevard West
St. Paul, MN 55102-1906
Telephone: 651-259-3381
Fax: 651-297-2967
E-mail: paul.storch@mnhs.org

Paul S. Storch has been an objects conservator for the Minnesota Historical Society (MHS) since 1991. He is trained as an archaeological and ethnographic objects conservator and has two degrees in anthropology/archaeology. His M.A. is from George Washington University with a Certificate in Conservation from the Smithsonian Institution. He has done archaeological fieldwork in Ohio, West Virginia, Texas, South Carolina, and Israel. Prior to his position at the MHS, he was the objects conservator for the Texas Memorial Museum, University of Texas at Austin, and the chief conservator of the South Carolina State Museum, in Columbia. He is the managing editor of the *Leather Conservation News*, a technical publication on leather and skin items, and has written many articles and technical bulletins on various conservation subjects over the past twenty years.

Laine Thom (Shoshone/Goshiute/Paiute)
Park Ranger (Interpretation)
Colter Bay Indian Arts Museum
Grand Teton National Park
PO Drawer 170
Moose, WY 83012
Telephone: 307-739-3594
E-mail: laine_thom@nps.gov

Laine Thom was born in Tooele, Utah, of Shoshone, Goshiute, and Paiute heritage. He was raised by his mother, maternal grandmother, and maternal great-grandmother and was taught the traditions of his culture by his elders. He began doing beadwork at an early age and became a recognized artist in the 1970s. He works five months a year in the Grand Teton National Park at the Colter Bay Indian Arts Museum as a naturalist in the interpretive division. He is known as an author as well as a bead artist and has produced books on native ways.

Joan Celeste Thomas (Kiowa)
Registrar
Gilcrease Museum
1400 North Gilcrease Museum Road
Tulsa, OK 74127-2100
Telephone: 918-596-2765
Fax: 918-596-2770
E-mail: jthomas@ci.tulsa.ok.us

Joan Thomas is an enrolled member of the Kiowa Tribe of Oklahoma. She received a B.A. in political science from Southwestern Oklahoma State University and an M.A. in history with an emphasis in museology from Oklahoma State University. She began her career with internships at the Oklahoma Museum of Higher Education and in the Anthropology Lab at the National Museum of Natural History in Washington, D.C. She also spent time at the Biltmore House, Asheville, North Carolina. After graduation she worked at the U.S. Army Center of Military History in Washington, D.C., as registrar and collections manager for the U.S. Army Art Collection. Before assuming responsibilities as registrar at the Gilcrease Museum in Tulsa, Oklahoma, she spent three years working as registrar/collections manager for the Mashantucket Pequot Museum and Research Center, Mashantucket, Connecticut. While there, she established the registrar and collections management department and oversaw the move of the collection into its new storage space.

Marjorie Waheneka (Confederated Umatilla Tribes)
Exhibits and Collections Manager
Tamástslikt Cultural Institute
72789 Hwy. 331
Pendleton, OR 97801
Telephone: 541-966-1909
Fax: 541-966-9927
E-mail: waheneka@uci.net

Marjorie Waheneka is the exhibits manager and conservation technician at Tamástslikt Cultural Institute, owned and operated by the Confederated Umatilla Tribes, near Pendleton, Oregon. She is an enrolled tribal member descendent of the Palouse, Cayuse, Umatilla, and Warm Springs Indian tribes. She joined the permanent staff in May 2001, leaving the National Park Service after eighteen years of service in interpretation. She was with the "Oregon Trail" project, as it was first titled, from its conception in 1987, serving on the Research and Resource Committee.

INDIVIDUALS QUOTED

Kathryn "Jody" Beaulieu (Anishinabe/Ojibwe)
Director and NAGPRA Representative
Red Lake Tribal Library and Archives
PO Box 297
Red Lake, MN 56671
Telephone: 218-679-3341
Fax: 218-679-3378
E-mail: sovrn@hotmail.com

Felton Bricker Sr. (Mohave Indian Tribe)
10489 McDowell Circle
Mohave Valley, AZ 86440

Marcella Cash (Sicangu Lakota)
Director/Archivist
Sicangu Heritage Center
Sinte Gleska University
Box 675
Mission, SD 57555
Telephone: 605-856-4901
Fax: 605-856-5027

Randall J. Melton (Creek/Seminole)
Registrar
Tamástslikt Cultural Institute
72789 Hwy. 331
Pendleton, OR 97801
Telephone: 541-966-1985
Fax: 541-966-9927

Char Tullie (Diné/Navajo)
Registrar
Navajo Nation Museum
PO Box 1840
Window Rock, AZ 86515
Telephone: 928-810-8536
Fax: 928-871-7942

Index

Note: Page numbers followed by *p* indicate photographs or photo captions.

Picture Credits

Page 178—Buffalo Bill Historical Center, Cody, Wyoming, Thomas Marquis Collection, P.165.1.49.

Page 182—The Minneapolis Institute of Arts, gift of Jud and Lisa Dayton.

All other pictures and items are from the collections of the Minnesota Historical Society. Many of them have accession or catalog numbers.

The accession numbers for items from the museum are as follows:
Page 15 (pipe: 1562.A, B), 24 (shirt: 1990.506; hoe: 7059.39), 25 (basket: 1994.247.81; drum: 6333.2), 33 (fragment: 6158.1), 43 (blouse: 1989.4.1; sash: 10,000.708), 44 (headdress on mount: 10,000.718; headdress in poor condition: 10,000.590), 45 (rolled roaches: 10,000.201.1 & 2 and 10,000.202.1 & 2; flat roach: 10,000.1245; roach on mannequin: 10,000.732), 46 (arrows: 6333.5), 55 (robe: 69.54.1), 59 (bag: 521/E146), 89 (sash: 6091.1; shirt: S1266; leggings: SH1268.a-b), 93 (moccasins: 75.35.a-b; bag: 68.116.2), 96 (sash: 8976; pouch: 6158.5), 124 (game: 10,000.386), 127 (necklace: 1981.4.52), 132 (scraper: 4080.A3024.1), 137 (leggings: 10,000.758B), 139 (bag: 10,000.152; necklaces: 10,000.171; pin cushion: 519.E144), 145 (leggings: 10,000.1179A), 147 and 152 (quilt: 1990.150.1), 150 (lace: Sibley Box 87), 156 (kettle: 9906.10 of 17; breachcloth: 10,000.1180), 158 (leg bands: 10,00.1026A&B), 162 (bowl: UC1978.56.127; makuk: 6522), 166 (ceramics: 10,000.1030), 168 (pot: 1997.294.1), 171 (pipe bowl: 10,000.3000), 187 (Snana: AV2002.169.447), 189 (Ma-Has-Kah: AV1999.216.2), 194 (baskets: 9598.18 and 10,000.1300), 195 (bag: 10,000.475)

Catalog and negative numbers for historic pictures and catalog numbers for books are as follows:
Page 29 (book: PM1024.R47 1839), 31 (book: PM1024.R51 1850 v. 1), 111 (MM6.7Mr56, neg. 62718), 114 (Zozed:E97.34p10, neg. 10895-A; boat: E95r86, neg. 7634), 120 (E94r6, neg. 8394), 127 (E99.1p16, neg. 12135), 131 (woman and child: E99.31r3; woman and hoe: E94p4, neg. 21612), 135 (E97.1.r14, neg. 28155), 136 (woman and child: I.164.8, neg. 95184; women: E445.6r14), 144 (child: E97.1r66, neg. 34435; women: E99.1r50, neg. 95128), 154 (E93.1r4, neg. 12145), 155 (E97.32Mr4, neg. 49125), 160 (E97.33r1, neg. 65233), 161 (Grand Medicine Lodge: E97.37r48, neg. 40458; Indians and canoes: E97.31r95, neg. 64914; Winnebago Indian: E98p19, neg. 20485; Indians and maple sugar: E97.32Mr3, neg. 19571), 165 (MM6.7Mr61, neg. 35758), 170 (Collection IV.3.53, neg. 56450), 171 (Collection IV.3.79, neg. 89981), 190 (newspaper: Folio E99.D1A66), 191 (E97.34p14, neg. 13204), 192 (family: E97.31r131, neg. 50909; wigwam: E97.31p50)